Psychoanalysis
and
Discourse

The New Library of Psychoanalysis is published in association with the Institute of Psycho-Analysis. The New Library has been launched to facilitate a greater and more widespread appreciation of what psychoanalysis is really about and to provide a forum for increasing mutual understanding between psychoanalysts and those working in other disciplines like history, linguistics, literature, medicine, philosophy, psychology, and the social sciences. It is planned to publish a limited number of books each year in an accessible form and to select those contributions which deepen and develop psychoanalytic thinking and technique, contribute to psychoanalysis from outside, or contribute to other disciplines from a psychoanalytical perspective.

The Institute, together with the British Psycho-Analytical Society, runs a low-fee psychoanalytic clinic, organizes lectures and scientific events concerned with psychoanalysis, publishes the *International Journal of Psycho-Analysis* and the *International Review of Psycho-Analysis*, and runs the only training course in the UK in psychoanalysis leading to membership of the International Psychoanalytical Association — the body which preserves internationally-agreed standards of training, of professional entry, and of professional ethics and practice for psychoanalysis as initiated and developed by Sigmund Freud. Distinguished members of the Institute have included Wilfred Bion, Anna Freud, Ernest Jones, Melanie Klein, John Rickman, and Donald Winnicott.

NEW LIBRARY OF PSYCHOANALYSIS
2
General editor: David Tuckett

Psychoanalysis and Discourse

PATRICK J. MAHONY

BRUNNER-ROUTLEDGE
ALERE FLAMMAM
Taylor & Francis Group

First published in 1987 by
Tavistock Publications Ltd
11 New Fetter Lane, London EC4P 4EE

Reprinted 2001
by Brunner-Routledge,
11 New Fetter Lane, London EC4P 4EE

Published in the USA and Canada by
Brunner-Routledge, 325 Chestnut Street,
Suite 800, Philadelphia, PA 19106, USA

*Brunner-Routledge is an imprint of the
Taylor & Francis Group*

© 1987 Patrick J. Mahony

Set by Hope Services, Abingdon
Printed in Great Britain
by TJI Digital, Padstow, Cornwall

British Library Cataloguing in Publication Data
Mahony, Patrick J.
Psychoanalysis and discourse. – (The New
library of psychoanalysis; 2)
1. Psychoanalysis
I. Title   II. Series
150.19′5   BF173
ISBN 0–422–61030–5

Library of Congress Cataloging-in-Publication Data
Mahony, Patrick, 1937–
Psychoanalysis and discourse.
(New library of psychoanalysis; 2)
Bibliography: p.
Includes indexes.
1. Psychotherapy patients – Language.   2. Psycho-
analysis.   3. Psychoanalysis and literature.   I. Title.
II. Series.
RC489.P73M34 1987   616.89′17   86–30175
ISBN 0–422–61030–5

Contents

Contents

Introduction

My aim in the following pages is to present some of my reflections on the ever more timely topic of psychoanalysis and discourse. Referring to Breuer's famous patient, Anna O., analysts frequently speak of their therapy as a 'talking cure'—yet historically, we should mind, analysis also had its origins in a 'writing cure,' for Freud analyzed his dreams in writing them through. It is genetically appropriate, then, that my book deals with both spoken and written discourse. In the light of such inexhaustible scope, the reader will not be surprised to find a mixture of suggestive and comprehensive investigations; in addition, I must firmly hope that he will meet with ample matter for future wide-ranging considerations.

The book is divided into two parts: One: Discourse and the clinical context and Two: Non-clinical discourse and psychoanalysis. Part One fittingly begins with a chapter on translation, which bears the import of nothing less than a unified field concept in that it is applicable to the interaction of intrasystemic, intersystemic and interpsychic phenomena. Freud should indeed be ranked among the world's major theoreticians of translation, for he ascribed to the concept a scope and depth that had appeared nowhere before in history. Through the use of the German *Übersetzung* in its literal meanings of translation and transposition, Freud explicitly envisioned the following as translations: hysterical, obsessional, and phobic symptomatology; dreams; screen memories; parapraxes; the choice of suicidal means; the choice of fetish; the analyst's interpretations; and also the transposition of material from the unconscious to the conscious. The examination of the sorely neglected concept of translation, especially in the last mentioned meaning, logically leads into Chapter 2, which attempts a comprehensive study of psycho-analytic literature on free association. Accordingly I move the term through a whole series of far-ranging categories, from symptomatology and transference to resistance and structural issues. Whereas verbalization *per se* is but one of the many categories considered in the survey of Chapter 2, it is duly given chief focus in Chapter 3. Here I specify the verbal nature of the patient's free association, indicate its optimally transformational interaction with the analyst's interpretations, and define the whole as a unique event within the entire history of verbal discourse.

The generic perspectives on clinical discourse in the first three chapters prepare us for the topic of dreams, which of course enjoyed a perennial attention in classical psychoanalysis. Accordingly, Chapters 4 to 6 concern what might be called oneiric discourse. Sharing in the current discussion over Freud's *Interpretation of Dreams* and its relation to semiology and Chomskian linguistics, Chapter 4 appropriately serves as a general orientation to the theory of dreams and their chiefly visual and verbal contents. Then Chapter 5 turns to concrete interpretation, and in doing so, takes as a suitable specimen the most pivotal dream in all of psychoanalysis, Freud's Irma dream; based on the indispensable original German text of that written dream, a formalistic study uncovers unexpected meanings in various features, ranging from grammar, punctuation and typography to orthography, and so on. In Chapter 6, I take up a complementary subject, the oral reporting of a dream, whose possible peculiarity involves interesting theoretical ramifications.

Indicative of the diptych structure of the book, the clinical focus of Part One is matched by the non-clinical focus in Part Two. The latter starts with Chapter 7, which offers an overview of Freud's writing. Despite the enormous amount of available psychoanalytic commentary, the subject of Freud's writing *qua* writing still remains untapped to a considerable extent; an adequate appreciation of the matter would involve how Freud read and wrote and—it can hardly be overstressed—how Strachey translated him. Meanwhile, by broadening our frames of reference and by deepening our awareness of the nuances and implications of the manner in which Freud wrote, we correspondingly increase our knowledge of his original mind and the way he understood psychoanalysis. Resaid briefly, as we enlargen our vistas, Freud's genius looms larger. With Chapter 8 we pass on to a particular example of Freud's writing, *Totem and Taboo*, whose fourth book Freud judged to be the finest piece he ever composed. A scrutiny of the historical context pertinent to Freud's relationship with Jung proves indispensable in order to appreciate

Totem and Taboo as an instance of enactive discourse: it not only says but also does in a self-reflexive way.

Next in consideration is literary discourse, the subject-matter of Chapters 9 to 12. Here I examine the very 'art-work' through which form and content attain a higher complex integration than is present in dream-work, joke-work, or in the free association of clinical discourse. Keeping in mind the dynamic factor greatly pervading content and form, one can understand the literary object relating to a symbolic nuclear principle. My thesis receives additional reinforcement by the chronological and linguistic spread of the texts I have chosen for analysis, which go from modern German to Renaissance English to medieval French. Finally, the thirteenth chapter grapples with the much debated question in both English and French circles, the particularity of women's discourse and literature within the framework of natural or cultural determinants.

It is evident from the preceding remarks that my psychoanalytic reflections on discourse has, over the years, been moving along various lines of convergence. With the exception of the extensively rewritten essay on Villon, I have been content to make relatively minor modifications upon the other essays, all of which have been previously published. I wish lastly to thank the editors of the following journals for their courteous permission to reprint my work: *American Imago, The International Review of Psycho-Analysis, Contemporary Psychoanalysis, The Psychoanalytic Study of the Child* (Yale University Press), *Journal of the American Psychoanalytic Association,* and *Psychoanalysis and Contemporary Thought.*

PART ONE

Discourse and the clinical context

Towards the understanding of translation in psychoanalysis*

That outstanding figure in the history of linguistics, Roman Jakobson, postulated that there were in effect three kinds of translation (1971). First, intralingual translation or rewording within the same language; in short, paraphrase. Second, interlingual translation or rendering via another language; this is the most common use of the word. Third, intersemiotic translation, that is, the verbal signs are recoded into nonverbal sign systems; nonverbal highway signs are a ready and clear example of this category. The fact is, however, Jakobson's attempt at all-embracing categories does not take into account Freud's enormous contribution to the critique of translation. Moreover, its central importance in Freud's writings has been unfortunately neglected in subsequent psychoanalytical commentary.

Because of its widespread and multi-leveled meanings, translation is truly a nodal word, or, in the terminology of modern physics, a unified field concept which illustrates the interaction of intrasystemic, intersystemic and interpsychic phenomena. A thorough understanding of the concept of translation will enable us to appreciate a new coherence in Freud's works as well as to acknowledge his historical eminence as one of the great thinkers and innovators in the domain of translation. Indeed, Freud merits to be ranked among the major theoreticians of translation for he gives the concept a scope, extension and depth in his work that had appeared nowhere previously in history. In exploring Freud's innovative concept of translation, I thereby hope to contribute to the recent laudable attempts in various languages to relate psychoanalysis and semiotics or the study of signs in their dimensions both of meaning and communication (e.g. Bär, 1975; Gear and Liendo, 1979; Lacan, 1966; Liberman, 1970; Rosen, 1970; Verdiglione, 1975).

This point merits some brief consideration. In the most literal sense, semiotics embraces any discipline that theorizes about signs, going from linguistics, kinesics, communication theory, information theory, to proxemics or the study of spatial concepts and experiences. The breadth of semiotics is also reflected in the complexity of the six species of signs comprising symbols, signals, symptoms, icons, indexes, and names (Sebeok, 1975). More specifically to our own interest, I should briefly mention some of the connections between psychoanalysis and semiotics conveniently outlined by Liendo (1979): we may use semiotics as a technological instrument to examine semantic, syntactic and pragmatic features of both free associations and the analyst's interventions; next, semiotics as a syntactic structure stripped of its semantic contents can serve as a theoretical model applicable to the logical formulation of psycho-analytic theory, much as the hydrodynamic and amoeba models formerly were; and finally, we might utilize semiotics to study the intrapsychic code with which the patient codifies and decodifies messages[1] (for a further penetrating elaboration of these ideas, see Liendo [1979]). Because of its particular intrapersonal and inter-personal scope, Freud's notion of translation is truly a semiotic contribution and justly merits examination. In what follows, I shall first trace the recalcitrancy inherent in the nature of language in general, a recalcitrancy that Freud had inevitably to contend with. Reflection on this fact prepares us better to esteem Freud's insights into the dynamics of translation, the main concern of this chapter.

Given the intrinsic elusiveness of verbal language, the principal communicative medium in psychoanalytic treatment, Freud's dis-coveries become all the more amazing. We know that a translated word most rarely enjoys a congruence of denotation and connotation in the source and target languages and that even within the rare congruence of figurative and literal meanings for the same word, distributions of usage are skewed differently. Neither can we choose to ignore that if denotation and connotation are problematic in interlingual translation, they are likewise in intralingual context. Obviously, due to each individual's unique personal history, the meanings he assigns to words are distinctive and all the more so as the form word is more common. Alongside this obstacle, there is the essential distortion of psychic reality, condemned as we are to translate it into the language of perception, a situation Freud twice bemoans (*S.E.* 22: 90 and 23: 196); then again, there is the added

4

obscurity in the figurative language particular to psychological investigation itself (*S.E.* 18: 60).

In still other ways we might profitably pursue our subject: To begin by Laffal's judicious distinction, 'Although auditory perceptions were given pre-eminence by Freud as the vehicle for consciousness, he recognized other sensory modalities as also capable of contributing to consciousness *but in a relatively limited fashion* as compared to verbally mediated consciousness' (1969, p. 159 n. 1). When that verbally mediated consciousness is touched by pathological conflict, the verbal sign's components—the signifier and the signified—as well as appropriate effect are variously subject to disruption. Laboring under the communicative obstacles presented by the individual patient and contending *with* and *in* a lexical heritage of broken signs, part of Freud's grand solution was one of reintegrating translation, which can be also understood as a repatriation of the alienated signifiers (see Nicolaïdis and Cornu, 1976). True enough, Freud's self-analysis, upon which his crucial findings in translation depended, had an influential source completely bypassed in Jones's and Schur's biographies: it had as its medical counterpart Fliess's auto-therapy (auto-therapeutischen Versuche, *Aus den Anfängen*, p. 134) and was influenced by the daily chart which Fliess encouraged him to make of his symptoms. These factors notwithstanding, Freud's unifying and centralizing enterprise of translation is an extraordinary and important step in the history of man.

We can recognize Freud's victorious struggle through the linguistic barrier from a slightly different perspective. In spite of a communicative commitment, analysis is interminable and absolute clarity is a dangerous illusion. Thanks to ambiguity itself, talking is possible, human verbal communication is possible. In the latter half of the seventeenth century there was a gargantuan effort, spearheaded by the famous John Wilkins, to eliminate ambiguity and hence create a univocal language in which there would be a different word for every conceivable and perceptible entity (Knowlson, 1975). Of course this towering gesture of folly came babbling down as it would have been necessary to create an infinite language to be adequate to the infinite variety of human experience. Even repetition is never the same, is never duplicated exactness, if for no other reason than that each repetition represents an accumulation. So language has a finite number of words to communicate the endless variety of human experience.

In connection with this, there is a scene in Lewis Carroll's wonderland where Alice explains to the March Hare that to say what you mean and to mean what you say are not the same thing. To this

5

well-known citation it could be added: we are saying much more
than we mean, and we are meaning much more than we say. These
reflections harmonize with George Steiner's observation that from
the dual or subsurface phenomenology of speech

> Humboldt derived his well-known axiom: "All understanding is
> at the same time a misunderstanding, all agreement in thought and
> feeling is also a parting of the ways." Or as Fritz Mauthner put it,
> it was via language, with its common surface and private base, that
> men had 'made it impossible to get to know each other' [1975, p.
> 173].

Freud would be the first to endorse this stance, and *a fortiori* in the
clinical setting: 'Every single association, every act of the person
under treatment must reckon with the resistance and represents a
compromise between the forces that are striving towards recovery
and the opposing forces' (*S.E.* 12: 103). It would be difficult to find a
stronger statement: the patient's every single gesture, act, word, is
not pure expression, but is compromise. Such were the communicative
obstacles Freud surmounted and out of which came his comprehension
of translation in an extended depth and complexity hitherto
unsuspected.

To follow in a more specific way Freud's understanding of
translation or *Übersetzung*, one should ideally abide or at least
recheck with the original texts, whose German term is obscured by
such English renderings as 'convey' and 'transpositions' (cf. *S.E.*
5: 610 and *Gesammelte Werke* 2/3: 615; *Origins*, p. 120; and *Aus den
Anfängen*, p. 130).[2] A survey of the notion of translation in the
Freudian corpus reveals its inclusive scope, giving an imposing
coherence to seemingly disparate phenomena; and yet we must not
forget that however suggestive were Freud's verbal reformulations
of paranoid delusions (*S.E.* 12: 62–64), of negation (*S.E.* 19: 235–
239) and beating fantasies (*S.E.* 17: 185–198), he understandably never
spelled out any detailed grammar that would comprehensively
account for conflicts, defenses, and compromise formations. In the
most basic sense, more interesting for the lexicographer than for the
psychoanalyst, Freud uses *Übersetzung* merely as the equivalent of
verbalization either on the literal (*S.E.* 20: 29) or theoretic
(*S.E.* 18: 59) level. More importantly, neurotic symptoms as in the
case of hysteria might be translations of unconscious material; and
the manifest or pictorial dream is nothing but a kind of internalized
intersemiotic translation of the previous verbal latent dream. Many
of the analyst's interventions are also translations, and even more
than this, the very movement of material in the psychic apparatus as

6

such is understood as translation whereas repression is a failure in translation. Freud's literal use of the German *Übersetzung* as 'translation' and 'transposition' shows us that he conceived as a concomitant unifying activity the translation of ideas and affects into words and the translation or transposition of psychic materials from the unconscious to the conscious levels. Pursuing that insight further, we may recall the philological observation that etymologically the terms 'translation,' 'metaphor,' and 'transference' are synonymous; said otherwise, transference is an unconscious translation and metaphor, or as the early Freud would have it, 'a false connection.' Since all the patient's utterances are proximately or ultimately related to this transference, we may logically conclude that, operationally speaking, psychoanalytic treatment is truly a semiotics of approximations, indeed derivations, orbiting around that false connection. Since ambiguous meaning characterizes the analytic patient in his talking and his listening, no wonder Winnicott said that he never had a patient (counting Guntrip) who could give back exactly what he heard as an interpretation.

It is worthwhile to elaborate some of the ideas in the previous paragraph. Freud observed that hysterical phantasies can be translated into the motor sphere and portrayed in pantomime (*S.E.* 9: 229); the dreams and hysterical phobias of a certain patient were translations into different languages of a psychic reaction to the same idea (*S.E.* 4: 259–260); screen memories are also to be accounted as translations (*S.E.* 3: 321). Avoiding a word for word or sign for sign equivalence, dream-work does not preserve the distinctions proper to the original text but rather translates into another script or language (*S.E.* 15: 172–173), or more accurately, translates into picture writing (*S.E.* 15: 229); the symbols in dreamwork are 'stable translations' (*S.E.* 15: 151). Although the manifest dream is mostly a translation of latent thoughts into visual frames (*S.E.* 18: 242; 20: 43–44), yet in order to avoid reductionism it must be remembered that dreams are not just translations of thoughts into archaic form but also represent allocations of libidinal and object cathexes which might be forced into the background during waking life (*S.E.* 16: 457; cf. 18: 230). In Letters 46 and 52 to Fliess (cf. also *S.E.* 23: 96), Freud conceives of the individual as a series of 'successive transcripts' representing 'the psychical achievement of successive epochs of life. At the frontier between any two such epochs a translation of the psychical material must take place.' But a pathological reaction, writes Freud, may interrupt this developmental continuity; that reaction of 'failure of translation is what we know clinically as "repression"' (*Origins*, p. 175; actually 'repression,' the English

7

equivalent of *Verdrängung*, is not the best rendition of the term Freud employed here—*Versagung*, countersaying, denial).

If the patient to some extent can be psychically represented as a vicissitude of translations, and here we recall the hysteric suddenly turned obsessional as a bilingual document (*S.E.* 12: 319), so the complementary role of the analyst is that of translator. The analyst interprets or translates dreams (*S.E.* 9: 60, 110) into a rational process (*S.E.* 22: 220); this includes the present tense of the manifest dream being translated into a wish, into an 'I should like' (*S.E.* 15: 129). The analyst's more general aim is to effect via his translations a translation and transposition of what is unconscious into what is conscious (*S.E.* 14: 166; 16: 435; 23: 159, 286) and verbally conscious at that, for thinking in pictures is a very incomplete form of becoming conscious.

Freud's contribution is especially outstanding with respect to Jakobson's third category of inter-medium or intersemiotic translation. While ample attention has been given to the endopsychic semiotics of the rebus used by the manifest dream to translate some verbal material of the latent dream,[3] no unifying treatment has ever been accorded to the various externalized and physically expressed translations of verbal material that is a subject throughout Freud's works. In them I have found three different cases where words are the final determinant in a physical and externalized translation of the unconscious:

1. Generalized hysterical, obsessional and phobic symptomatology. Concerning the ' "symbolic" relation between the precipitating cause and the pathological phenomenon' (*S.E.* 2: 5) in hysteria, Freud makes some very shrewd distinctions (*S.E.* 2: 176, 178–181; 3: 34), based on what we may call primary and secondary symbolization. In primary symbolization, an idea gives rise to the sensation: after feeling her grandmother's 'piercing' look, Frau Cäcilie developed a penetrating pain between her eyes. In secondary symbolization, the sensation gives rise to the idea: among her multiple leg pains, Frau Cäcilie selected the one in her right heel, gave it a psychic value, and then complained about not finding herself 'on a right footing' with the other patients in the sanatorium. Not only is it sometimes difficult at large to discern whether the idea or the sensation has precedence, but even in the particular instance of primary symboliz-ation there may be actually the restoration of a primary literalism! If this be so, primary symbolization is often less of an idiosyncratic expression than an indication that hysteria and linguistic practice take their material from a common origin. Hence the slighted hysteric who speaks of being 'stabbed in the heart' and who attendantly has

precordial sensations may in effect be phenomenologically accurate. Although admittedly problematic, instances of 'pure' primary symbolization[4] are semiotically the more interesting and involve a concrete elaboration which, *inter alia*, sets them off from the organ speech of schizophrenics (*S.E.* 14: 198–199). Freud further holds that such an occurrence of concrete primary symbolization in adult life must partly depend for its force and realizability upon an infantile prototype. Thus Dora's dragging her leg, due immediately to having made a 'false step' at the lake scene, was based on a childhood incident of having twisted the same foot as she was going downstairs (*S.E.* 7: 103).

In this realm of intersemiotic symptomatology, care must be taken to distinguish between the gesture-language of hysteria and the thought-language of obsessional neurosis typically manifesting itself in protective measures (*S.E.* 13: 177–178). Hysterical attacks, moreover, may assume added symbolic complexities in that the patient might take on a multiple identification (the active and the passive partner), exhibit an antagonistic inversion of innervations (the *arc de cercle* repudiating a copulating posture), and by a sequence of convulsiveness and placidity could reverse the chronological order of seduction (*Minutes* 1: 371; *S.E.* 9: 230–231).

2. Specific choice of (a) suicidal means and of (b) fetish. For example, a man hangs himself and thereby is pendant like a penis, or a woman by jumping out a window is both falling down and lying in delivery, *niederkommt* (*Minutes* 2: 183; *S.E.* 18: 162). Then again, there was the patient for whom a 'shine on the nose' (Glanz auf der Nase) meant a '*glance* at the nose' which the patient endowed with a luminous shine (*S.E.* 21: 152).

3. Intersemiotic parapraxes, which in effect combine elements of the bungling or faulty act and the verbal lapsus. An excellent case of this is one of Ferenczi's reactions to having committed a technical error in treatment: throughout the day he stumbled several times, thereby translating into action his *faux pas* (*S.E.* 6: 156 n.).[5] This striking correspondence between verbal elements and external movement contrasts with its absence in the greater number of parapractic acts. Four possibilities for a richer and intended consideration of intersemiotic parapraxes deserve special mention. First, Silberer's functional phenomenon, whereby the dreamer's mode of functioning is caught red-handed and represented in the dream might obtain in an intersemiotic parapraxis. Thus when Freud awkwardly wrote *für* twice in quick succession and then substituted *bis* for the second occurrence (*S.E.* 22: 233–235), the *bis* and the crossing out of the second *für* are an attempt to undo the mental trace of having given a similar gift to the same party. Second, although neither Freud nor, as far as I can ascertain, anyone else in analytical literature has furnished an example of intersemiotic parapraxis based on the opposite, such an entity undoubtedly exists and is in essential accord with the unconscious. In his own private notation (*S.E.* 6: 49 n.) Freud singled out a dream in which ice symbolized by antithesis an erection; in spite of having no real instance at hand, I can conjure up an intersemiotic parapraxis in which a person mistakenly and 'with open arms' bumps into his enemy, thereby cloaking diametrically opposite feelings. I am sure that this new and unpopulated parapractic category could be readily overflowed with incidents hitherto unnoticed. Third, Erikson's programmatic for dream investigation—that it deal with the dreamer's style of representability —might also be valuably applied to the intersemiotic parapraxis. Fourth, the comparative study has yet to be done of Freud's drawings and diagrams for along with the accompanying commentary they present an intersemiotic manifestation of Freud's psychic operation. In such a venture, care must be taken always to compare even the illustrations in the English version with the original; Erikson (1954, p. 9) caught such an error in the transcription of the *Origins.* For purposes of revealing Freud's own parapraxis, Strachey should have reproduced the map in *G.W.* (7: 432). Freud asks that his structural diagram be mentally rectified by the reader in one place (*S.E.* 22: 79) and in another place classifies a similar one as simply heuristic (*S.E.* 19: 24). Fisher (1957) has pointed out the inconsistency between Freud's diagrammatic location of the system Pcs. in Chapter 7 of the *Interpretation of Dreams* and the explanatory prose text.

Freud's concept of translation is indeed an extensive one when we remember that, after formulating the analyst's task as translating what is unconscious into what is conscious, he equated that formula with two others, namely, lifting repressions and filling in the gaps of memory (*S.E.* 16: 435). But in spite of the fact that Freud from time to time identified translation with interpretation (*S.E.* 15: 135, 151) and even seemed to use them both as synonyms for transformation (*S.E.* 15: 129), one might insist upon some distinction. For instance, within the framework of personality development, interpretation rather than translation would aptly pertain to the establishment of meanings and connections which never existed or could exist given the developmental immaturity of a certain child. The question remains as to what kind of distinction might be legitimately maintained between translation and transformation. The latter term is the one properly applicable to a developmental process (see Part

Three of *Three Essays on Sexuality* and 'On the Transformations of Instinct as Exemplified in Anal Eroticism'). On the other hand, one might equally choose to call transformation or translation the phenomena of displacement and condensation that attend the passage from secondary to primary process in dream construction. Addressing himself to *The Interpretation of Dreams* Roman Jakobson (1966) considers displacement and condensation as metonymic and synecdochic procedures respectively. From this we may accordingly postulate that translational operations, apart from adhering closely to the specific units of a code, may be of a tropological order.

I should like to conclude by a short, suggestive framing of Freud's contribution within a larger historical context. We lack the kind of chronicle of human consciousness that could better serve to situate Freud's own technical vocabulary as a blend of personal genius and its deeper interaction with the history of the sensorium and of the communication media. For example, how much would a phenomenological study of psychoanalytical concepts reveal their terminological reliance on tactile as opposed to other kinds of sensorial experience (cf. Ong, 1967, pp. 92–110)? There is also the important reflection that different epochs and cultures varied in the authority ascribed to language, in the perceived relations between word and object, in the amount of taciturnity and prolixity and therefore in a redistributed 'speech mass,' in their inhospitality or openness to new metaphors, in locutory conventions as to how much was concealed or implied or equivocated, and in the ratio between inward and public discourse. Born at a time in European sensibility when techniques of meditation and introspection favoring an inward discourse of analytic argument had shriveled up, psychoanalysis now lives through a period when public verbalization and publicity seem to have greatly reduced internal language (Steiner, 1975, 1976). In this uncharted area of flux, and semi-assisted, semi-impeded by the treacherous tools of ambiguous language, Freud made his most famous discovery that may be construed on another level of reference: man and woman are Oedipal translators, Oedipal traitors. And that is no metaphor.

The stage is now set for us to investigate free association, Freud's principal technical discovery, which is a quintessential distinction of psychoanalytic treatment. The vast secondary literature on free association seems partially to mimic the very meaning of the term and to substantiate its resistance to circumscription, an exegetical situation reminiscent of the recalcitrance of hysteria to diagnostic definition as opposed to the relative diagnostic stability of obsessional neurosis.

11

Notes

* First published in the *Journal of the American Psychoanalytic Association* (1980), 28: 461–473.

1 I cannot avoid taking the occasion here to repeat the appreciative appraisal of the logician Rulon Wells: 'The power to express negation marks the highest achievement of semiosis; without it, even human semiosis lacks the power to express abstract thought. Philosophers had made this point from time to time, but it was most forcibly brought to the world's attention by Freud' (1977, p. 16).

2 Given Freud's reputed literary style and also his pioneering awareness of verbal detail, it is surprising that in the beginning he cared little about the poor way in which his works were translated (Jones, 1955, p. 45), an indifference perhaps motivated by his greater concern that the bulk of his scientific insights be conveyed, for as time went on he paid tribute to the translation of nuance. And yet, as admirable and fluent as Strachey's translation is, it falters frequently enough in scientific accuracy and more consistently in affective quality (Brandt, 1961; Brull, 1975; Mahony, 1977). Since, as with all eminent authors, the time will come when Freud will be fully translated anew in English, it is hoped that such a translation, probably taking place in the next century, will be as lexically sensitive as This and Thève's 45-page translation and commentary on 'Negation' (1975) (*S.E.* 19: 235–239).

3 For hallucinations coming about in the same way, cf. Freud (1893–1895, p. 181 n.).

4 For various examples, see Freud (1887–1892, p. 198; 1909a, p. 128; 1909b, pp. 188–189, 213–215; 1913a, p. 308; 1941, p. 187); Nunberg and Federn (1962, pp. 346, 404; 1967, pp. 80, 460–461). I should like to add the example of one of my French-speaking patients who cheated her mate (*tromper*) and developed a pseudoinfection in her fallopian tubes (*les trompes*).

5 See also Freud (1901b, pp. 48–51, 164–165, 172–173, 177–178, 182, 199–203, 206 and 214). Mention might also be made of another one of my patients, a middle-aged woman who in some ways was remarkably dependent and immature; her massive maternal transference onto me was attended by disavowed crises dealing with separation. Several days before I was about to begin my summer vacation, she had gone into a knitting store, which was certainly not her habit, and bought some *patch* and *pattern* work to do over the vacation. She was unaware that her choice of object was determined by my first name, so that choosing patch and pattern work was her original way of finding a latter-day transitional object.

References

Bär, E. (1975) *Semiotic Approches to Psychotherapy*. Bloomington, Indiana: Indiana University Press.

Brandt, L. (1961) Some notes on English Freudian terminology. *Journal of the American Psychoanalytic Association*, 9: 331–339.

Brull, F. (1975) A reconsideration of some translations of Sigmund Freud. *Psychotherapy: Theory, Research and Practice*, 12: 273–279.

Erikson, E. (1954) The dream specimen of psychoanalysis. *Journal of the American Psychoanalytic Association*, 2: 5–56.

Fisher, C. (1957) A study of the preliminary stages of the construction of dreams and images. *Journal of the American Psychoanalytic Association*, 5: 5–6.

Freud, S. (1893) On the psychical mechanism of hysterical phenomena. *Standard Edition*, 2: 3–17. London: Hogarth Press, 1955.

—— (1893–1895) Studies on hysteria. *Standard Edition*, 2. London: Hogarth Press, 1955.

—— (1899) Screen memories. *Standard Edition*, 3: 303–322. London: Hogarth Press, 1962.

—— (1900) The interpretation of dreams. *Standard Edition*, 4 and 5. London: Hogarth Press, 1953 [Die Traumdeutung. *Gesammelte Werke*, 2/3. Frankfurt: Fischer, 1973].

—— (1901a) The psychopathology of everyday life. *Standard Edition*, 6. London: Hogarth Press, 1960.

—— (1901b) A case of hysteria. *Standard Edition*, 7: 7–122. London: Hogarth Press, 1953.

—— (1906) Psychoanalysis and the establishment of the facts in legal proceedings. *Standard Edition*, 9: 103–114. London: Hogarth Press, 1959.

—— (1907) Delusions and dreams in Jensen's *Gradiva*. *Standard Edition*, 9: 7–95. London: Hogarth Press, 1959.

—— (1909a) Some general remarks on hysterical attacks. *Standard Edition*, 9: 229–234. London: Hogarth Press, 1959.

—— (1909b) Analysis of a phobia in a five-year-old boy. *Standard Edition*, 10: 5–149. London: Hogarth Press, 1955.

—— (1909c) Notes upon a case of obsessional neurosis. *Standard Edition*, 10: 155–318 [Bemerkungen über einen Fall von Zwangsneurose. *Gesammelte Werke*, 7: 381–463. Frankfurt: Fischer, 1927].

—— (1911) Psychoanalytic notes on an autobiographical account of a case of paranoia (dementia paranoides). *Standard Edition*, 11: 3–82. London: Hogarth Press, 1958.

—— (1912) The dynamics of transference. *Standard Edition*, 12: 99–108. London: Hogarth Press, 1958.

—— (1913a) Two lies told by children. *Standard Edition*, 12: 305–309. London: Hogarth Press, 1958.

—— (1913b) The claims of psychoanalysis to scientific interest. *Standard Edition*, 13: 165–190. London: Hogarth Press, 1953.

—— (1915) The unconscious. *Standard Edition*, 14: 166–204. London: Hogarth Press, 1957.

—— (1916–1917) Introductory lectures on psychoanalysis. *Standard Edition*, 15 and 16. London: Hogarth Press, 1963.

—— (1919) A child is being beaten: a contribution to the study of the origin of sexual perversions. *Standard Edition*, 17: 177–204. London: Hogarth Press, 1955.

—— (1920a) Beyond the pleasure principle. *Standard Edition*, 18: 7–64. London: Hogarth Press, 1955.

—— (1920b) The psychogenesis of a case of homosexuality in a woman. *Standard Edition*, 18: 147–172. London: Hogarth Press, 1955.

—— (1923a) The ego and the id. *Standard Edition*, 19: 12–66. London: Hogarth Press, 1961.

—— (1923b) Two encyclopaedia articles. *Standard Edition*, 18: 235–259. London: Hogarth Press, 1955.

—— (1925a) Negation. *Standard Edition*, 19: 235–239. London: Hogarth Press, 1961 [Die Verneinung, tr. B. This and P. Thèves. Le *Coq-Héron* (1975), 52: 1–45].

—— (1925b) An autobiographical study. *Standard Edition*, 20: 7–74. London: Hogarth Press, 1959.

—— (1927) Fetishism. *Standard Edition*, 21: 152–157. London: Hogarth Press, 1961.

—— (1932) My contact with Josef Popper-Lynkeus. *Standard Edition*, 22: 219–224. London: Hogarth Press, 1964.

—— (1933) New introductory lectures. *Standard Edition*, 22: 7–182. London: Hogarth Press, 1964.

—— (1935) The subtleties of a faulty action. *Standard Edition*, 22: 233–235. London: Hogarth Press, 1964.

—— (1939) Moses and monotheism: three essays. *Standard Edition*, 23: 7–137. London: Hogarth Press, 1964.

—— (1940a) An outline of psychoanalysis. *Standard Edition*, 23: 144–207. London: Hogarth Press, 1964.

—— (1940b) Some elementary lessons in psychoanalysis. *Standard Edition*, 23: 281–286. London: Hogarth Press, 1964.

—— (1941) Psychoanalysis and telepathy. *Standard Edition*, 18: 177–193. London: Hogarth Press, 1955.

—— (1950) *The Origins of Psychoanalysis*. New York: Basic Books, 1954 [*Aus den Anfängen der Psychoanalyse*. London: Imago Books, 1950].

Gear, C. and Liendo, E. (1975) *Sémiologie psychanalytique*, tr. D. Glauser and M. Tulien. Paris: Editions de Minuit.

Jakobson, R. (1966) Two aspects of language and types of aphasic disturbances. In: R. Jakobson and M. Halle, *Fundamentals of Language*. The Hague: Mouton, pp. 55–82.

—— (1971) On linguistic aspects of translation. In: *Selected Writings*, 2: 260–266. The Hague: Mouton.

Jones, E. (1953–1957) *The Life and Works of Sigmund Freud*, 3 vols. New York: Basic Books.

Knowlson, J. (1975) *Universal Language Schemes in England and France: 1600–1800*. Toronto: University of Toronto Press.

Lacan, J. (1966) *Ecrits*. Paris: Editions du Seuil.

Laffal, J. (1969) Freud's theory of language. *Psychoanalytic Quarterly*, 33: 157–175.

Liberman, D. (1970) *Lingüística, interracción, communicativa y proceso psico-analítica*. Buenos Aires: Editorial Galerna.

Liendo, E. (1979) Metapsychology as a semiotic model. Unpublished paper, presented to the Canadian Psychoanalytic Society (Toronto), January 10, 1979.

Mahony, P. (1977) Towards a formalist approach to dreams. *International Review of Psycho-Analysis*, 4: 83–98.

Nicolaïdis, N. and Cornu, F. (1976)) Etude du signifiant psychanlytique à travers les 'Cinq Psychanalyses' de S. Freud. *Revue Française de Psychanalyse*, 40: 325–350.

Nunberg, H. and Federn, E. (eds.) (1906–1915) *Minutes of the Vienna Psychoanalytic Society*, 4 vols. New York: International Universities Press.

Ong, W. (1967) *The Presence of the Word*. New Haven: Yale University Press.

Rosen, V. (1970) Sign phenomena and their relationship to unconscious meaning. *International Journal of Psycho-Analysis*, 50: 197–207.

Schur, M. (1972) *Freud: Living and Dying*. New York: International Universities Press.

Sebeok, I. (1975) Six species of signs: some propositions and structures. *Semiotica*, 13: 233–260.

Steiner, G. (1975) *After Babel: Aspects of Translation and Language*. London: Oxford University Press.

—— (1976) A note on language and psychoanalysis. *International Review of Psycho-Analysis*, 3: 253–258.

Verdiglione, A. (ed.) (1975) *Psychanalyse et sémiotique*. Paris: Union Générale d'Editions.

Wells, R. (1977) Criteria for semiosis. In: T. Sebeok (ed.) *A Perfusion of Signs*. Bloomington, Indiana: Indiana University Press, pp. 1–21.

2

The boundaries of free association[*]

I have found it very difficult to gather material on free association and present an orderly account of it, for the pertinent psychoanalytical literature frequently consists of random comments, sorts of free associations about free associations. Given Freud's readiness to say that for many people the technique of free association was 'the most important contribution made by psychoanalysis' (letter to Stefan Zweig, Feb. 7, 1931),[1] it becomes all the more surprising that, relative to every other psychoanalytical topic, there are so few sustained studies of free association. This topic presents many pitfalls and little comfortable terrain to the probing adventurer. In any treatment of free association, a methodological challenge imposes its presence from the very beginning, for ultimately free association embraces so much—transference, symptomatology, the economic system, etc. And yet to include everything in the term is to render one's task unfeasible from the very outset. Hence as an initial approach I have elected to follow some vague consensus and thereby track down the term and its partial synonyms (basic or fundamental rule) as a rubric listed in bibliographies and book indexes. I have preferred, too, to avoid dealing with rigorous definition of the term at the very beginning and rather to coast into the topic through a historical sketch of the practice of free association. It will be seen that my general orientation to free association is guided by its meaning as a therapeutic technique of uncovery and not as a philosophical theory about ideas (the history of the latter was partly traced by Rapaport's doctorate dissertation written in 1929, and translated and republished in 1974).

The amazing thing about the history of free association up to

16

Freud is its cryptomnesic fate, its isolatedness, its non-linking in the flow of events. Mindful of the problematic factual reliability of imaginative literature, one may nevertheless posit that something like free association was used as early as Athenian Greece (5th–4th c. B.C.). In Aristophanes' comedy *The Clouds* there is a scene in which the dishonest Strepsiades consults Socrates about business matters. Socrates bids him to lie down; this he does and he associates despite the pestering bed bugs, while Socrates draws inferences and indicates his inconsistencies (see Menninger, p. 45 and fn., and Dracoulides). The next instance of free association achieving mention happens in medieval Judaism. There are

> three grades of the method of free association as it appears in the Jewish tradition. First is the rabbinic literature which has the *ad locum* feature that stays relatively disciplined. Second is the type represented by the *Zohar*. The *Zohar* has its own fundamental idiom, largely sexual-cosmological, whereby its *ad locum* interpretations are less literal and more 'free.' Third, in Abulafia [a thirteenth-century Jewish mystic and one of the leading figures in modern Kabbala] . . . we have the most unlimited use of the associative methods. Instead of using Biblical text as the starting point of his meditations, he uses his own written productions. Freud, when interpreting dreams, follows the pattern of the *Zohar*. In his general practice of psychoanalysis, however, he is closer to the pattern of Abulafia [Bakan, 1958, p. 257].

Of more recent vintage, Freud in 'A Note on the Prehistory of the Technique of Analysis' (1920) cites as precedents both Schiller (as indicated in 1788 in correspondence with Körner) and Dr. Garth Wilkinson (as described in his 1857 essay). Subsequently Francis Galton expatiated on his own method of free association in a series of three articles published with the periodical *Brain* in 1879 (Zilboorg, 1952). Freud in his own youth read and afterwards forgot Ludwig Börne's anticipatory essay of 1823, 'The Art of Becoming an Original Writer' (see Trosman, 1969).

On the clinical side, it is noteworthy that three female hysterics occasioned enormous contributions to free association: Anna O. (Breuer's patient from Dec. 1880 to June 1882); Frau Emmy, who started treatment with Freud in 1889; and Fräulein Elisabeth, who began with Freud in 1892. Anna O. is the well-known inventor of Breuer's cathartic method, which she called 'chimney sweeping' and 'talking cure.' Although Breuer told Freud of his method in 1882, Freud waited years before he used it. In fact, his first use of hypnotism in 1887 predated by some two years any recourse on his

17

part to the cathartic method. It was perhaps in that year, 1889, with Frau Emmy that occurred the first appearance of the free association technique (see *S.E.* 2: 56; Jones 1: 223–234, 241 ff.). Freud perceived that Frau Emmy herself was establishing a continuity, 'apparently unconstrained and guided by chance, as a supplement to her hypnosis.'[2] This early perception by Freud was monumental, for as Rosner has stated so well and briefly:

> Psychoanalytical technique is based on the assumption that there is a connection between each succeeding session (if not in manifest, then in latent content). Thus the content, affects, and ideas from one session can be the stimulus for the idea that presents itself at the beginning of the next hour. The transfer or carry-over from one session to the next is related to the previous discussion of the set [Rosner, 1973, pp. 558–575].

Before arriving at full maturation, Freud's insight of 1889 had to undergo the further vicissitudes of directed association. Freud first used the technique of hand-pressure probably with Fräulein Elisabeth (*S.E.* 2: 110 fn.). At any event, it was with her that he began to apply the concentration technique, inviting her to lie down and associate to aspects of her symptoms.[3]

In 1895 Freud for the first time systematically associated to every element of his own dream. Five years passed, however, before we have with the Dora case the earliest recorded instance of Freud's directing a patient's associations to a dream as he himself had done to his Irma dream. Some eight years elapsed, then, before the technique of directing a patient's associations to symptoms was applied to the patient's dreams. Non-directed association culminated only in 1907 with the analysis of the Rat Man, the matured technique being announced by Freud to the Vienna Society on November 6, 1907 (Gedo and Pollock, 1976, pp. 230–231; Trosman, 1969, pp. 497–498). There was concurrently a noticeable shift away from uncovering 'complexes' to the rooting out of resistances. In 'The Future Prospects of Psycho-Analytic Therapy' (1910) Freud announced that technical change; with his subsequent work on the ego, especially from 1920 on, a scientific study of resistance became a possibility. A historical landmark is Anna Freud's *The Ego and the Mechanisms of Defense* (1936) in which practical measures to analyze resistances were published in schematized form (cf. Compton, 1975, pp. 26–29). A still later phase in managing free association (Bergmann, 1968, pp. 271–273) occurred with the attempt to widen the application of psychoanalytic therapy beyond classical neurosis. More precisely, Federn in his book on psychosis (1952) indicated the

danger of free association toward weakening the ego of a preschizo-
phrenic's hold on reality, and Eissler's article (1958) maintained that
delinquents, if induced to free-associate, would produce only
undisguised id-derivatives, a discharge not contributing to the
amelioration of delinquency.[4]

Historically, Freud revolted against hypnosis since it concealed
resistance and transference. He arrived at the same function of
hypnosis by supplementing free association with interpretation (cf.
S.E. 19: 196, 243), and in doing that he simultaneously widened the
boundaries of therapy as a freer psychic and linguistic enterprise. It
was that freedom that he availed himself in his self-analysis. I should
incidentally venture an answer as to why Freud's own analysis, as
that of his few historical predecessors, was not conducted orally but
consigned to writing. Since true oral association done strictly in
isolation may present certain difficulties of control, Abulafia, Börne,
Freud and others might have unconsciously realized this and, as a
counter-move, controlled the 'freedom' of association by writing.
Writing is much slower than speech and could well have acted as a
security device for those solitary forerunners who were fascinated
and yet anxious before the torrential movement of an unleashed
unconscious. The medium controls, massages the message.

The formulation of any definition necessitates, by the very
etymology of the word, the imposition of limits or boundaries (Lat.
fines). Certainly the task of drawing up the boundaries around free
association is a ticklish one, given its intrinsic nature. As a start, one
may underscore that free association and the basic or fundamental
rule are mutually influential but not identical aspects of the analytical
process:

> In correspondingly reassessing the analytic method, the funda-
> mental rule is contemplated in its determining effects upon 'free
> association.' The imperative and idealizing aspects of the former
> are contrasted with the supposedly unfettered course of the latter.
> Where free association predisposes to withdrawal and narcissistic
> states, the fundamental rule involves a two-person relationship
> with historical and functional antecedents in hypnosis [Kanzer,
> 1972, p. 265].

There is surely some element of contradiction about ruling that the
other be free.[5] In analytic practice this contradiction may be softened
or aggravated, depending on the verbalization of that rule to the
patient. A remarkable distance obtains between an explanation
couched in the grammatical third and second persons respectively:
between 'There is a basic requirement that the patient . . . ' and the

analyst who *orders* his patient to *perform* free association (the latter form apparently used by Okonogi [1959, pp. 119, 121]). An imperious superego quality also characterizes Lacan's conception of the basic rule which he divided into the 'loi de non-omission' and the 'loi de non-systématisation' (1966, pp. 81–82). A necessary corrective to the basic rule—and one which I hope gains permanent acceptance —was proposed by Epstein in a recent communication. Briefly, the basic or fundamental 'condition' should replace 'rule' in the psychoanalytic lexicon. Epstein pointed out that the relation between analyst and analysand is neither that of parent and child or surrogate parent and child, but alternate parent and child; and it is within that context that one should postulate the fundamental condition (which addresses the ego and enlists its cooperation) rather than the fundamental rule (which addresses the superego and provokes its resistance).

The epithet 'free associations' likewise presents complications. Freud repeatedly said that the aim of saying all—however unimportant, irrelevant, indiscreet, nonsensical, or disagreeable that it may be—rests on the substitution of conscious purposive ideas by abandoned, concealed, purposive ones (*S.E.* 5: 531; 16: 287, etc.). Hence free association is not free but determined (*S.E.* 19: 195); 'free' is but a conscious reference, entailing the rejection of conscious or preconscious interference. The concealed purposive ideas that determine the patient's associations are many, ranging from those with roots in the infantile past to those arising from the psycho-analytical treatment itself. In the latter sense associations are not free 'because the patient remains under the influence of the analytical situation even though he is not directing his mental activities on to a particular subject. We shall be justified in assuming that nothing will occur to him that has not some reference to that situation' (*S.E.* 20: 40–41).

One cannot refuse to be ever amazed at the drama of the analytical situation where in its unique way every single association is determined, every single association is a compromise and contains resistance,[6] and every resistance continually fluctuates, for 'Unequal inhibition is . . . the essence of every action' (Ferenczi, 1926, p. 405). Within this relativism, we may better appreciate Kelman's provocative question: 'The question, "What is freer association?" prompts more and other dimensions of responding, requires newer ways of thinking, more comprehensive models of symbolizing, and fresh vistas regarding the doctor–patient relationship than does the question "What is free association?" ' [1967, p. 176].

Just as in a dream where one wish may be a defense against another wish, so one level of free association may be a defense against another, freer level. A further paradox is that analytical free association is not a natural but a 'learned process' during treatment (Kanzer, 1972, p. 247), and therefore 'the analyst is the guardian of free associations just as dreams are the guardian of sleep' (Lewin, 1955, p. 189). Even at that, 'true free associations are not easily come by, and make up only a small portion of any analytical session' (Kubie, 1950, p. 48). In fact, 'We may say that when the patient really is apt to associate freely (in the analytic sense) his case is finished' (Merloo, 1952, p. 21). The upshot of this is analysts hear comparatively little true association, which is maybe another reason that not much is written about it.

Considered as a totality, the epithet 'free association' is at best a lame expression in English and does injustice to the German *freier Einfall* though we must not overlook the fact that Freud sometimes did use the alternate and more restricted phrase *freie Assoziation*. On three occasions James Strachey expatiated on the question-begging and circular meaning inherent in 'association' and concomitantly proposed some paraphrase such as 'the idea that occurred' as a more adequate rendering of *Einfall*:

> If a person is thinking of something and we say that he has an '*Einfall*', all that this implies is that something else has occurred to his mind. But if we say that he has an 'association', it seems to imply that the something else that has occurred to him is in some way connected with what he was thinking of before. Much of the discussion in these pages [the three chapters on parapraxes in vol. 15] turns on whether the second thought is in fact connected (or is necessarily connected) with the original one—whether the 'Einfall' is an association [*S.E.* 15: 48 fn.; see also 11: 29 fn.; 18: 264 fn.].

In similar fashion Niederland bemoaned the English rendering 'association', with its administrative and organizational connotations, whereas the German *Einfall* denotes a spontaneous and coincidental falling out into the open; furthermore, there existed in Freud's perspective a revelatory phonetic link between *Einfall* and *Einsicht*, insight (Seidenberg, 1971, p. 109).[7] True, everything is determined and therefore an association, but on the surface there is the experience of *Einfall*, chance thoughts, some kind of ideational serendipity.[8] Having alluded to these lexical clarifications, I prefer if for no other reason than convenience to retain the epithet 'free association,' though this is not without even other pitfalls. To those that contend that everything in analysis is free association, Glover flatly replies: 'Not everything in analysis is free association;

suppressing conscious ideas is not free association' (1955, p. 300). And yet 'associations' by itself is a general rubric currently used to apply to everything a patient says in analysis. More restrictedly, referring to Freud's identification of transference as a 'false connection,' Green classifies transference as an association (1974, p. 418). Rycroft (1968), on the other hand, distinguishes between free associations and mere associations, insisting that whatever replies to an analyst's interpretations belongs to the latter. To summarize the discussion thus far in Saussurean terms, the syntagmatic coloring of the English phrase 'free association' does not contain the linguistic freedom of the German *Einfall*. Then again, there are those analysts, like Rycroft, who would stress the full lexical value of 'free.' In any event, whether or not we think of interpretations as limiting in some sense the patient's associations, we are aware of the wider scope in analysis than in the usual laboratory association tests which impose sequence upon the patient and in effect, give him paradigmatic but not appreciable syntagmatic freedom (cf. Hartmann, 1927, p. 62).

The more one reflects on free association, the more one is aware of its paradoxes and seeming contradictions. Some of them, even if obvious, are worth enumerating:

1. In order to associate, the patient must first dissociate, split the ego (cf. Sterba, 1934). On the level of affect, moreover, an anguished patient narrating the most excruciating memories may concomitantly feel gratified that they are due part of analytical work and please the analyst. Loewenstein has emphasized that simultaneous with regression there is an enhancement and intensification of some normal secondary process and autonomous ego functioning, such as self-observation and candid verbalization (1956, 1963, and also in the Seidenberg report, 1971).

2. Though the associating patient is passive in nature, within that passivity there is a feeling of omnipotence in telling *all*; the omnipotence has its roots not only in the positive transfer but also in the nature of the analytical association (see J.-C. Sempé, 1968, esp. p. 1042).

3. On one plane the initial analytical contract is not between two equal people, for one party is subordinate and asks for help, a crucial factor in determining future free associations.[9] And then, as the analysis progresses, a reward and punishment situation takes place largely unbeknown to the analyst, for he will respond more to certain kinds of associations (those about childhood) and not to others (Bellak, 1961, p. 12). Such a clarification explains why elements of Jungian archetypes and Eastern nirvana feelings

occur in the deeper associations of Kelman's patients (1962, pp. 190, 191, 199). The analyst simply becomes introjected as part of the intrapsychic as well as external communicative system of the dreamer-patient (Kanzer, 1955). Or, as Ellenberger observed, citing Gabriel Tarde's dictum that 'genius is the capacity to engender one's own progeny,' Freudian patients will have 'Freudian' dreams and Jungian patients will have archetypal ones (1970, p. 891).

4. On one hand, the patient is encouraged to express himself spontaneously, to follow the Pleasure Principle verbally, but then he is countered with non-gratification and the Reality Principle. The id is invited to speak, but its emerging derivatives are held to word representations and are not allowed to take charge of the motor apparatus (see A. Freud, 2: 13).

5. The analytical setting modifies free association, not only in the sense that the patient feels in an inferior regressive supine position next to the sedentary analyst, but also, I would say, because he is aware of his spatially inferior position to the analyst looking down. Tourists may experience an analogous feeling when visiting Lenin's Tomb. Immediately upon entering the monument, one is impressed for the added reason that one must first look up in order to see the remarkably elevated sarcophagus.[10]

Having considered free association from the point of view of history, definition, and its attendant paradoxes, we may now reach out to grapple with its structural, dynamic, and other characteristics. Freud dealt extensively with the association of ideas internally, as elaboration within the psychic apparatus, and externally, as evidenced in parapraxes, jokes, and dream reports. But it is thoroughly surprising that in dealing with associations verbalized within analytical treatment, Freud repeated himself on this important topic, and though he came back to it again and again throughout his life, he never got far beyond some early core ideas; and it is just as surprising how often these same ideas have been reiterated in psychoanalytical literature with relatively little advance beyond them. For Freud the two basic pillars of psychoanalytical technique are the theorems that the abandonment of conscious purposive ideas is replaced by concealed purposive ones and that superficial associations are substituted displacements for suppressed deeper ones. These superficial associations, moreover, may disguise either the *contents* of thoughts or the connection between them (*S.E.* 5: 530–531). False connections covering up lacunae, symbolism, condensation, displacement, nodal points, clusters of associations, common features running through groups of apparently disparate ideas—these are the outstanding devices that Freud used in formalistic descriptions of free association. Significantly he said, only once, that 'the most important sign' of a connection between two thoughts is the length of the patient's hesitation between them (*S.E.* 9: 109).

Perhaps a way of further investigation could be made through the setting up and tracing of linguistic correlates for the primary and secondary process. On a most superficial level, qualifiers as 'more probably,' 'possibly' and 'maybe,' and syntactical subordination are alien to primary process as adjectival and adverbial superlatives are congenial to it: the task would not be a simple one, especially since, as is now generally held, there is a continuum rather than a rigid dichotomy between the two processes (see Gill, 1967). Such a linguistic project would ideally entail plotting out the syntactical as well as semantic and phonological aspects of condensation and displacement, and drawing up a linguistic model of the defenses similar to the mathematical model of them worked out by Suppes and Warren (1975). Attention could also be given to the styles of associative narration (via induction, causality, comparison and contrast, etc.)[11] and to the vagueness or precision of spatial and chronological relationships.[12] Another important area of research would be tracing the differences of a patient's verbalization in his dream reports, his associations to the dream, and other associations in general. What happens to the text of an id-dream reported the next day by the patient in a markedly 'ego state'? Or what happens to the so-called ego–dream or 'dream from above' reported the next day by a changed id–directed patient? In investigating associations or dreams, what will be the unit of analysis?[13]

In this comprehensive survey of psychoanalytical literature on free association, one of the most thought-provoking statements that I found comes from Anna Freud: 'The attitude of a particular individual toward his free associations in analysis and the manner in which, when left to himself, he masters the demands of his instincts and wards off unwelcome affects enable us to deduce *a priori* the nature of his symptoms' (2: 34; see also pp. 32, 35). In other words, free associations are both a window and a mirror. Now given the fact that the ego at its nethermost and uppermost levels is a body ego, may we not push Anna Freud's statement further and say that the body percept is ultimately the source of free associations and the patient's attitude to free-associating? Related evidence for a positive answer to this question issues from studies postulating the body percept as fundamental in dreams, meaning apprehension, art, and language acquisition. For Schilder, the 'body image'[14] plays an

24

essential part in nearly all, if not all dreams (1942, see esp. pp. 116, 124); Székely finds that archaic meaning schemata are the results of those apprehensive processes by which the child incorporates optical impressions into his body schema (1962, esp. pp. 303–304); Fisher (1970) established a correlation between an artistic orientation and a special awareness of one's own body; extending Greenacre's idea that the artist's body imagery amalgamates with other forms in the world, Gilbert (1963) cites evidence that the canvas may indeed be a skin-representative for the painter. In her theory of language acquisition Sharpe (1950, pp. 155–169) claimed that during childhood development the very

> activity of speaking is substituted for the physical activity now restricted at other openings of the body, while words themselves become the very substitutes for the bodily substances. Speech secondly becomes a way of expressing, discharging ideas. So that we may say speech in itself is a metaphor, that metaphor is as ultimate as speech. [15]

If it is true that free association closely corresponds to the infant's uninhibited and unselected reactions rendered in movement, sound or silence to the processes of his own organism (Spitz, 1956, p. 382), and if it is true that free association in itself represents the full polymorphous perverse activity of a child (Stern, 1966, p. 146), might not a profitable working hypothesis be that free association at its primitive level could be modified in its semantic, syntactic and other components by the body percept?[16] Most to the point, Lewin revealed the bodily and infantile origins of both the room metaphor Freud employed for the topographical system (1971, esp. pp. 14–16, 21)[17] and the famous train metaphor Freud employed to describe free association itself (1970)—*Q.E.D.*!

If we grant that an infantile body percept is useful as a point of reference by which the relative regression of free association may be situated, we must nonetheless be wary about outrightly privileging later 'body language' over verbalization as a closer approximation to that body percept. In a fascinating report of recent research on body movement, Gottschalk (1975, esp. pp. 285–290) refers to mounting solid evidence against Deutsch's advocacy of the dependency for meaning by body movements on their contiguity with specific verbalization. Together with the fact that 'A patient's free associations . . . are not entirely revealed by his speech,' one must think of a complicated interaction: body movement may influence or replace a thought, or vice versa; motor activities may add to or subtract from the content of verbal associations. Gottschalk has further data

25

showing that in some cases touching the hand to the mouth evokes oral memories, and in other instances the oral content of the free associations follows from the motor activity.

To be sure, free associations are not some static entity, but arise from a psyche fluctuating from wakefulness to a state of sleep. Ordinarily, however, the patients' 'state is an intermediate one, or they would not be analyzable' (Lewin, 1954, p. 508). This position can be joined to that of Beres (1957) and Bellak (1961) who see a parallel between the creative and psychoanalytical process,[18] each characterized by two phases that may intermingle or succeed one another:

Phase I, the relaxation of ego control. This relatively passive act in psychoanalysis is similar to the artist's inspiration and is directly influenced by the primary process. Whereas the patient tolerates these id-derivatives through transference or through changes in his superego, the artist uses his creative genius to soften the egoistical nature of his fantasies and thereby partially decrease his guilt and anxiety; sharing those fantasies will further allay his perturbance. Even at this phase it is likely that the artist is addressing himself, consciously or unconsciously, to an audience. A fine description of this first phase where temporal, spatial, and hierarchical relationships are reduced is found in Kretschmer's *Textbook of Medical Psychology* (cited by Dalbiez, 1941 p. 92):

> The more completely we relax into passivity, the more nearly does free association approximate to the psychic mechanisms of dreams and hypnosis. Linkage by sentences begins to loosen, the verbal formulation of thoughts yields noticeably to concrete imagery, to the direct contemplation of living figures as scenes which rise into the mind's eye. The temporal framework also loosens *pari passu* with the consciousness of the complete passivity of our inner experience. Memories of the past and desires for the future are experienced with the vividness of actual current events. That is about the extreme limit of waking thought. With a further increase of psychic relaxation, consciousness becomes more vague and nebulous. After the dissolution of the temporal framework, the spatial objectivity of things begins to weaken; exuberantly fantastic elements, i.e. asyntactical catathymic imaginal agglutinations, begin to insert themselves between the scenically arranged groups.

Phase II, passivity replaced by activity. In psychoanalysis this occurs by working through, and in art by preconscious elaboration (in attributing artistic form exclusively to secondary process, Schnier

[1960, pp. 71–72], seems also to see it as a product of conscious elaboration). In this second phase there is

> an *increase* in adaptive and synthetic ego functioning. As in the artistically creative process, so in associating the temporarily decreased boundaries permit fusion of new *Gestalten*, new emergencies or hitherto unperceived relations between the ideational content of different temporal, logical, and other orders; *insight* emerges, partly as spontaneous necessary wholes, partly by trial and error, as a result of oscillation from regression of certain ego functions to an increase in others [Bellak, 1961, p. 14][19]

In other words, there is an oscillation from extreme asyntactic to hierarchical perceptions and conceptions, or in linguistic terms, a swing from parataxis to hypotaxis. Parataxis itself is of two sorts: the more radical kind, the telegraphic style without any conjunctions; and the biblical style, where there are conjunctions but loosely used and deprived of logical value. In this connection, incidentally, I think that part of the universal appeal of Genesis and its treatment of cosmic and human origins is that the biblical style in various translations of that book is appropriately childlike, paratactic; likewise, this same style, favoring regression, is an apt instrument for the evangelical message 'By ye children' and certainly accounts, to some degree, for the literary fascination of those writings to readers of the most divergent persuasions.

The vacillation between the two phases is stimulated by the lifting of suppression and the censor between the conscious and preconscious, leaving repression and the censor between the preconscious and the unconscious to be contended with.[20] Or as Alexander imagistically says (1948, p. 279): the situation is analogous to a spring held down by two weights, and when one is removed the spring moves accordingly. The attendant free associations, a controlled regression in service of the ego, is—in spite of its secondary process nature because it is speech—that speech which comes closest to indicating or reflecting primary process (see Kanzer, 1958; Loewenstein, 1963). Yet the end of free association is not to give full reign to primary process as such but rather to bring to light new connections or significant lacunae in the analysand's discourse and reveal the prior and current absence or presence of psychic elaboration (Laplanche and Pontalis, 1968, pp. 130–131, 221–224, 399; cf. Rapaport, 1967, p. 197). In phenomenologically accounting for these features, Spiegel (1975, pp. 381–383) proposes the term 'psychoanalytic field' in analogy to the behavioral field of Gestalt psychology: previously unconscious derivatives enter that field with meanings incompatible with it; elements are unmoored from their former links and either obtain new ones or stay isolated, and the analyst's interpretations assist the ego's synthetic capacity to restructure that field, for if it remains destructured too long, there ensues an acting out with elements striving for primitive satisfaction.

Concomitant with the constant restructuring of that field the superego changes equilibrium with the id and ego and pursues a major role in the production of free associations right to the end of the analysis. As Kanzer explains, regressively mental illness is experienced by the patient as punishment, and health as a gift won through appeasing offended parents and deities; the submission to honest verbalization and the existence of external restrictions 'lend an aura of confession to the flow of associations, make an inquisition of the analyst's quest for data, find condemnation in his silences, and sense accusations in his interpretations.' Functions of auxiliary ego and also superego are delegated to the analyst, and furthermore, the healthy normal cooperative superego is operative within the positive transference and the working alliance as it and not the infantile passivity of the experiencing ego supports the emergence of painful conflicts. The final analytic goal includes not only making the ego more independent of the superego but also making a normal superego (Kanzer in Seidenberg's panel report, 1971, pp. 105–107; Kanzer, 1972, esp. pp. 255, 258–260, 264).

If the superego is vital in our understanding of free association, so also is affect. Glover states outrightly that the most valuable indication of the analysand's unconscious state is the affective tone of his associations (1955, p. 27). Kanzer, insisting on the important distinction between nonverbal and preverbal, maintains that the nonverbal elements of affect and patient behavior are greater clues to resistance than is verbalization (1961, pp. 330, 348). However the value of affect as an indicator may exceed verbalization, it does not obviate the desirability of verbalizing the affects themselves. If Freud assumed that ideas become conscious via words and affects become conscious directly, Koff goes on further to say that to be fully conscious affects must be put in words (Edelheit, 1972, p. 155). Thinking in a similar vein consistent with the topographical model whereby affects must be verbalized in order to enter secondary process, Loewenstein spells out certain dynamic implications:

> But the mere experiencing of affects in analysis must be followed by their verbal expression. Moreover, although in the analytic process such verbal expression may be a necessary step, this process is not completed until the connection of the affects with

specific contents has been re-established. Only thus can the affects be re-integrated as a part of the defenses as well as instinctual drives; in other words, in their place within the structural framework of id, ego, and super-ego, The establishment of these connections is likewise achieved with the help of verbalization. . . . Affects expressed in words are henceforth external as well as internal realities [1956, p. 464].

Another complexity of free association is involved here: the simultaneity of thought, feeling, and body sensation should be verbalized; but since the nature of language is a verbal string, and if affect which is carried in paralinguistic phenomena is also to be verbalized, the linearity of the utterance is by necessity temporally at odds with its pre-enunciated contents (much as a string of Crest toothpaste is very unlike its appearance inside the tube). Indeed, in other ways too the temporal complexity of analytic associations is remarkable, dealing as they do with the past, present, and future. The verbal description of a fantasy or episode may take shorter, the same time, or longer and accordingly have an *added* effect on the associations themselves. And then again, the temporal sequence of the analyst's understanding usually does not coincide with what he hears. Thus Freud: 'It must not be forgotten that the things one hears are for the most part things whose meaning is only recognized later on' (*S.E.* 12: 112).

Free association may also be characterized by the requisite that they not only express but express understandably.[21] Free association is discourse addressed to another, with the immediate aim of letting it make sense first to the analyst and subsequently to the speaker (Knapp, 1975, p. 20).[22] Kris makes the point that if the patient's associations are not addressed to the analyst but are overheard by him, this is to be understood as a departure from the analytical contract:

While the patient is referred to free association, he has to learn to establish in his contact with the analyst at which point that which he says or thinks can be grasped by his silent listener. It is always of crucial significance when we observe that a particular patient tends to lose this contact, that when invited to follow the pressure of his thoughts and images, as they impose themselves upon his mind, he retires into soliloquy and mental isolation [1956, pp. 450–451].

The requirement of understandableness ordinarily entails the patient's having to tag and label quotations if possible and to supply

29

grammatical subjects and verbs to his utterances. In this sense analytical free association is grammatically and lexically different from interior monologue. The conventions of stream of consciousness literature allow more consistent freedom to the writer to approximate the linguistic structure of interior monologue. As an example I can do no better than cite a passage from James Joyce's *Ulysses* and a recent grammatical commentary on it:

> Weak joy opened his lips. Changed since the first letter. Wonder did she write it herself. Doing the indignant; a girl of good family like me, respectable character. Could one meet Sunday after the rosary. Thank you: not having any. Usual love scrimmage. Then running round corners. Bad as a row with Molly. Cigar has a cooling effect. Narcotic. Go further next time. Naughty boy: punish; afraid of words, of course. Brutal, why not? Try it anyhow. A bit at a time.
>
> Fingering still the letter in his pocket he drew the pin out of it. Common pin, eh? He threw it on the road. Out of her clothes somewhere: pinned together. Quite the number of pins they always have. No roses without thorns.

Apart from three sentences of narrative, distinguishable by their use of the third person, this is Bloom's monologue throughout. But no graphological signals separate monologue from narrative, Bloom's own thoughts from Martha Clifford to be thinking or saying ('a girl of good family like me, respectable character'), or Bloom's memory of words in Martha's letter ('Naughty boy: punish') from his mental comment on them ('afraid of words, of course'); nor does the passage contain a single reporting clause or verb of saying. The resemblance to 'spoken' speech shows even more clearly if we replace the omitted subjects and auxiliaries: '*She's* changed since the first letter. *I* wonder did she write it herself. *She's* doing the indignant. *We* could meet one Sunday after the rosary. No thanks: *I'm* not having any [Bickerton, 1967, p. 237].[23]

Appreciable insight may be further obtained into free association if approached from the perspective of resistance. We must agree that a patient who does not associate is not analyzed, that a good deal of the analyst's work consists in holding the patient to free association up to the very end, and that throughout the treatment the patient's capacity to free-associate is an index of his analytical progress (Glover, 1955, p. 27; Greenson in Seidenberg, 1971, p. 104). Yet there is ample evidence that free association itself may be utilized as a resistance. Ferenczi counseled that if an analyst observes that free associations are used by a patient to avoid rational painful considerations, the patient should be induced 'to free' the latter (1926, p. 284). And one of Loewenstein's patients began the hour with, 'I was going to free associate, but I'd better tell you what is really on my mind' (Seidenberg, 1971, p. 100). In effect, the patient may have recourse to free association as a verbal disguise to repress or suppress anxiety, guilt, aggressive or libidinal impulses, physical sensations and motoric impulses (Merloo, 1964, pp. 15–16). More particularly, free association may be employed in the service of resistance by virtue of (1) its activity as utterance and (2) the form and the content of its utterance.

First it is essential to underscore the clinical meaning of free association as an enunciatory activity in itself. One of the basic effects of the enforcement of free association is the reactivation of infantile neurosis and the displacement of erotogeneity upon the speech-apparatus itself (Fliess, 1949, pp. 27–28). Since in early language acquisition words 'become the substitutes for the bodily substances' (Sharpe, 1950, p. 157), the result is that later on, 'There are obstacles to free associations which arise from the symbolic value which words themselves, or the mere act of uttering them, may have for certain patients' (Kubie, 1950, p. 49). To put it differently, a desideratum of psycho-analytical therapy is that the patient's associations not only be free but *freeing* as acts, apart from consideration of their content. Eidelberg (1951, pp. 50–51) and other authors have spoken of those associations by anally aggressive or narcissistic patients which can be resistances to the psychoanalytic process; though such associations may be free, they fend off the freeing and dyadic aspects of analytic communication. Accordingly free associations may be an acting in, resisting transference or dramatizing a negative transference.[24] Depending on the case, free association could well be equated with flatulence (Abraham, 1927, p. 308); in the associative abuse by narcissists there may be a satisfaction in recalling biographical events, a kind of narcissistic reverie, but unattended by insight or rational synthesis (Bellak, 1961). Fliess describes a urethral erotogenity where verbalization represents a displaced urinary aggressive performance, and also alludes to a transferential importance of verbalization as phallic exhibition, gift, impregnation, etc. Accordingly, 'the release of regressive affect through the erotogenic employment of the speech-apparatus in verbalization is . . . capable of *initiating alterations in the pleasure-physiological constitution of the body-ego*' (1949, pp. 29–30).[25] Especially in the instances where the very act of enunciating free associations is a narcissistic or aggressive

31

defense, the necessity of meta-associations or associations about associating is called for.[26]

Free associations are similarly distinctive in terms of their content and form, but one should immediately make the difference by taking into account various aspects of identity. For instance, consideration about variation in free association ought to take into account the conclusions that visual thinkers are closer to their thoughts than are auditory thinkers (Galinsky and Pressman, 1963, p. 166) and that, comparatively speaking, women and artists have more facility to free-associate (Hendrick, 1966, p. 30). There are also the facts of genderlect, e.g. the speech of American women is characterized by rising intonations, and tags such as 'Don't you?' or 'Isn't it?' (see R. Lakoff's [1975] book-length study and McConnell-Ginet's review). It would also be most profitable to discern free association differences according to Jung's four types, the thinking, the feeling, the intuitive, and the sensate, and then again, to pair any of the four with extroversion or introversion in Jung's sense of those terms—the attitude of one who derives motivation from outside or inside himself.

From a conflictual point of view, one may note the resistive selection of free associations representing one psychic system to the exclusion of the others: the ego (typical of character neurosis), the superego (obsessive neurosis), or the id (psychopathy and border-line).[27] Freud distinguished obsessional and hysterical associations this way:

> Obsessional neurotics understand perfectly how to make the technical rule almost useless by applying their over-conscientious-ness and doubts to it. Patients suffering from anxiety hysteria occasionally succeed in carrying the rule *ad absurdum* by producing only associations which are so remote from what we are in search of that they contribute nothing to the analysis [*S.E.* 16: 289].

Zetzel generalized that obsessives have noticeable problems with the analytic process and primary process, but little so with the analytic setting and the therapeutic alliance, whereas the exact opposite obtains with hysterics: much difficulty with the setting and little difficulty with the process (Zetzel and Meissner, 1973, p. 255). Supplementary to this is Glover's corollary of temporality and free association: if the obsessional is wont to obscure the real issue with historical opacities and elaborations, the hysteric selects present events for elaboration. This sweep forward by the hysteric and concern for the present eventuate in a thinking blockage due to the immediate transference situation (1955, p. 113). Variations in the anally obsessive verbalized comportment range from rounding off each session with a finished discourse (Glover, 1955, p. 28) to one case where hypermnesia was a defense against the emergence of painful memories of, especially, his father's sexual life (Friedman, 1967). Summarily, free association for the obsessional is doubly difficult, for he is not only reticent like the hysteric toward free association because of its content,[28] but also because of its form; the suspension of logical control in expression constitutes an additional obstacle for the obsessional.[29]

There is a certain resistance to free association that deserves to be set apart in special mention. One of the commonest problems in free association occurs when the patient tells *about* rather than tells *as it is* or as it is happening. Telling about lacks immediacy and points to a certain self-awareness on the part of the speaker. In this connection we recall the postulate of medieval mystics: if one is aware that one is praying, it's not the perfect prayer. Ferenczi judged, 'So long as the patient introduces every idea with the phrase, "I think that", he shows that he is inserting a critical examination between the perception and the communication of the idea' (1926, p. 180). In this connection, what I call framing devices are indicators of the ego's manifest control in associating: 'This leads me to another subject. . . . From here I'd like to go on to another topic. . . . Now I'm wondering about . . .' The question involved here is one of degree and relation between expression, self-observation, their concomitance and sequentiality; there is certainly some lack of nuance in Spiegel's categoric position that the patient cannot simultaneously free associate and observe its sequence (1975, pp. 384–385). A related matter concerns the grammatical way of, say, past trauma which continue into the present, for in such instances, descriptions retaining exclusively the past tense are defensive. Indeed, we must admit that the use of grammar as a defensive device is neglected in psycho-analytical commentary. That area of fruitful research is vast, starting from the relevant consideration that 'The present [tense] . . . has the property of conveying most readily . . . "the feeling of presence"' (Perelman and Olbrechts-Tyteca, 1970, p. 60).[30]

Finally, an important kind of resistance is silence which, however, is a less frequent defense than loquacity (Galinsky and Pressman, 1963, p. 153; Glover, 1955, pp. 295–296). The extreme case of loquacity is found in some obsessionals who free-associate easily, and yet, because of their resisting doubts, no analytic progress occurs and the symptoms remain (*S.E.* 16: 289). Four types of silence in the patient have been discerned, and I would like to interpolate that the

33

patient himself may attribute different or correspondent meanings to
the analyst's silence:

1. Urethral-erotic silence, the most normal type, resembling the
   silence happening in everyday conversation.
2. Anal-erotic silence, occurring grammatically at odd places and
   disruptive of syntax, with the patient tense and struggling.
3. Oral-erotic silence, not an interruption like urethral silence or a
   disruption like anal silence, but a replacement of speech by oral
   erotogeneity. In its pure type, it is one of intra-uterine fantasy
   (Fliess, 1949, pp. 23–25; see also Van der Heide's 'Blank Silence
   and the Dream Screen' [1961]). Merloo (1964, p. 21) includes in
   this category the patient's silent vague meditations on death and
   eternity. The patient longs to be understood without talking
   when the ultimate paradigm, the child–mother relationship,
   prevails in the analysis (Loewenstein, 1963, p. 467). In Freud's
   own outlook, when the patient stubbornly insists that nothing
   comes to his mind, he is in effect thinking of the transference
   (*S.E.* 18: 126 fn.).[31]
4. Genital silence, which 'represents the taboo against a direct sexual
   wish' (Merloo, 1964, p. 21).

A connected matter is the speaker's awareness of his own voice as
an influence on his free association. In a pioneering research, Mahl
(1972, see esp. pp. 257–261) administered masking noise which
prevented subjects from hearing their own voices. The laboratory
results were very suggestive. Subjects reported that the noise
appeared to be less loud when they talked. Though showing no
grammatical change, their speech registered a decided phonological
change, including social class dialect shifts of a regressive nature,
meaningless vocal noise, slurring; meanwhile, their behavior transformation involved freer associative response, cognitive confession,
negative affects, and even 'thinking out loud' or unintended,
unconscious utterance often slightly above the audible threshold.
From these results Mahl draws some provocative implications. An
inverse relationship is evident in the fact that talking decreases rather
than increases the perceived intensity of receptor stimulation. Hence
when a person talks, he is less aware both of cues coming from his
interlocutor and stimulation emerging from within himself. One
intrapsychic consequence of talking is that free association as a vocal
activity may be implemented by a patient as a defense against silently
directing attention toward anxieties. In an experiment tangentially
related to Mahl's, Holzman and others perceived associative con-
strictions that subjects displayed to play-backs of their own voice. In

brief, listening to one's own voice simultaneous or subsequent to its production disrupts free associations.

As a last topic, there remains the paradoxical management of free associations. It is not enough to say that the evenness of the analyst's floating attention constitutes an asymmetrical counterpart of the volatility and imbalance of the analysand's discourse. Through his interventions the analyst is concerned primarily not with the enforcement of the Fundamental Counsel for its own sake but the conflicts which issue from it (A. Freud, 2: 14–15). And yet Anna Freud had been quick to point out that 'not all repressed psychic content is capable of emerging in the states of widened consciousness as promoted by free association or available in dreams' and that such material may be unobtainable except in the transference (7: 98). Marmor for his part finds that in certain instances psychic disturbances are revealed neither in free associations nor in the transference: a cooperative analysand in treatment may act thoroughly otherwise outside the therapy and be not even subliminally aware of it (1970, pp. 162–165). On the other hand, Greenacre (1973), alludes to primal scenes witnessed in fact before the second year, that thereby elude any verbalizable and direct memory representation, though they are 'deposited in the physical components of emotional reactions';[32] the storage of such an event in the patient's body memory, his body expression, opens up the possibility of construction and interpretability. On a larger order, Rosen with his typical perspicacity asked several searching questions about the adequacy of language as a communicative instrument:

> First, if thought is language dependent, what are the problems for treatment of language-impaired individuals? Is it possible that some of the deviant kinds of therapy with which we are currently deluged might be viewed somewhat more benignly as efforts to deal with this particular question? Second, if thought and language are relatively independent, can we say that we have truly tapped a patient's thought processes when we instruct him to tell us everything he thinks. Finally . . . schizophrenia might serve as the prototype for an important question implicit in the discussion, for might not schizophrenia be considered as much a language disorder as it is a disorder of thinking? [Edelheit, 1971, p. 155].

The formulation of the Fundamental Condition or Counsel is much more complex than one would think offhand. Merton Gill (1967) simply tells the patient 'You may say whatever you want,' and Leon Altman says, 'You are entitled to say anything here' (Anecdotes during discussion of Epstein's paper [1975]). Heimann

(1975) nevertheless believes that the patient would be tacitly inclined to conform to social decorum, and hence she has made it a practice to tell patients to feel free to interrupt her *during* an interpretation. Heimann's point is insightful though there is an unfortunate wording in her suggestion that such practice be adopted as a second Fundamental 'Rule.' Glover (1955) made the following general criticism:

> The form of the association rule most frequently communicated to patients seems to be: 'Say what is in your mind.' And this is taken by the patient to mean: 'Say what you are thinking.' Whereas if the instruction were: 'Tell me also all about your *feelings* as you observe them rising into your conscious mind,' in a great number of cases the ideational content would follow of necessity [p. 300].

However valuable Glover's emendation is, one in turn may cavil about his lexical choice of 'feelings,' for as a plural form it customarily applies to feelings and omits bodily sensations, which are more often referred to by the singular 'feeling' and which are so important in free association (cf. Ferenczi, 1926, p. 179). A limitation with the formulations of Glover, Gill and Altmann is that they leave no room for nonverbal sounds; these are one of the indications of discourse between people as they become less formal and more intimate with each other. As an adjunct to this, I would suggest that one way of initially wording the Fundamental Counsel or Condition might be 'The progress of your analysis depends on how much you give voice to (express) all that comes to you.' Although any mechanical practice is harmful, it is to be noted that current formulas insistently stressing 'say' might skew the response. Actually a person does not *say* sounds but makes them, and so to urge repeatedly a patient to say whatever comes to him might, at times, influence him away from making nonverbal sounds, from becoming less formal or even regressing to a pre-lexical state.

Standing apart is Roy Schafer's program of action language in psychoanalysis and its implications for free association (1976, esp. pp. 147–152; 1978, pp. 29–66). Judging that a mechanistic model should be replaced by his action model as being more adequate to the theory of the psychoanalytical process, Schafer ascribes a monumental value to language: 'It is wrong to think of the choice of words as a part of the interpretative technique that follows understanding. In psychoanalysis the words *are* the understanding.' Referring to the identification of disclaimed action or masked activity as pivotal in psychoanalytic therapy, Schafer accordingly proposes an interpretative vocabulary that confronts the analysand's strategy of disclaiming action. Schafer objects to such formulas as 'Say everything that comes to mind' or 'Say what occurs to you' on the grounds that these statements are residues of hypnotic technique and indicators of an anti-therapeutic collusion with the patient's resistance, passivity, desire for regressive gratification, and disavowal of responsibility for his or her own thought-actions. In line with this, to say that the patient is overtaken by change or that an action happened to him or her is an inappropriate mechanistic explanation. Hence Schafer's first instructions in treatment are: 'I shall expect you to talk to me each time you come. As you talk you will notice that you refrain from saying certain things' (1976, p. 147). And instead of 'What comes to mind?' Schafer prefers, 'What do you think of in this connection?' or 'What do you now connect with that?' or 'If you think of this, what do you think of next?' (1976, p. 148). Drawing out the logical implications of Freud's statements that the dreamer in effect is responsible for his or her dream and that conflictual negations are really disguised affirmations, Schafer concludes that 'responsibility emerges as a defining feature or constituent element of mental acts and not as a logically independent causal factor' (1978, p. 45). Although influenced by context and situation, free association is a thought-action originating in itself. If unconscious, preconscious, and conscious are considered not as topographical referents but rather as terms indicating mental qualities, then thought-actions can be understood as being performed according to those modes and the rules characterizing them. For Schafer, this perspective furnishes a clearer and more coherent understanding of the analytic process. Whereas Freud assumes that our primary cognitive operation is incoherent and initially follows no rules, Schafer contends that any bodily actions, in contradistinction to reflex responses and bodily reactions to physical force, is a rule-guided performance; even in the very beginning, the infant follows rules—rules which are archaic, subjective, unrealistic, uncoordinated, but nevertheless rules of coherence. On the part of the analysand, his or her free association as ruled action is carried out not in a stereotyped, but in a creative self-presentational situation; the analyst, for his or her part, 'observes these creative actions which state or imply definition of self and other in relationship, and makes surmises about the rules the analysand is following, the situations that are implied by these rules, and the conflictual historical antecedents and prototypes that may be the background of this conduct' (1978, p. 52). In short, from this view, 'the genius of the free-association method lies not in its establishing suspension of rules but in its making plain the rules embodied in the analysand's associating' (1978, p. 58).

37

Schafer's comprehensive position has many implications ranging from metapsychology to clinical practice, but I shall restrict myself to a lexical commentary within the latter area. In support of Schafer's approach, I refer to the German *Abwehr*, which indeed has a much more active meaning than the English *defense* (cf. also Strachey, 1966, p. xxiii). On the other hand, there is more of a passive meaning in *Einfall* than in the English 'association.' Furthermore, the German *bewusst* and *unbewusst* as past participles have a much more passive sense than the English 'conscious' and 'unconscious,' which are more commonly active; Freud used *bewusst* in its active sense to indicate awareness of pain, and in its passive sense to indicate awareness of hatred (cf. 1915, p. 165 fn.; 1915–1917, p. 21 fn.; 1926b, p. 197 fn.). My point is not one of semantic niggling, although it is useful to return to the original German to find out Freud's conception of free association, which is somewhat latent in the English translation. The chief issue arising from implications of the foregoing is that I find in some instances a thin line between Schafer's tenets and some aspects of the concentration technique that Freud abandoned in his option for free association. Traditionally understood, free association widens consciousness; on the other hand, 'if one endeavours by conscious attention to fathom a symptom or an idea, the censorship is only spurred on to increased wakefulness' (Ferenczi, 1926, p. 401). Whether Schafer's technique, which has a confrontational tinge and is liable to intensify censorship, is as successful as standard Freudian technique in summoning up a wealth of deeper unconscious derivatives, should hopefully be decided by the ongoing experience of the psycho-analytic community.

Analysts have also described other preliminary steps they have taken in guiding free associations.[33] Kelman (1962) conducted a ten-year experiment during which time he was hardly ever the first to mention the couch. He began treatment face-to-face and waited for the patient's lexical or gestural references to the couch, thus entering the couch and the analytical setting as much as possible into a larger parameter of spontaneity and free association (pp. 183–185). Greenson prefers a slow careful explanation introducing the patient to free association that is apt to last several preliminary interviews. To evaluate the patient's capacity to free-associate, Greenson will ask the patient to associate to any part of an adduced dream, or will notice how the patient answers vague, unstructured questions. It cannot escape our observation, however, that Greenson's clarification to the patient has a cognitive bent: free association 'consists of trying to let your *thoughts* drift and to say, to the best of your ability, whatever comes into your *mind* . . . it's the same kind of *thinking* that might occur if you are driving in a car alone and not worrying about the road' (Seidenberg, 1971, pp. 102–103, italics mine). This travel metaphor, by the way, is reminiscent of Freud's classic analogy: 'Act as though, for instance, you were a traveller sitting next to a window of a railway carriage and describing to someone inside the carriage the changing views which you see outside' (*S.E.* 12: 135). Transportation gets an up-dating in Stern's preliminary explanation that 'the therapist's chamber is like a control-room in a submerged submarine with the patient looking into the periscope and describing to the analyst what he sees there' (1966, p. 642).[34]

I shall finally mention several varying methods of directing free association once the analysis is under way. Jungian analysts use a more or less directive method promoting 'circular' rather than free associations. Considering the Freudian approach to dreams as one which stresses their repressed meaning and is causal-reductive, Jungians favor a synthetic-constructive method, which aims at an understanding of the dream as a certain kind of symbolic message. To that end, they focus on an amplification of a circular type around a dream, evoking further fantasy to the fantasy in the dream (Adler, 1967, pp. 356–358). Fromm (1955) advocates pointed and direct intervention to stimulate associations:

> I find it helpful to stimulate free association at various times during the session by asking the patient in a definite way: 'Tell me what is in your mind *right now*.' The difference sounds small, yet it is considerable. What matters is the *now*, the urgency of the request. Usually the patient will answer this request more spontaneously than the general question, 'What comes to mind?' [p. 4].

Two analysts, Ferenczi and Voth, describe an invariable technique they have in managing free association: hearing a generalization Ferenczi was wont to reply 'For example' (1926, pp. 184–186); Voth advises that the analyst should always ask a patient to associate to a metaphor he uses. Thinking strictly within Voth's position, I wonder why he singles out metaphor from the other kinds of semantically typed figurative language. As for Freud, he changed his technique in the management of dream associations. Freud's subsequent looser practice was preceded by the original classical method according to which the patient associates to the dream elements in the chronological order of the dream dreamt (*S.E.* 19: 109). One could say that an added advantage to associating to a dream in a haphazard manner is that thereby the associator avoids the reactive sequence imposed on the dream by elaboration and secondary process; it is puzzling why Freud continued to regard abidance by the chronological sequence as the best way to analyze one's own dreams. Reference might also be made to Felix Deutsch's concern with posturology. Basing himself on the rationale that 'Every person returns finally to a basic posture which expresses the psychosomatic homeostasis,' Deutsch directs free association to posture when there is undue resistance (1952, p. 212).

One of the curious aspects about analysis is that the analyst himself is also managed by language due to the ineluctable development in the informative nature of the patient's associations. It is paradoxically ambiguous that the analyst is often like a child acquiring new information given him by the patient-verbal adult (Rosen, 1967, pp. 483–484). As such, there grows a dyadic linguistic bond so that 'towards the last third of their analysis, patient and analyst usually develop a sort of shorthand language of their own, one mainly concerned with some outstanding moral problems which they work with certain minimal references to reality events as starting-points' (Bellak, 1961, p. 12).

In this category of managing free association, I cannot bypass the full citation of a peculiar technique which was employed by Ferenczi in all seriousness and which, nevertheless, has something undeniably comic about it:

> some patients take up the whole hour with a monotonous series of hypochondriacal and querulous ideas which are a substitute for free association. Having allowed them a certain amount of latitude, I sometimes make the suggestion that instead of repeating the boring sequence over again, the patient should make a prearranged gesture to indicate that he is busy with the familiar train of thought. In this way he is unable to gain relief, with the result that the underlying material is more rapidly brought to light [1926, p. 284].

In conclusion I am full of wonderment before the complexities of free association. Its modalities of communicativeness and non-communicativeness are many and partially traceable in a series of prepositions: the subject may associate for, at, to, with, into, against, and so forth. Truly numerous factors of utterance alone bear upon free association—the patient's ascription of diverse meanings to the analyst's speech and silence; the overdetermination of the patient's vocalization; the different or similar meanings of the content and the form of that vocalization; the patient's ascription of correspondent or different meanings to his own silence and speech as he perceives them and/or as he imagines that the analyst perceives them. Given the defensively progredient and retrogredient possibilities, there may be, for instance, a phasically anal act of utterance with phallic contents, followed by erotogenically oral silence, etc. In this diagnostic enterprise affect is all-important. Yet we must regret that although tone is a choice revealer of affect and the patient's unconscious state and that a change into a vague, soft wandering tone frequently accompanies deepest association, tone apparently has not been the object of any prolonged psychoanalytic study whether in scientific or evocative language.

I want lastly to point out that in Latin *socius* means 'ally' and is etymologically bound up with the word 'associate.' Hence there is an original link between free 'associate' and therapeutic 'alliance.' Ideal free association involves a therapeutic alliance. And through this there flourishes the developmental aspect of free associations, for they not only disclose unconscious connections but also, in the process of cure, create new connections, new boundaries. In the next chapter, however, we shall somewhat retract those boundaries as we focus on verbalization proper, mainly the patient's, within the historical uniqueness of the clinical setting.

Notes

* First published in *Psychoanalysis and Contemporary Thought* (1979), 2: 151–198.
1 Cf. Jones (1: 241): The devising of 'free association was one of the two great deeds of Freud's scientific life, the other being his self-analysis through which he learned to explore the child's early sexual life, including the famous Oedipus complex.'
2 Methodologically speaking, Freud also profited from Frau Emmy's rebuke that he interrupted her train of thought (*S.E.* 2: 62 fn.). In describing this incident, Jones erroneously names Fräulein Elisabeth (1: 243–244 and fn.).
3 From Freud's description of the three different structures of psychical material that may join a symptom, one may infer the three different ways that Freud directed free associations at the time (see *S.E.* 2: 288–292).
4 Bergmann and other critics commit the frequent error of saying that it was with Anna Freud's classic text that central attention was accorded to resistances alongside id-derivatives. Freud at an early date explicitly recognized the capital importance of dealing with resistances, as Compton shows in his well-selected citations. Freud's awareness, though, had to await the technical refinement elaborated by his daughter.

41

5 For technical interventions at the other end of the spectrum, cf. Laforgue who counseled that we must not insist on the rule with an obsessional afraid of pronouncing certain magical words; Laforgue also advocates forbidding strict observance of the rule in order to deprive a certain type of patient of a cherished way of self-torture and humiliation and thereby manage to 'cause him perversely to give free associations' (1936, p. 373)!

6 Cf. Merloo (1964, p. 14): resistance is never dissolved or eliminated but changes position; ultimately all life's patterns from the lowliest to the poet's lofty goal of immortal fame are resistances against deeper obscure fears towards death and the unknown.

7 The German, on the other hand, is not without its own difficulty. Literally *Einfall* is a fall-in, thus causing a vertical paradox in the usual account about ideas as *emerging* from the unconscious.

   I have in fact come across an extraordinary passage in which Freud gets phonetically carried away in talking about *Einfall* and which goes unperceived in the *Standard Edition*. In the two initial paragraphs of the essay 'Negation,' Freud seven times employs *Einfall* in its verbal or substantival forms. And in the same context he describes a convenient method of eliciting spontaneous associations, whereby a 'patient falls into the trap' (*S.E.* 19: 235); the German text is phonetically and thematically much more revelatory: 'Geht der Patient *in die Falle*' (italics mine).

8 In an admirably clear exposition of Lacan, Bär (1974, p. 499) offers a collateral reason for the linguistic confusion that unconscious material is liable to have as it appears into consciousness; alongside Freud's theory of the repressed, Bär resorts to information theory and talks about a 'traffic jam' that causes a distortion in material going from the unconscious to the conscious (cf. also Bär, 1971). Bär's position, I think, receives support from telepathic phenomena. Once I had the occasion of listening to the performance of a renowned telepathist on the CBC network. I remarked that as anonymous callers phoned in to the studio (and there were two selected by CBC itself), the telepathist said, significantly, that he was trying to *link* up with the caller and proceeded to grope sometimes letter by letter, syllable by syllable, till he got the caller's full name, address, and so forth. Obviously the various linguistic distortions that the telepathist was mentally sorting out were due more to informational jamming than to any return of the repressed. Conceivably, the analysand's difficulty in psychically retrieving past data in his life could be due simultaneously to dynamic conflict and informational overloading.

9 Compare Fenichel (1941, p. 25): '. . . "free associations" of analysands always retain an aspect determined by the conscious awareness of the whole purpose of analysis . . . the wish for recovery' and Kanzer's more

nuanced picture (1961, esp. pp. 333, 348): being intermediate between dream and waking activity, free association is governed not by the wish to sleep but by the wish for recovery; the analyst's interventions point to resistance when the patient is deflected from the fundamental purpose of recognizing his illness and working at its cure.

And yet there are sleep-like elements in the free association setting, for a psychical state is established in which energy is more mobile and maybe cathected onto 'involuntary ideas' (*S.E.* 4: 102). Pursuing the analogy between the analytic setting and dream, Lewin calls the analyst an arouser as well as a day-residue of the subject's manifest content (1955, p. 193).

10 Two researched examples concerning the influence of setting are worth mentioning. In having subjects free-associate into a tape-recorder, Colby (1960) discerned that their imago system was influenced by the occasional presence of a male observer. In the second instance, Winck analyzed 183,000 free association messages typed by some 60,000 passers-by on a publicly placed typewriter in midtown N.Y. during a three-year period. As could be expected, those messages typed between 5 P.M. and 9 A.M. had a noticeable rise in references to sex, masochism, and hostility. On the other hand, there were six central human concerns that were hardly ever expressed in day or night messages: money, work, clothing, married love, proverbs, and traditional folklore.

11 To my knowledge, only once does Freud expatiate on the patient's order of associative presentation (*S.E.* 2: 288–292).

Rapaport has made a fine corrective contribution to the interpretation of causality and associative sequence (1967, p. 216): ' . . . if one idea follows another in a chain of free associations, the analyst will assume *post hoc ergo propter hoc* (after it thus because of it). I believe that this rule goes without an explanation. What is the justification for psychoanalysis taking such a stand? Perhaps the *propter* is somewhat too narrow a term, because frequently the causal relationship just referred to is reversed like this: 'The cause of it, therefore after it.'

12 A deictic, or for Jackobson, a shifter, is a linguistic term designating those lexical items whose referent can be determined only in connection with the speaker (e.g. here, that, yesterday, now, tomorrow). Apart from the importance these words take on during the analytic session when the patient's spatial and temporal boundaries are loosened, their effect even extends to metapsychology. The id in English and *das Es* in German are spatially neutral and can be equally rendered as 'it'; the French translation, however, is *ça*, a deictic having repercussions in Lacan's naming of the Freudian unconscious as *l'Autre*. Contrary to the German and English terms, *ça* is a spatial placement, and therefore a displacement.

43

13 In a tentative effort Reynes isolated what he called regressive imagery; in his study, strangely enough, though primary process words occurred with higher frequency in 'working hours,' there was no such discrepancy in the middle phase of analysis, when regressive imagery was expected. Opposed to the linguistic categories of Reynes and Gottschalk (whose unit of analysis is the sentence) Knapp favors 'attentional categories' (shift of focus concerning time and modes of experience). If his analytical categories for free association (1974, p. 18) are compared with Erikson's schematic outline for dream analysis (1954, pp. 22–23), we note many resemblances though, curiously, there's no counterpart in Knapp for Erikson's separate linguistic category! In terms of larger patterns Freud merely spoke of deepening versus broadening associations (*S.E.* 19: 110). Glover attended to the associational 'drift' mainly regarding time and affect. We can only await the psycho-analytical usefulness of the concerted effort of trying to pinpoint the narrative unit or 'narreme,' and abiding concern of the newly formed field of narratology, whose recent origins date from Barthes' 'Introduction à l'analyse structurale des récits' (1966). For English readers, convenient introductions to narratology are the works by Culler (1975), Scholes (1974), and *New Literary History* (1975).

14 Though 'image' (used by Schilder) is currently used in a generic sense both in literary criticism and psychoanalysis, I prefer the term 'percept' which is not sensorially biased; etymologically as well as semantically 'image' is first of all a visual reference.

15 With the contents of Chapter 1 in mind, one may conceive of the whole analytic treatment to be metaphorical. 'Translation' comes from the Latin, 'carried across'; the infinitive of that most irregular verb is *trans ferre*, from which comes 'transference.' What's more, the Greek for *transferre* is *metaphorein*! On one level, consequently, metaphor, transference, and translation are identical.

16 Cf. Milner (1957, p. 151): 'Thus it seems to me that in the analysis of the artist (whether potential or manifest) in any patient, the crucial battle is over the 'language' of love, that is to say, ultimately, over the way in which the orgasm, or the orgastic experiences, are to be symbolized.'

17 Attempting a 'psychoanalysis of psychoanalysis,' Whitehead compared the horizontal layering of Freud's topographical theory with Klein's vertical splitting and cleavage (1975, pp. 384, 391), and wondered whether there was a link between the Kleinian verticality and the external appearance of the female genitalia. With this reflection I find it somewhat amusing that the time-honored phallically symbolical line has now become bisexual.

18 For further comments on this parallel, cf. Anna Freud's foreword to Milner's *On Not Being Able to Paint* (1957, pp. xiii–xiv) and Kubie (1958,

pp. 57–58). On the inhibitory forces hindering the productive imagination, stimulating remarks are made by Kubie (pp. 60–61), and Rosen (1960, pp. 229, 242–243).

19 In a nuanced addendum to Kris's teaching that in the creative act there is an oscillation between ego regression and full functioning, Bellak (1961, p. 13) prefers to say that there is an oscillation from regression to vigilance, the latter being a greater than normal operation of cognitive, adaptive, and synthetic functions. Since enhanced, intensified secondary process is inherent in artistic creation (Bellak) and the analytic situation (Loewenstein), it gives us pause to think that these are also the two moments which, readily associated with fantasy and primary process, yet give an unhabitual climate for fantasy production. The question immediately arises, To what degree do we thereby obtain a distorted fantasy 'text'? This textual problem echoes considerations of relativity dear to modern physics.

20 For a comparative topographical and structural description of 'the widening of attention' and its effect on free association, see Coltrera and Ross (1967, pp. 19–20).

21 Though this comprehensibility is seen as an unexceptionable requisite by Rosen (1967) and Loewenstein (in Seidenberg, 1971, p. 100), Winnicott (1971) believes that the analyst must have enough of a flexible and creative technique to countenance nonsense associations in certain cases (pp. 55–56). For Freud, free associations are diametrically opposite to the dream which is 'a completely asocial product; it has nothing to communicate to anyone else' (*S.E.* 8: 179; see also 4: 377, 15: 231). On the other hand, Ferenczi (1926, p. 349) and Kanzer (1955) consider patients' dreams as communications to the analyst. In a different light, Hartmann (1927, pp. 61–63) differentiates analytical associations from daydreaming insofar as the latter contains wish-fulfilment and purposeful elements.

22 Compare child analysis, where the child's games take place *before* the analyst but only gradually, in the course of therapy, can they be interpreted as an address to the analyst (Lagache, 1964, p. 1077).

23 The *Ulysses* passage fits into the third of Joyce's techniques of discourse: (1) language to be read, pure and simple; (2) language written to be read, as if heard; (3) language written to be read, as if overheard, as if eavesdropping on the distinctive inner voice of a person musing (Spencer, 1965, p. 41).

24 Of course, not all resistances are resistances against free association. For example, a particular pathogenic make-up of certain conflicts or resistances against realizing that the transference is a repetition of past response to others may not necessarily create an obstacle to comply with free association (Loewenstein, 1963, pp. 460–462).

45

25 By the same token, the patient may attribute pre-genital meanings to the analyst's speech 'or alternatively will endow listening to it with oral, masochistic or voyeuristic significance' (Rycroft, 1958, p. 413).

26 Meta-associations are far from being restricted to these situations. During analytic treatment, for instance, the repressing patient may re-enact early stages of language development. It is no wonder that verbalization itself can become an object of examination much as it was during childhood when much communication between parent and child was about language. In free association, though, there may be a suspension of such paralinguistic phenomena as gestures and facial expression which clarify verbal expression in many speakers and may be so effective as to hide the reasons making them necessary in the first place (Rosen, 1967, pp. 469–470, 488).

27 Merloo goes on to add that a peculiar kind of resistance is a paradoxical clarity disguising guarded secrets and he glosses this with the pertinent Chinese proverb 'Those who talk about Tao don't know Tao' (1964, pp. 15, 19). Rycroft (1958, p. 414) tells of a particular patient who coined abstract tortuous neologisms to ward off physical sensations and concrete perceptions that conversational, metaphorical speech would occasion in her.

28 As far as content is concerned, Freud favors concrete over conceptual words because the former have richer associations due to their historical development (*S.E.* 5: 340). While acknowledging that free association promotes the substitution of ideas by images, Kanzer stresses the ambiguity of concrete language which may indicate regression instead of therapeutic progress, much as memories of the past in free association are often defenses in warding off present stimuli (1958, esp. pp. 465–466, 471, 475, 482).

29 To the obsessional who triumphantly protests he is cooperating in giving only senseless associations, Ferenczi simply replies: 'The patient, it is true, is asked to say everything, even the senseless things, that occurs to him, but certainly not to repeat only meaningless or disconnected words' (1926, p. 178).

30 Another kind of distant reportage is the intellectual resistance of some patients. Due to the paucity of their verbs choice, they have recourse to many verbs 'to be.' But their most eminent trait is the absence of temporal adverbs, replaced by such epithets as 'this is homosexuality' or 'this is a father figure.' Such statements 'are not adequate to describe any concrete psychological phenomenon which, in order to be placed into its genetic and dynamic content, requires qualification by a temporal adverb' (Loewenstein, 1957, p. 147).

31 Collateral evidence for Freud's conclusion is in Luborsky and Minz's research project on momentary forgetting during psychoanalysis,

which established a striking correlation between the forgetting and high involvement with the analyst (1975, p. 257). Luborsky elsewhere concluded that after a momentary forgetting, 'the recovered thought is likely to be a derivative toned-down version of the originally emerging threatening thought' (1964, p. 133).

32 Cf. Gedo and Goldberg (1973, p. 186): 'The question of the subliminal registration of external percepts remains unresolved. If such registration does exist, then only a model such as that of the *Project* can account for it. In other words, separate systems must be postulated for registration and consciousness rather than a unitary one (the *Pcpt.-Cs.* of Freud's later writings on this issue).'

Piaget, incidentally, rejects the child's capability within his first year of voluntarily or purposefully constructing an organized wish-fulfilling fantasy or thought (Sandler, 1975, pp. 367–368).

33 It might be well to stress here that associationists, with their tools, cannot duplicate psychoanalytic perception. Along with Hartmann (1927) and Freud (1906), Rapaport has written some of the finest comments on what escapes associationists:

> That somebody could never forget something he saw only once. There is no place for this in an observation system in which everything depends on observing how things occur together. . . . Another thing which they will never understand because there is no place for it: *déjà vu*. . . . In explaining this the occasionists have just never gotten to first base [1967, p. 170].

Schafer also distinguishes trenchantly between Freud's orientation and the associationistic theory of the academic psychology prevalent in his time:

> According to that theory, factors such as primacy, recency, contiguity, and frequency of occurrence determine the linear sequence of thoughts, arranging them like links in a chain. One does observe phenomena that suggest the play of such factors, and in his explanatory propositions Freud did seem to include these factors and the mental model they implied. But for the most part his making that inclusion played a superficial or incidental role in his explanations. What was primary for Freud was the organizing influence of unconscious conflict in which infantile wishes and fears figure decisively [1978, pp. 40–41].

34 In one of the rare experimental projects on free association, Colby (1961) found a greater amplifying power of causal-correlative over interrogative inputs on free association. To use Colby's examples, subjects associated more to a comment such as 'You can't concentrate because she might

47

find another guy' than to 'Do your parents object to the marriage?' On the opposite side, talking from her own experience, Heimann (1975, p. 14) prefers clarifications to explanations and 'because' statements since the latter do not challenge the patient's creative functioning. Actually, for purposes of not interfering with a patient's regression, the advantageous use of paratactic interpretation might be considered. Parataxis is the style that most adequately describes the dream dreamt. Upon training himself to write automatically at night so as to record reveries and dreams, Rapaport perceived that he left out conjunctions more and more as he proceeded to the dream state (1967, p. 395).

References

Abraham, K. (1927) *Selected Papers of Karl Abraham*. London: Hogarth Press.

Adler, G. (1967) Methods of treatment in analytical psychology. In: B. Wolman (ed.) *Psychoanalytic Techniques*. New York: Basic Books, pp. 338–378.

Alexander, F. (1948) *Fundamentals of Psychoanalysis*. New York: Norton.

Appelbaum, S. (1966) Speaking with the second voice: evocativeness. *Journal of the American Psychoanalytic Association*, 14: 462–477.

Bakan, D. (1958) *Sigmund Freud and the Jewish Mystical Tradition*. New York: van Nostrand.

Balken, E. and Masserman, J. (1940) The language of phantasy: III. The language of the phantasies of patients with conversion hysteria, anxiety state and obsessive-compulsive neuroses. *Journal of Psychology*, 10: 75–86.

Bär, E. (1971) The Language of the unconscious according to Jacques Lacan. *Semiotica*, 3: 241–268.

—— (1974) Understanding Lacan. In: *Psycho-analysis and Contemporary Science*, vol. 3. New York: International Universities Press, pp. 473–544.

Barthes, R. (1966) Introduction à l'analyse du récit. *Communications*, 8: 1–27.

Bellak, L. (1961) Free association: conceptual and clinical aspects. *International Journal of Psycho-Analysis*, 42: 9–20.

Benveniste, E. (1956) Remarques sur la fonction du langage dans la découverte freudienne. *La Psychanalyse*, 1: 3–16.

Beres, D. (1957) Communication in psychoanalysis and the creative process: a parallel. *Journal of the American Psychoanalytic Association*, 5: 408–423.

Bergmann, M. (1968) Free association and interpretation of dreams: historical and methodological considerations. In: E. Hammer (ed.), *Use of Interpretation in Treatment: Technique and Art*. New York: Grune & Stratton, pp. 270–279.

Bickerton, D. (1967) Modes of interior monologue: a formal definition.

Modern Language Quarterly, 28: 227–239.

Bordin, E. (1963) Response to the task of free association as a reflection of personality. Unpublished paper, delivered at the International Congress on Scientific Psychology, Washington, D.C.

—— (1966) Free association: an experimental analogue of the psychoanalytic situation. In: L. Gottschalk and A. Auerbach (eds.) *Methods of Research in Psychotherapy*. New York: Appleton-Century-Crofts, pp. 189–208.

Boring, E. (1953) A history of introspection. *Psychological Bulletin*, 50: 169–189.

Bouvet, M. (1954) La cure type. In: *Encyclopédie Médico-Chirurgicale*, 37812, A (10–40). Paris.

Carroll, J. (1958) Some psychological effects of language structure. In: P. Hoch and J. Zubin (eds.), *Psychopathology of Communication*. New York: Grune & Stratton, pp. 49–68

Chrzanowski, G. (1969) On the nature of therapeutic dialogue in psycho-analysis. *Contemporary Psychoanalysis*, 6: 39–47.

Colby, K. (1960) Experiment on the effects of an observer's presence on the imago system during free-association. *Behavioral Science*, 5: 216–232.

—— (1961) On the greater amplifying power of causal-correlative over interrogative inputs on free association in an experimental psycho-analytic situation. *Journal of Nervous and Mental Diseases*, 133: 233–239.

Coltrera, J. and Ross, M. (1967) Freud's psychoanalytic technique—from the beginnings to 1923. In: B. Wolman (ed.), *Psycho-analytic Techniques*. New York: Basic Books, pp. 13–50.

Compton, A. (1975) Aspects of psychoanalytic intervention [Kris Study Group of the New York Psycho-analytic Institute, Monogr. VI], ed. B. Fine and H. Waldhorn. New York: International Universities Press, pp. 23–97.

Culler, J. (1975) *Structuralist Poetics: Structuralism, Linguistics, and the Study of Literature*. London: Routledge & Kegan Paul.

Dalbiez, R. (1941) *Psychoanalytical Method and the Doctrine of Freud*, vol. 2, tr. T. Lindsay. London: Longman.

Deutsch, F. (1939) The choice of organ in organ neuroses. *International Journal of Psycho-Analysis*, 20: 252–262.

—— (1952) Analytic posturology. *Psychoanalytic Quarterly*, 21: 196–214.

Dracoulides, N. (1965) Origine de la psychanalyse et du psychodrame dans les 'Nuées' et les 'Guêpes' d'Aristophane. Unpublished paper, delivered at La Société Française d'Histoire de la Médecine, Paris.

Edelheit, H. (1972) Panel report: The relationship of language development to problem-solving ability. *Journal of the American Psycho-analytic Association*, 20: 145–155.

Eidelberg, L. (1951) *Encyclopedia of Psychoanalysis*. New York: Free Press. 'Basic Rule,' pp. 50–51.

Eissler, K. (1941) On: 'The attitude of neurologists, psychiatrists and psychologists towards psychoanalysis.' *Psychoanalytic Quarterly*, 10: 297–319.

—— (1958) Notes on problems of technique in the psychoanalytic treatment of adolescents: with some remarks on perversions. *Psychoanalytic Study of the Child*, 13: 223–254.

Ellenberger, H. (1970) *The Discovery of the Unconscious: the Evolution and History of Dynamic Psychiatry*. New York: Basic Books.

Epstein, G. (1975) A note on the semantic confusion in the 'Fundamental Rule' of psychoanalysis. Unpublished paper, delivered at the Fall Meeting of the American Psychoanalytic Association, New York.

Erikson, E. (1954) The dream specimen of psychoanalysis. *Journal of the American Psychoanalytic Association*, 2: 5–56.

Federn, P. (1952) *Ego Psychology and the Psychoses*, ed. E. Weiss. New York: Basic Books.

Feldmann, S. (1948) Mannerisms of speech. *Psychoanalytic Quarterly*, 17: 356–367.

Fenichel, O. (1941) *Problems of Psychoanalytic Technique*. New York: Psycho-analytic Quarterly, Inc.

Ferenczi, S. (1926) *Further Contributions to the Theory and Technique of Psycho-analysis*. London: Hogarth Press.

Fisher, S. (1970) *Body Experience in Fantasy and Behavior*. New York: Appleton-Century-Crofts.

Fliess, R. (1949) Silence and verbalization: a supplement to the theory of the 'analytic rule.' *International Journal of Psycho-Analysis*, 30: 21–30.

Freud, A. (1936) The ego and the mechanisms of defense. *The Writings of Anna Freud*, 2. New York: International Universities Press, 1966.

—— (1954) Problems of technique in adult analysis. *The Writings of Anna Freud*, 4: 377–406. New York: International Universities Press, 1968.

—— (1957) Foreword to M. Milner, *On Not Being Able to Paint*, pp. xiii–xv.

—— (1968) Acting out. *The Writings of Anna Freud*, 7: 94–109. New York: International Universities Press, 1971.

Freud, S. (1893–1895) Studies on hysteria. *Standard Edition*, 2. London: Hogarth Press, 1955.

—— (1900) The interpretation of dreams. *Standard Edition*, 4 and 5. London: Hogarth Press, 1953.

—— (1905) Jokes and their relation to the unconscious. *Standard Edition*, 8. London: Hogarth Press, 1960.

—— (1906) Psychoanalysis and the establishment of the facts in legal proceedings. *Standard Edition*, 9: 97–114. London: Hogarth Press, 1959.

—— (1910) Five lectures on psychoanalysis. *Standard Edition*, 11: 1–56. London: Hogarth Press, 1957.

—— (1912) Recommendations to physicians practising psycho-analysis. *Standard Edition*, 12: 109–120. London: Hogarth Press, 1958.

—— (1912) Recommendations to physicians practising psychoanalysis. London: Hogarth Press, 1958.

—— (1915) The unconscious. *Standard Edition*, 14: 159–215. London: Hogarth Press, 1957.

—— (1916–1917) Introductory lectures on psychoanalysis. *Standard Edition*, 15 and 16. London: Hogarth Press, 1961.

—— (1920) A note on the prehistory of the technique of analysis. *Standard Edition*, 18: 263–265. London: Hogarth Press, 1955.

—— (1921) Group psychology and the analysis of the ego. *Standard Edition*, 18: 67–143. London: Hogarth Press, 1955.

—— (1923) Remarks on the theory and practice of dream-interpretation. *Standard Edition*, 19: 107–121. London: Hogarth Press, 1961.

—— (1924) A short account of psychoanalysis. *Standard Edition*, 19: 189–209. London: Hogarth Press, 1961.

—— (1925a) Negation. *Standard Edition*, 19: 233–239. London: Hogarth Press, 1961.

—— (1925b) Die Verneinung. *Gesammelte Werke*, 14: 11–15. London: Imago, 1948.

—— (1925c) An autobiographical study. *Standard Edition*, 20: 1–74. London: Hogarth Press, 1959.

—— (1926a) Inhibitions, symptoms and anxiety. *Standard Edition*, 20: 75–175. London: Hogarth Press, 1959.

—— (1926b) The question of lay analysis. *Standard Edition*, 20: 177–258. London: Hogarth Press, 1959.

—— (1931) Letter to Stefan Zweig, no. 258. *Letters to Sigmund Freud*, ed. Ernst Freud and tr. T. and J. Stern. New York: Basic Books, 1960.

Friedman, D. (1967) Obsessive hypermnesia and free association as a transference resistance. *American Journal of Psychotherapy*, 21: 105–111.

Fromm, E. (1955) Remarks on the problem of free association. *Psychiatric Research Reports*, 2: 1–6.

Galinsky, M. and Pressman, M. (1963) Intellectualization and intellectual resistance. *Bulletin of the Philadelphia Association of Psychoanalysis*, 13: 153–172.

Gedo, J. and Goldberg, A. (1973) *Models of the Mind: A Psycho-analytic Theory*. Chicago: University of Chicago Press.

—— and Pollock, G. (eds.) (1976) *Freud: the Fusion of Science and Humanism*. New York: International Universities Press.

Gilbert, R. (1963) Body ego and creative imagination. *Journal of the American Psychoanalytic Association*, 11: 775–789.

Gill, M. (1967) The primary process. In: R. Holt (ed.) *Motives and Thought:*

Psychoanalytic Essays in Honor of David Rapaport. New York: International Universities Press, pp. 260–298.

Glover, E. (1955) *The Technique of Psychoanalysis*. New York: International Universities Press.

Gottschalk, L. (1975) The psychoanalytical study of hand–mouth approximations. In: L. Goldberger and V. Rosen (eds.) *Psychoanalysis and Contemporary Science*. New York: International Universities Press, pp. 269–291.

Green, A. (1974) Surface analysis, deep analysis (the role of the preconscious in psychoanalytical technique). *International Review of Psycho-Analysis*, 1: 415–423.

Greenacre, P. (1973), The primal scene and sense of reality. *Psychoanalytic Quarterly*, 42: 10–41.

Hartmann, H. (1927) *Die Grundlage der psychoanalyse*. Leipzig: Georg Thieme.

Heimann, P. (1975) Further observations on the analyst's cognitive process. Unpublished paper, delivered to the Canadian Psycho-analytic Society, Montreal.

Hendrick, I. (1966) *Facts and Theories of Psychoanalysis*. New York: Dell Publishers.

Holzman, P., Rousey, C. and Snyder, C. (1966) On listening to one's own voice: effects in psychophysiological responses and free associations. *Journal of Personal and Social Psychology*, 4: 432–441.

Jaffe, J. (1958) Communication networks in Freud's interview technique. *Psychiatric Quarterly*, 32: 456–473.

Jakobson, R. (1963) *Essais de linguistique générale*. Paris: Editions de Minuit.

Jones, E. (1953–1957) *The Life and Works of Sigmund Freud*, 3 vols. New York: Basic Books.

Kanzer, M. (1955) The communicative function of the dream. *International Journal of Psycho-Analysis*, 36: 260–266.

—— (1958) Image formation during free association. *Psychoanalytic Quarterly*, 27: 465–484.

—— (1961) Verbal and nonverbal aspects of free association. *Psychoanalytic Quarterly*, 30: 327–350.

—— (1972) Superego aspects of free association and the fundamental rule. *Journal of the American Psychoanalytic Association*, 20: 246–265.

Kelman, H. (1962) Freer associating: its phenomenology and inherent paradoxes. *American Journal of Psychoanalysis*, 22: 176–200.

Knapp, P. (1974) Segmentation and structure in psychoanalysis. *Journal of the American Psychoanalytic Association*, 22: 14–36.

—— (1975) Dimensions of free association: some clinical and experimental observation. Unpublished paper, delivered to the Canadian Psycho-analytic Society, Montreal.

Kris, E. (1952) *Psychoanalytic Explorations in Art*. New York: International Universities Press.

—— (1956) On some vicissitudes on insight in psycho-analysis. *International Journal of Psycho-Analysis*, 37: 445–455.

Kroth, J. (1970) The analytic couch and response to free association. *Psychotherapy: Theory, Research and Practice*, 7: 206–208.

Kubie, L. (1950) *Practical and Theoretical Aspects of Psychoanalysis*. New York: International Universities Press.

—— (1958) *Neurotic Distortion of the Creative Process*. New York: Noonday.

Lacan, J. (1966) *Ecrits*. Paris: Editions du Seuil.

Laforgue, R. (1936) Exceptions to the basic rule. *Psychoanalytic Quarterly*, 5: 369–374.

Lagache, D. (1964) La méthode psychoanalytique. In: ed. L. Michaux *et al.*, *Psychiatrie*. Paris: Vrin, pp. 1036–1066.

Lakoff, R. (1975) *Language and Woman's Place*. New York: Harper & Row.

Laplanche, J. and Pontalis, J. (1968) *Vocabulaire de la psychanalyse*. Paris: Presses Universitaires de France. 'Association,' pp. 36–38; 'Elaboration psychique,' pp. 130–131; 'Liaison,' pp. 221–224; 'Libre association,' pp. 228–229; 'Règle fondamentale,' pp. 398–400.

Leavy, S. (1973) Psychoanalytic interpretation. *The Psychoanalytic Study of the Child*. 73: 305–330.

Lewin, B. (1955) Dream psychology and the analytic situation. *Psychoanalytic Quarterly*, 24: 169–199.

—— (1954) Sleep Narcissistic Neurosis and the Analytic Situation. *Psychoanalytic Quarterly*, 23: 487–510.

—— (1970) The train ride: a study of one of Freud's figures of speech. *Psychoanalytic Quarterly*, 39: 71–89.

—— (1971) Metaphor, mind, and manikin. *Psychoanalytic Quarterly*, 40: 6–39.

Loewenstein, R. (1956) Some remarks on the role of speech in psychoanalytic technique. *International Journal of Psycho-Analysis*, 37: 460–468.

—— (1957) Some thoughts on interpretation in the theory and practice of psychoanalysis. *The Psychoanalytic Study of the Child*, 12: 137–150.

—— (1963) Some considerations on free association. *Journal of the American Psychoanalytic Association*, 11: 451–473.

Luborsky, L. (1964) A psychoanalytic research on momentary forgetting during free association. *Bulletin of the Philadelphia Association of Psychoanalysis*, 14: 119–137.

—— and Mintz, J. (1975) What sets off momentary forgetting during a psychoanalysis: investigations of symptom-onset conditions. In: L. Goldberger and V. Rosen (eds.), *Psychoanalysis and Contemporary Science*, vol. 3. New York: International Universities Press, pp. 233–268.

McConnell-Ginet, S. (1975) Our father-tongue: essays in linguistic politics. *Diacritics*, 5: 44–50.

Mahl, G. (1972) People talking when they can't hear their voices. In: A. Stegman and B. Pope (eds.) *Studies in Dyadic Communication*. New York: Pergamon Press, pp. 211–264.

Marmor, J. (1970) Limitations of free association. *American Medical Association Archives of General Psychiatry*, 22: 160–165.

Martin, P. (1964) Psychoanalytic aspects of that type of communication termed 'small talk,' *Journal of the American Psychoanalytic Association*, 12: 392–400.

Menninger, K. (1958) *Theory of Psychoanalytic Technique*. New York: Harper & Row.

Merloo, J. (1952) Free association, silence, and multiple function of speech. *Psychiatric Quarterly*, 26: 21–32.

—— (1959) Psychoanalysis as an experiment in communication. *Psychoanalysis and the Psychoanalytic Review*, 46: 75–89.

—— (1964) *Unobtrusive Communication: Essays in Linguistics*. Assen, Netherlands: Van Gorcum.

Milner, M. (1957) *On Not Being Able to Paint*. London: Heinemann, 2nd edition.

New Literary History (1975) Whole issue entitled 'On Narrative and Narratives.' Vol. 6, no. 2.

Okonoki, K. (1959) Studies on free association and analytic process. Abridged trans. of report on the 4th Ann. Gen. Meeting of Japan. Psychoanal. Ass. *Japan Journal of Psychoanalysis*, 6: 52–56.

Perelman, C. and Olbrechts-Tyteca, L. (1970) *The New Rhetoric*. South Bend, Indiana: Notre Dame University Press.

Pressman, M. (1961) On the analytic situation: the analyst is silent. *Bulletin of the Philadelphia Association of Psycho-analysis*, 2: 168–182.

Rado, S. (1958) Psychotherapy: a problem of controlled communication. In: P. Hoch and J. Zubin (eds.), *Psychopathology of Communication*. New York: Grune & Stratton, pp. 214–226.

Rapaport, D. (1967) *The Collected Papers of David Rapaport*, ed. M. Gill. New York: International Universities Press.

—— (1974) *The History of the Concept of Association of Ideas*. New York: International Universities Press.

Reider, N. (1972) Metaphor as interpretation. *International Journal of Psycho-Analysis*, 53: 463–469.

Reyner, J. and Smeltzer, W. (1968) Uncovering properties of visual imagery and verbal association: a comparative study. *Journal of Abnormal Psychology*, 73: 218–222.

Reynes, R. (1975) Variations in regressive imagery during psychoanalysis. Unpublished paper, delivered at the Fall Meeting of the American

Psychoanalytic Association, New York.

Rosen, V. (1960) Some aspects of the role of the imagination in the analytic process. *Journal of the American Psychoanalytic Association*, 8: 229–251.

—— (1967) Disorders of communication in psychoanalysis. *Journal of the American Psychoanalytic Association*, 15: 467–490.

Rosner, S. (1973) On the Nature of Free Association. *Journal of the American Psychoanalytic Association*, 21: 558–575.

Rubenstein, B. (1972) On metaphor and related phenomena. In: *Psychoanalysis and Contemporary Science*, vol. 1, ed. R. Holt and E. Peterfreund. New York: Macmillan, pp. 77–108.

Ruesch, J. (1952) The therapeutic process: IV. The therapeutic process from the point of view of communication theory. *American Journal of Orthopsychiatry*, 22: 690–700.

—— (1957) *Disturbed Communication*. New York: Norton.

Rycroft, C. (1956) The nature and function of the analyst's communication to the patient. *International Journal of Psycho-Analysis*, 37: 469–472.

—— (1958) An enquiry into the function of words in the psychoanalytical situation. *International Journal of Psycho-Analysis*, 39: 408–415.

—— (1968) *A Critical Dictionary of Psychoanalysis*. New York: Basic Books.

Sandler, A. (1975) Comments on the significance of Piaget's work for psycho-analysis. *International Review of Psycho-Analysis*, 2: 365–378.

Schafer, R. (1976) *A New Language for Psychoanalysis*. New Haven: Yale University Press.

—— (1978) *Language and Insight*, New Haven: Yale University Press.

Schilder, P. (1942) The body image in dreams. *Psycho-analytic Quarterly*, 29: 113–126.

Schnier, J. (1960) Free association and ego function in creativity: a study of content and form in art. *American Imago*, 17: 61–74.

Scholes, R. (1974) *Structuralism in Literature*. New Haven: Yale University Press.

Seidenberg, H. (1971) Panel report: The basic rule: free association—a reconsideration. *Journal of American Psychoanalytic Association*, 19: 98–109.

Sempé, J. (1968) Du discours associatif dans les rapports avec la toute-puissance de la pensée au silence et à la parole de l'analyste comme effets de la toute-puissance. *Revue Française de Psychanalyse*, 32: 1041–1048.

Shands, H. (1960) *Thinking and Psychotherapy: An Inquiry into the Process of Communication*. Cambridge, Mass.: Harvard University Press.

Sharpe, E. (1950) *Collected Papers on Psycho-Analysis*, ed. M. Brierley, London: Hogarth Press.

Sheiner, S. (1967) Free association: compiled and edited from lectures on psychoanalytic technique given by Karen Horney. *American Journal of Psychoanalysis*, 27: 200–208.

Southwood, H. (1974) The communicative relationship. *International Journal of Psycho-Analysis*, 55: 417–423.

Spencer, J. (1965) A note on the 'steady monologuy of the interiors.' *Review of English Literature*, 6: 32–41.

Speigel, L. (1975) The functions of free association in psychoanalysis: their relation to technique and theory. *International Review of Psycho-Analysis*, 2: 379–388.

Spitz, R. (1956) Transference: the analytic setting and its prototype. *International Journal of Psycho-Analysis*, 37: 380–385.

Sterba, R. (1934) The fate of the ego in psycho-analytic therapy. *International Journal of Psycho-Analysis*, 15: 117–126.

Stern, H. (1966) The truth as resistance to free association. *Psycho-analytic Review*, 53: 642–646.

Strachey, J. (1966) Notes on some technical terms whose translation calls for comment. Standard Edition, 1: xxiii–xxvi. London: Hogarth Press.

Suppes, P. and Warren, H. (1975) On the generation and identification of defence mechanisms. *International Journal of Psycho-Analysis*, 56: 405–414.

Székely, L. (1962) Symposium: the psycho-analytic study of thinking: meaning, meaning schemata and body schemata in thought. *International Journal of Psycho-Analysis*, 43: 297–305.

Trosman, H. (1969) The cryptomnesic fragment in the discovery of free association. *Journal of the American Psychoanalytic Association*, 17: 489–510.

Van der Heide, C. (1961) Blank silence and the dream screen. *Journal of the American Psycho-analytic Association*, 9: 85–90.

Viderman, S. (1972) Comme en miroir, obscurément . . . *Nouvelle Revue de Psychanalyse*, 5: 131–152.

—— (1974) Interpretation in the analytical space. *International Review of Psycho-Analysis*, 1: 467–480.

Voth, H. (1970) The analysis of metaphor. *Journal of the American Psycho-analytic Association*, 18: 599–621.

Weigert, E. (1955) Special problems in connection with the termination of training analyses. *Journal of the American Psychoanalytic Association*, 3: 630–640.

Whitehead, C. (1975) Additional aspects of the Freudian-Kleinian controversey: towards a 'psychoanalysis' of psychoanalysis. *International Journal of Psycho-Analysis*, 56: 383–396.

Winck, C. (1962) Thoughts and feelings of the general population as experienced in free association typing. *American Imago*, 19: 67–84.

Zetzel, E. and Meissner, W. (1973) *Basic Concepts of Psychoanalytic Psychiatry*. New York: Basic Books.

Zilboorg, G. (1952) Precursors of Freud in free association: some sidelights on free association. *International Journal of Psycho-Analysis*, 33: 489–495.

3

The place of psychoanalytical treatment in the history of discourse *

No doubt 'in the beginning was the deed' [Goethe's *Faust*] and the word came later [The question of lay analysis, *S.E.* 20: 188].

Nothing takes place in a psychoanalytic treatment but an interchange of words between the patient and the analyst. . . . Words were originally magic and to this day words have obtained much of their ancient magical power. By words one person can make another blissfully happy or drive him to despair, by words the teacher conveys his knowledge to his pupils, by words the orator carries his audience with him and determines their judgements and decisions [Introductory lectures, *S.E.* 15: 17].

Not only is psychoanalysis unique among therapies but it also stands apart as a speech event in the history of discourse. In this chapter I shall examine and situate the discourse in psychoanalytical therapy within the four modes of discourse: the expressive, the aesthetic, the rhetorical, and the referential. I shall define the end as well as the surface, formal elements of each discourse and then trace its appearance in the psycho-analytical setting. In a global sense I believe that my undertaking is original—Loewenstein (1956) briefly touched on the subject in part of an article; Entralgo (1970) devotes his chief attention to certain historical connections between rhetoric and psychotherapy at large; there are also provocative ideas by Eng (1923), Simon (1972, 1973a and b), and Mortimer Adler (1927) about rhetoric, the Platonic Dialogues, and modern psychotherapy. In terms of discourse theory, I am greatly indebted to that most extraordinary work, James Kinneavy's *The Theory of Discourse* (1971, esp. pp. 58–68, 218–226, 393 ff.).[1]

I shall be quite explicit at the outset: neither analysts nor historians of ideas nor literary theorists have been aware of the outstanding novelty of psychoanalysis in the history of world discourse, of whatever has been spoken, heard, written or read. Nowhere previous to psychoanalysis was there a setting or literary genre in which each of the four kinds of discourse figured prominently. And more than that, each of these discourses acquires new traits in psychoanalysis. And more than that again, there is a dynamic interaction between these four discourses in psychoanalytic treatment and they constitute one of the verifications of the success of the treatment. My enterprise in the text that follows will be to elaborate and justify these vast claims for psychoanalysis.

As a preliminary step, I shall orient my general subject within the framework of communication. In a deep sense, communication is a misnomer of a quixotic sort, for it must always be understood in terms of its opposite, counter- or miscommunication. Miscommunication exists on three levels, and the first two of them have been affected by psychoanalysis in a spectacular way:

1. *The intrapersonal.* The Freudian typology of the id, ego and superego is also a communication system in which, for example, the mechanisms of displacement and condensation function as agents of counter-communication and defence, which prevent unconscious material from becoming directly conscious. Such a model is adaptable to the semiology of meaning but radically opposed to the unfortunately named semiology of communication, which insists on a voluntary act to communicate.[2]

2. *The interpersonal.* One of the most powerful statements that I have found in the Freudian canon serves to divest interpersonal communication: '*Every* single association, *every* act of the person under treatment must reckon with the resistance and represents a *compromise* between the forces that are striving towards recovery and the opposing ones which I have described' (*S.E.* 12: 103; italics mine). Or as Richelieu once declared, we use words to hide our thoughts. The very nature of language, furthermore, is partially counter-communicative, a phenomenon summed up in the Bergsonian insight that language increases as well as decreases awareness. We may readily recall the modern educative interest in body expression as an effort to neutralize the counter-communicative factor inherent in group verbalization.

3. *The intercultural level.* Propaganda agencies are a dramatic example of selective information and control of receptor response. In its own way, Francis Bacon's declaration three and a half centuries

ago in his *De Dignitate et Augmentis Scientiarum* (1623) has contemporary relevance as a gloss on the incessant indoctrination organized by political regimes:

> In that tale of Orpheus are finely described the nature and morals of men, who are carried away by various uncontrolled desires of money, lust and revenge. However, as long as men lend their ears to religious, legal and academic precepts and counsels eloquently and delicately modulated in books, sermons and public discourses—just as long as men shall honor peace and society. *But if these media be silent* or if sedition and tumult disrupt them, all things will dissolve and relapse into anarchy and confusion [Italics mine].[3]

Communication and counter-communication are divided into verbal and non-verbal categories. With specific reference to the verbal, I shall have recourse to the well-known communication triangle:

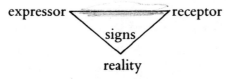

In any use of language there is one who expresses (expressor), one who receives (receptor), the sign-message itself, and the 'reality' to which it refers. The four types of discourse are definable with respect to the focus directed onto any one component of the communication triangle. Right away, it is important to bear in mind that the four discourses differ by their emphasis: they overlap and are not mutually exclusive. Referential discourse obviously involves a receptor and to that extent is rhetorical, yet its essential feature is its stress on the referent. And that holds true for referential discourse in its two varieties—the scientific, characterized by its closed nature, and the open-ended dialectic. Rhetoric, the art of persuasion, emphasizes the receptor. Nevertheless argumentation to some degree pervades all discourse; everything we say, Aristotle has pointed out, is more or less argumentative. Expressive discourse focuses on the expressor; and aesthetic discourse, on the structure of signs worthy of appreciation and contemplation in itself.

How, then, do these discourses appear in the psychoanalytical cure? At this point, I shall sketch out a brief answer, which will be useful as a general orientation for my subsequent exposition. The analyst's speech is referential discourse of its dialectical kind; closed scientific discourse with its much higher degree of certitude is, as explicit verbalization, rather alien to the analytical setting. The patient's discourse is harder to place. To make the broadest of generalizations, his associations start out as an admixture of the rhetorical and the expressive. As the analysis proceeds, on one hand he tends to relinquish a rhetorical stance and accede to the analyst's dialectic, and on the other hand the expressive nature of his associations take on certain aspects of aesthetic discourse; he becomes a poet. I find so pertinent to psychoanalysis the ideal quality that John Keats required of a poet: ' . . . at once it struck me what quality went to form a Man of Achievement especially in Literature and which Shakespeare possessed so enormously—I mean Negative Capability, that is when man is capable of being in uncertainties, Mysteries, doubts, without any irritable reaching after fact and reason.'[4] Simplified schematically, the progress of a patient's associations may be indicated this way:

Progress in the analysis: dialectical, expressive and aesthetic discourse

Beginning of the analysis: rhetorical and expressive discourse.[5]

In the pages that follow, I shall explore each of the modes of discourse, and in each instance trace its specific relationship to psychoanalysis. Because of the traditional and critical questions particular to each discourse and its application to the analytic setting, my treatments will noticeably vary in length. Expressive and aesthetic discourse, as a matter of fact, are combined in the first section. Due to its long intimate history with psychotherapy and its intrinsic complexity, rhetoric has a section to itself. In Section III, I try to elucidate dialectical discourse, which is so often a vague woolly notion, and then I use that elucidation toward a better historical and inherent understanding of analytical intervention.

I. Expressive and aesthetic discourse

Expressive discourse stands apart from other discourses insofar as it has no long critical tradition behind it. Although expressive discourse is genetically prior to all other uses of language, comparatively less has been written on it. With affect as a basic though not exclusive component, with its focusing on the expressor, expressive discourse is the least organized of all, as shown through its appearance in autobiographies, journals, diaries, the effusion in encounter groups, and ordinary conversation. Relative to the other discourses, expressive discourse gives prominence to the first person pronoun *I*. Even if ideally this style is distinctively individual, conforming to Buffon's maxim 'The style is the man,' yet its trademarks are repetitiveness, very emotionally charged words, a tendency to superlatives, ambiguity, transforming things into persons (personification), and making persons into things. Relevant also to this topic is the question of sound symbolism, the attribution of psychological meaning to phonemes. From a psychoanalytical perspective, the most interesting research in this domain has been done by the phonostylistician Ivan Fónagy (1970–1971), professor at the University of Paris and author of many psychoanalytical interpretations of articulation. For Fónagy, each person has an individual phonological style that can both echo and liberate various zonal tensions.

Another feature of expressive speech is 'associative rhythm,' which is one of the three primary rhythms of verbal expression (Frye, 1963, esp. pp. 18–29). First there is verse, the rhythm of a regularly repeated pattern of accent or meter; verse is closely related to song and dance as well as to a child's speech, replete with chanting and singing. Secondly there is the rhythm of prose, whose unit is the sentence; reflecting directed thinking, prose is not simply ordinary speech but ordinary speech at its best behavior. Whereas prose is governed by the syntactical relation of the subject and predicate, verse is governed by recurrent rhythm and sound, and being a more simple and more primitive type, verse is historically earlier than prose. And lastly there is associative rhythm, that of ordinary speech, which is more prolix than prose and whose unit is the short phrase revolving around a central word and largely wanting in syntax. Frye (1963) suggestively continues:

> Traditionally, the associative rhythm has been used in tragedy to represent insanity, as in some speeches in *King Lear*, and in comedy to represent the speech of the uneducated or the mentally confused. Mrs. Quickly and Juliet's nurse are Shakespearean examples. But it is only within the last century or so, with the rise of mimetic fiction, that literature has made any systematic effort to explore the rhythms of ordinary or of inner speech. . . . We notice that associative speakers have a great aversion to the definiteness and full close of the sentence: if they produce a sentence by accident, they will add unnecessary words to the end as an apology for having uttered it, like [pp. 23, 29].

Further clarification of expressive discourse comes from William Howarth's solid study, 'Some Principles of Autobiography' (1974).

61

Though to all appearances autobiography should be a bona fide example of expressive discourse, such in fact was not always historically the case. As a genre, autobiography had been utilized primarily for aesthetic or rhetorical ends. Then with Rousseau (1712–1778) autobiography was enlisted in the service of expressive discourse. Authors in this category—Rousseau, Thoreau, Whitman, Yeats, Agee—expose their perplexity and frequently change motive, purpose and reference in the course of their writing.

Due to the recollection of lost memories, dramatic regression, overdetermined abreaction, and the like, expressive discourse acquires new dimensions in psychoanalysis. And yet, expressive discourse does not constitute all of free association. However much expressive discourse and its 'associative rhythms' overlap free association, there remains the crucial area of difference. In quintessential expressive discourse, there is no driving effort to win acceptance from the audience.[6] Such insouciance must contend with the transference in the analytical setting and its demanding constraints. No wonder, then, as Kubie (1950, p. 47) wrote: 'The most spontaneous of all forms of thinking, which in solitude is also the easiest, proves in the analytical situation, to be the most difficult.' Amplified by positive transference, the desire to gain the analyst's approval incites the patient constantly to shift from self-expression and self-exposure to rhetorical manoeuvres in all its varieties: silence, defensive logic, hesitation, rambling associations . . .

Although aesthetic discourse may be expressive and even tendentious (see Booth's *The Rhetoric of Fiction*, 1961), it is unique among discourses for the emphasis on its own structure as worthy of appreciation. Now of the many kinds of aesthetic discourse, poetry is the one usually singled out as relating to dreams and free association. In English we unfortunately do not realize the close connection between condensation and poetry, which in German are *Verdichtung* and *Dichtung* respectively. The obvious carry-over to psychoanalysis is that free association is a discourse 'in which multiple meanings appear more clearly and which is closer to poetry than to scientific language' (Loewenstein, in Seidenberg, 1971, p. 109). Collaterally, one of the institutional obstacles in psychoanalysis is that it requires of the therapist a trait that cannot be taken for granted—a way of thinking in symbols which is innate in a poet and 'carefully avoided in scientific thought' (Jung, 1906, p. 289).

A more specific entrance into our topic is by way of an observation of the eminent linguist Emile Benveniste: a veritable inventory of stylistic figures is present in a Freudian interpretation of dreams (1956, p. 15). It was left for Roman Jakobson (1960) to note that two of those figures, metaphor (based on similarity) and metonymy (based on contiguity), play a very important role in dreams and the most important role of being principally constitutive of all sign systems whether verbal or nonverbal. In a further step, Lacan (1966) in his famous essay 'L'instance de la lettre dans l'inconscient' equated metaphor with condensation, and metonymy with displacement. Jakobson's seminal thought was also developed by Rosen (1967). Although Jakobson posited metaphor and metonymy as the two fundamental linguistic operations, he noted that figures of similarity were dominant in lyric poetry while figures of contiguity are inherent to epic verse. Rosen observed that most patients free-associate with either a preponderantly lyric style or epic style. There may even be a preponderance of one style accompanied by a disorder in the other. For instance, the patient with a lyric style may actually have a contiguity deficiency indicated by problems with narrative sequences, which are based on spatial and temporal contiguity (Jakobson, 1960, pp. 476, 478).

Another element linking poetry and free association is sound. It is essential to bear in mind that the operational principle governing the paradigmatic or vertical axis of language, as explained by Saussure (1916), is lexical substitution which occurs either through meaning (synonymous or antonymous) *or* sound. As a principle of substitution, the role of sound varies, depending on the discourse. Poetry itself may be defined as a structure in which sound has a value roughly coordinate to that of meaning (LaDrière, 1948). The use of sound is poetically evident in rhythm, in the many kinds of full and imperfect or slant rhymes, in the repetition of the same consonant (alliteration) or vowel (assonance), in the harmony of prefixes (*re-, im-*) and suffixes (*-ity, -tion*) and so on. In psychoanalytical literature there is comparatively little attention paid to sound, in spite of Jones's stand that it is a major feature of free associations in general (1913, pp. 208–209, 216). In the analytical situation one should naturally expect a linguistic regression alongside the psychic one—hence a pre-lexical, phonological regression, whose extreme point is clang association, in which sound is *the* main linking factor. Perhaps it is sound that is the defining constituent of the nonsense discourse described by Winnicott (1971, pp. 53–64) as needed by some patients to be accepted on its own right, thereby requiring a special reaction of creative play on the analyst's part.

We all have had occasion to be amazed at the extraordinary dramatic structure of free association—the distribution and reappearance of elements, suspense, climax and surprise. Our response of wonderment finds a good ally in the portrayal of the unconscious by the French literary critic Charles Maurron: 'Sous une église romane on n'est pas étonné de trouver une crypte ayant une valeur architecturale.' This portrayal is more apt than Kenneth Burke's account that psychoanalysis makes one look upon literature as an *ecclesia super cloacam,* a church above the cloaca (both critics cited by Mehlman [1970, p. 374]). Though there may be sheer beauty and intricacy of unconscious material as it rises to the surface, yet it is precisely that surface that constitutes a prime difference between aesthetic discourse and the dream. In the dream, of course, repressed ideas bypass the censor by using neutral or indifferent material for disguises, with the all-important consequence that there may be ideational connections in the dream-content that did not exist in the dream-thoughts (*S.E.* 5: 344). Such preconscious manifestations and day residues as thinking ahead and framing solutions also, when in dreams, testify to the discrepancy between dream-contents and dream-thoughts (*S.E.* 5: 580 fn.). Freud's conclusion is unambiguous: dream-contents are 'of no importance,' only 'dream-thoughts matter' (*S.E.* 5: 517).[7] In contrast to dreams, poetic discourse accords a supreme value to the surface text. The writer's experience is to destroy the arbitrariness which exists between the sign's components, the signified and the signifier. The post endeavors to banish the neutral and indifferent, to recreate language, to establish a necessary, motivated bind between the signified and the signifier.[8]

Whatever congruity occurs between aesthetic discourse and free association, there remains a difference, a difference which is crucial. Aesthetic structure is autotelic, self-purposive, existing as an end in itself, as an object of beauty. This is the writer's compensation for the anguish of his self-exposure, his sublimation, his regression. The analytical patient does not have this compensation. There is no relief that his associations, so fleeting and transitory, may be immortally enshrined on account of their admirable structure. For the patient, however, there is the transference, which is both a relief and a despair. It comes as no surprise that he is continually inclined to flee from the painful levels of free association to take refuge in rhetorical discourse.

II. Rhetorical discourse

It would be hard to exaggerate the historical and intrinsic significance of rhetoric for psychoanalysis. Aristotle's *Rhetoric* is the classic in its field and remains unsurpassed as a single work. Owing to the second of its three books, it also has the distinction of being the first major

64

psychological treatise in the West. As Aristotle defined it, rhetoric is the art of finding all the best available means of persuading or convincing an audience; the art is a conscious, active enterprise. The rhetoric of the analytic patient, however, assumes a new nature, for it is a conscious as well as unconscious effort to 'bribe' and 'manipulate' the analyst, to flatter him through the rearrangement of associations into a more pleasant and acceptable form (see Kubie, 1950; Weigert, 1955). Rhetoric should be part of an analyst's education (Lacan, 1966, p. 288), for it will further equip him to understand the patient's rhetorical strategy:

> C'est ainsi en effet que procède le discours pour *convaincre*, mot qui implique la stratégie dans le procès de l'accord. . . . Ce procès s'accomplit dans la mauvaise foi du sujet, gouvernant son discours entre la tromperie, l'ambigüité et l'erreur. Mais cette lutte pour assurer une paix si précaire n'offrirait pas le champs le plus commun de l'intersubjectivité, si l'homme n'était déjà tout entier *per-suadé* par la parole, ce qui veut dire qu'il s'y complaît de part en part [italics mine, p. 352].

By way of a preface to the pertinent complexities of rhetoric, I shall dwell for some time on its imposing place in history both as a force in itself and as the handmaid of psychotherapy from the beginning. In a long germinal essay Roland Barthes has carefully shown us the impressive sovereignty of rhetoric. With grammar excepted, rhetoric was the only system by which Western society recognized language. Rhetoric is no less than a gargantuan historical phenomenon, a veritable empire that by virtue of its dimensions and endurance has been vaster than any political empire. It has reigned in the Occident from the time of Hellenic Greece up to the present. It has witnessed the birth and disappearance of the Athenian democracy, Egyptian royalties, the Roman Republic, the Roman Empire, the great invasions, feudalism, the Renaissance monarchies, the French Revolution, and so on. Barthes outlined six ways in which rhetoric has functioned during its historical survival: as an art of persuasion; as institutionalized instruction of capital importance; as a proto-science or metalanguage; as a moral code on word usage; as a ludic practice turned against its institutionalized self; and as a social practice and privileged technique which assured the ruling classes of the ownership of the word, since historically one usually paid in order to master rhetoric (Barthes, 1970, pp. 173–174). To this impressive list we must add the essential role of rhetoric in the evolution of psychotherapy. As we are psychoanalytical practitioners who are interested in retrospection, ontogeny and phylogeny, we cannot afford to overlook the fact that the Greek rhetorical tradition anticipated psycho-analysis as a verbal therapy; the somatically oriented Hippocratic medicine did not anticipate psychoanalysis. The point is worth explaining.

The types of persuasive, therapeutic words found in the Homeric epics (9th? 8th c. B.C.?) include the *epôdê* or magical charm and the *thelktêrion* or persuasive and strengthening conversation with the patient.[9] Centuries later, Empedocles (*ca.* 490–430), both a poet and physician, was reputed for his power of verbal seduction and his cures by *epôdê*. Significantly enough, Empedocles was the teacher of Gorgias, the first great figure in the history of rhetoric. During the later decades of the fifth century, the Sophist doctor Antiphon attempted to relieve both physical and mental illness by a verbal persuasion. The patient was supposedly cured upon being told the causes of his malady.

In the fourth century of Hellenic Greece verbotherapy reached its zenith, and to Plato go the laurels as the inventor of the first rigorous technique. He concentrated on the *epôdê* but purified it of any magical element. This rationalized *epôdê* held a prominent place in the Platonic concept of health, according to which the body was ideally a responsive instrument to the sound psychological and moral order of the individual. Consequently, in Plato's eponymous dialogue, Charmides attempted to harmonize persuasion and belief[10] and to that end he had to trust and yield himself (*parechein*) to the physician Socrates. Aristotle (384–322 B.C.) took a further step. If Plato's conception of rhetoric was moral, Aristotle's was radically non-moral. Secondly, Aristotle's openness to emotional appeal differs from Plato's stance that limited persuasion to rational appeal and hence was inimical to poets who were emotionally provoking.

In any event, many fourth-century Greek physicians were deeply affected by the Hippocratic writings which, however, allowing for some vague unspecified psychotherapy, emphasized the somatic side of medicine. They practiced the 'muta ars' or mute art as Vergil subsequently called it. In the main, these doctors purportedly accepted Plato's proposed split in the *Phaedrus*: medicine should be assigned the task of curing the body, and rhetoric the psyche or soul. The *Corpus Hippocraticum* in turn influenced Galen (*ca.* 130–200 A.D.), whose selected works[11] determined university medical studies in Europe throughout the Middle Ages and the Renaissance. Entralgo goes so far as to maintain that 'The incapacity of Western medicine for verbal psychotherapy until a few decades ago depended ultimately on that great achievement and that great limitation of Hippocratic medicine' (p. 170).[12]

66

Strictly by virtue of his careful tracing of the patient's persuasive strategies, Freud figures as a landmark in the exploration of the rhetorical function in psychotherapy. But whether he had a clear, formal notion of a full-bodied rhetoric is open to speculation. He did promote the more general category of literary criticism as desired training for a psychoanalyst (*S.E.* 20: 246) and his work testifies to a well-known scrutiny of literature. The kind of evidence that exists for Marx—a youthful translation of Aristotle's *Rhetoric*—is missing in our knowledge of Freud. It would indeed require volumes of painstaking erudition to track down the appearances of classical rhetoric in the impressive upsurge of Romantic psychiatry and philosophy, including that great professor of classical philology and rhetoric, Friedrich Nietzsche. However diffused was the knowledge of rhetoric, Freud surely acquired some of it by osmosis.

The popular modern reduction of rhetoric to style is far from the richness of a classical and more or less Aristotelean model of rhetoric. The latter model classifies into five parts:

1. The invention or finding of arguments:
   (a) The logical argument, whose target is the reasonability of the message.
   (b) The ethical argument, which displays the character of the speaker.
   (c) The pathetical argument, which appeals to the emotions of the audience.
2. The arrangement or order in the speech.
3. Style.
4. Memory.
5. Delivery:
   (a) Voice.
   (b) Gesture.

This schema, apparently so simple, involves many complexities, and so I shall be quite selective in my explanation. First of all, we notice that classical argument consists of ethical, pathetic as well as logical means, whereas in modern parlance argument commonly designates the speaker's arsenal of logical means. The use of short-circuited reasoning and the replacement of firm induction by isolated example results in an *apparent* rather than solid reasonability of rhetorical logical argument and makes it less secure than the argumentation in referential discourse. Accordingly the ethical and pathetic arguments in rhetoric help bear the burden issuing from a weak logic. Aristotle goes so far as to say that the ethical argument or character of the speaker is the most powerful element in all of rhetoric, an insight borne out by the contemporary rhetorical industry of advertising which annually pours millions of dollars into 'image-making.' A basic distinction exists, however, between the classical orator who uses ethical argument to influence a known audience and the analytical patient who through the transference is creating an audience with an illusory identity.

The tripartite structure of rhetorical argumentation is actually quite a refined one, and in the cases of ethical and pathetical argument, involves further tripartite structures:

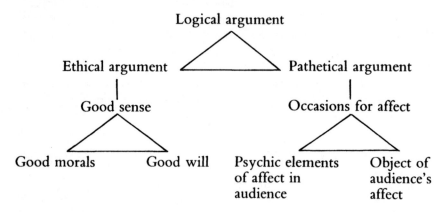

Aristotle required that if a speaker wants to elicit a certain emotion in the audience, he should bear six things in mind. To evoke fear, for example, the orator should know the psychic traits of people when fearful, the occasions that provoke that fear, and the kinds of people whom they will fear; concomitantly the orator must be aware of the opposite to the feeling of fear—confidence or assurance—and its characteristics, the occasions eliciting it, and the kinds of persons with whom it is felt. Although pathetical argument in the Aristotelean sense is a strictly conscious manipulation of the audience, it can at least serve as a contrastive model to describe the patient's persuasive discourse in the analytical situation.

I'll add just a few more comments about the other parts of rhetoric. The predetermined formal order of classical discourse is naturally alien to primary process, which ideally should determine free association. We readily see too the different value that style assumes in analysis. In more ways than one, there is in psycho-analysis a lexical 'matrix' by which words have a life which pales their momentary thinness in Aristotelean rhetoric. At any rate, it is an important factor to note that whether in an oration or therapy, the use of figurative language such as metaphor has always a rhetorical coloring. No referential discourse can ever use a metaphor and escape a rhetorical bias, for it is in the nature of metaphor to enhance or depreciate its subject. Analytically speaking, classical rhetoric has little to say of intrinsic interest about memory, although the ancient art of mnemo-technics is a fascinating story (see Yates, 1966). If memory in classical rhetoric is but an instrument, it is of course instrument and subject in analysis. Lastly, there is the obvious difference of delivery in that the rhetorician-patient receives no visual feedback from his gestural performance.

Within a novel therapeutic context, the scope of classical rhetoric as conscious discourse has been widened many times over. In effect, the analyst is often exposing as transferential and rhetorical what the patient thinks is sheerly referential or expressive discourse on his own part. And so Freud (1905) states:

> When a patient brings forward a sound and incontestable train of argument during psychoanalytic treatment, the physician is liable to feel a moment's embarrassment . . . But it soon becomes evident that the patient is using thoughts of this kind, which the analysis cannot attack, for the purpose of cloaking others which are anxious to escape from criticism and from consciousness. A string of reproaches against other people leads one to suspect the existence of a string of self-reproaches with the same content [*S.E.* 7: 35].

To a large degree the transference relationship entails a patient trying to persuade an audience that he himself has created. By contrast the therapeutic alliance, a cooperative effort with a real audience, is eminently dialectical.

III. Dialectical discourse

Like the other discourses, dialectical discourse is present, yet modified in the psychoanalytical situation. The analyst's discourse fits in the tradition of dialectical art and can be clarified by it to some extent. To be sure, however, any therapeutic use of language—choice of the 'right' meaning, diction, tone, stress, pitch—issues from a groping discipline, for as yet 'we do not possess even the beginnings of a technology of therapeutic talk' (Rado, 1958, p. 217). The journey from a groping discipline to a refined one is long, and longer again, if at all possible in our case, would be the journey to a technology of dialectics.

There were personal as well as professional reasons that led Freud to be so concerned with dialectical argumentation and psychotherapy. While customarily resisting influence from others (Jones, 1955, 2: 428–429), he also 'had little desire to influence his fellow men. He offered them something of value, but without any wish to force it on them. He disliked debates or even public scientific discussions, the object of which he knew was mainly controversial' (1951, 1: 31; see also 1: 257). Like Darwin, he preferred exposition rather than controversy; and as a response to opponents, he often counseled his militant followers simply to furnish more evidence (1: 120–121, 426; 2: 124). His delivery was never oratorical, for he favored an intimate conversational approach to the audience and gathered it close to him (1: 341–342). He had faith that the dialectical process could win out over instinctual resistances:

> Since men are so little accessible to reasonable arguments and are so entirely governed by instinctual wishes, why should one set out to deprive them of an instinctual satisfaction and replace it by reasonable arguments? It is true that men are like this; but have you asked yourself whether they *must* be like this, whether their innermost nature necessitates it? [*S.E.* 21: 47].

Rejecting hypnotism as a clinical technique and opting for a framework of maximum liberty, Freud did not so much persuade a patient as assist him in a dynamic self-persuasion. In effect, Freud saw a correlation between dialectical affectiveness and the sum of derivatives worked through. This correlation underlies Freud's (1909) justification of an interpretation which he gave to the Rat Man:

> It is never the aim of discussions like this to create conviction. They are only intended to bring the repressed complexes into consciousness, to set the conflict going in the field of conscious mental activity, and to facilitate the emergence of fresh material from the unconscious. A sense of conviction is only attained after the patient has himself worked over the reclaimed material, and so long as he is not fully convinced the material must be considered as unexhausted [*S.E.* 10: 181 fn.].

So much was Freud (1915–17) concerned with the ramifications of conviction that he began with that topic in each of the two years when he presented his *Introductory Lectures on Psychoanalysis* (Lectures One and Sixteen; see esp. *S.E.* 15: pp. 15–19, 16: 243–245).

At this point, several questions come to the fore: Just what is dialectical discourse and how does it differ from the referential? How does dialectical argumentation differ from rhetorical argumentation? We must answer these questions and spell out the characteristics of dialectical discourse before we can adequately grasp its meaningfulness to psychoanalysis.

Philosophically, dialectic has been habitually used in two senses: as a principle governing the historical process, as with Hegel and Marx, and as a certain kind of discourse. Dialectical discourse itself has two main activities, refutation and apparent demonstration: '. . . la dialectique réfute réellement . . . mais elle ne démontre qu'en apparence . . . La dialectique est donc légitime dans ce qu'elle nie, éristique dans ce qu'elle affirme' (Aubenque, 1962, p. 286 fn.). Historically, focus shifted from the more superficial to the more profound aspect of dialectic, from the overcoming of an opponent in debate (eristics) to the tentative exploration of truth.[13] With remarkable clarity and precision Otto Bird (1955) has outlined the four notes of this dialectic:

1. It is propositional, and therefore not factual or intentional as in Hegelian or Marxist dialectic. Whereas science is about things, dialectic is about statements concerning things.
2. It is interrogative. Science is directed to answers, and in that discipline, questions serve to be answered. By contrast, dialectic is directed to questions, and answers merely serve as occasions for other questions. Concordant with its interest in things, science orients its questions towards things, for example, what is the definition of man? Dialectical questions, on the other hand, are about propositions as, whether such and such is the definition of man, and then the dialectician answers on both sides.
3. It is controversial, but not in an eristical or rhetorical way. If rhetoric aims at overcoming the opposition, dialectic aims at the establishing of opposition and then proceeding through it.
4. It is interminable, which is to say, dialectic is interrogative, not demonstrative. On this fourth point mentioned by Bird, I have found Mortimer Adler's seminal book *Dialectic* (1927) very instructive (esp. pp. 34, 86, 101–107). Various instances that may contain some dialectical process—conversation, argument, intellectual deliberation—are never pure or perfect, for 'Infinite leisure would be required for the perfection of dialectic; and that could not be asked even of those who call themselves philosophers.' And yet, due to the variable meanings of words, dialectics is rendered possible, if not inevitable, in human discourse, and fulfils the double function of linguistically clarifying word usage and logically resolving difficulties. Hence the dialectical enterprise

71

is repeatedly involved in analysis and definition, that definition in turn being subject to further analysis, redefinition, and so on.

Summarily, whereas science is empirical and really demonstrative, dialectic is confined to the area of discourse and not to the entities outside it. Investigating rather than demonstrating the truth, dialectic aims at correct reasoning, logical inferences and conclusions, and explores rather than finalizes the truth. Guided by an element of play,[14] dialectics impartially gathers together opposite new outlooks, points out their harmony or disharmony, and entertains, but not absolutely asserts, that several positions may be equally valid, or then again—contrary to conclusive scientific demonstration—it may show two sides of an argument and indicate that no side is conclusive, although one is probable. Insisting that any conclusion is only tentative and gives rise to other questions and hypotheses with their presuppositions and consequences, dialectics is evidently invaluable for interdisciplinary ventures, beset with the task of reconciling discordant propositions.

The play of cognition is uppermost in the dialectical process. It is this play that enables the mind to be impartial, to be free from the exigencies of practice, and as well,

> to experience the apparent tragedy by being thoroughly and relentlessly dialectical, and also to stand apart from it, untouched, only smiling. In its impartiality before all ideas, in its freedom from what is really special pleading, in its ability to entertain any notion whether or not it be true or credible, such a mind enjoys the dialectical insight which makes controversy and reflection sane pursuits, and has those moments of quiet laughter which makes them what Plato called a 'dear delight' [Adler, 1927, p. 134].[15]

When this cognitive play, moreover, occurs in dialogue form, there is the added play of conversational rhythm and the responsive following of the interlocutor's powers of absorption and reference.

Such, then, is the nature of dialectic, not demonstrative like science,[16] but nevertheless operating on a higher level of appeal than rhetoric.[17] The logical argument is firmer in dialectic, its appeal to the emotions is more restrained than in rhetoric, and whereas the rhetorician will assume any ethical 'image' purely for its effectiveness, the dialectician's ethical argument is radically rooted in the quest for truth. This difference between rhetoric and dialectic can be traced in the evolution of Plato's dialogues.[18] In the early dialogues Socrates' kind of ethical and pathetical arguments suits his rhetorical ends, ranging from charming and seducing his audience to ridiculing and greatly discomfiting it. With the transition to Plato's middle and later dialogues, the protagonist assumes a dialectical approach: his pathetical argument consists of 'academic' emotions such as surprise, intellectual frustration, shame about ignorance, unease in recognizing contradictions in one's position, satisfaction in resolving a problem; and his ethical stance is strictly involved in striving to attain truth.

We have now arrived at the point when we are ready to see how dialectics, like the other discourses, appears in a somewhat transmuted guise in the psychoanalytic cure, and in the analyst's speech par excellence. We will follow carefully the changes which psychoanalytic intervention has contributed to dialectic discourse in its various traits, propositional, interrogatory, controversial, and interminable.

The dichotomy between dialectic as propositional and science as factual has necessarily to be adjusted to account for psychoanalysis. Psychoanalysis is propositional, yet deals with facts insofar as it interprets them. Ricoeur incisively insists that psychoanalysis is an exegetical enterprise dealing with meaning whereas the facts of behavior are the concern of observational science (1970, pp. 350–364; 1969, pp. 167–168). Attending to motives rather than causes (see also Rosen, 1975, pp. 203–208) and addressing itself not to facts as such but to their meaning in a patient's history, psychoanalysis operates in a semantic field of desire mediated by a language which distinguishes as well as interrelates presence and absence. For the behavioral psychologist, absence is only an independent variable, a lack of stimuli; for the analyst, that absence exists as a fragmental symbol redramatized within the analytic dialogue.[19] The lost object and its substitute object (the basic matter of psychoanalysis) attain, I might say, a new depth of meaning through and *in* the analyst's speech.

Like dialectic, psychoanalysis is interrogative. The various kinds of interventions are dominated by incompleteness and are preparatory to and culminate in interpretations (see Compton's report, 1975, pp. 30–31, 40), and in turn the whole import of the analyst's interpretations is essentially a question, whatever be the grammatical form used. As Lagache (1964) clearly states, 'la fonction de l'interprétation n'est pas de pétrifier ou d'endoctriner, mais d'éclairer et d'ouvrir la voie, et en ce sens elle est une question, même si elle n'en revêt pas la forme' (p. 1045). In terms of interrogative form itself,[20] analytical practice is very divided. On the one hand, there are the Horneyan analysts who consistently practice an outright preference for questions over declarative statements;[21] in a midway position is Eissler (1953) who holds that the two essential interventions are questions and interpretations. On the other hand, the case for a most hesitant, cautious use of questions has been well presented by Olinick (1954):

> one patient will welcome questioning as a form of active guidance, and his dependency may become a potently enhanced factor in the transference and a probable resistance to progress. Another patient, fearful of passivity, will resist questioning with his customary defenses against anxiety; still another, obsessively defensive about activity, will resist the definitive decision required in answering any question [p. 62].

On another score, it was part of Ferenczi's (1926) regular technique to have recourse to a question as a dynamically oriented response to an analysand's question:

> I made it a rule, whenever a patient asks me a question or requests some information, to reply with a counter interrogation of how he came to hit on that question. If I simply answered him, then the impulse from which the question sprang would be satisfied by the reply; by the method indicated, however, the patient's interest is directed to the sources of his curiosity, and when his questions are treated analytically he almost always forgets to repeat the original enquiries, thus showing that as a matter of fact they were unimportant and only significant as a means of expression for the unconscious [p. 183].

Actually the topic of interventions in interrogative form[22] is a complicated one, and I shall limit myself to two linguistic comments. First, an obstacle in studying interventions is that one cannot establish a one-to-one relationship between grammatical form and meaning. For instance, a request may be expressed in the imperative (Please lie down on the couch), the conditional (I should like you to lie on the couch), the indicative (Now the time has come for you to lie on the couch), and the interrogative (Will you lie on the couch right now?). Second, within the framework of pragmatics (the consideration of discourse in a specific time and place) the analyst's question tends to carry the weight of an imperative which the patient has relatively little choice but to acknowledge, as opposed to his being asked a question in the street by an accosting stranger. Briefly, any linguistic investigation into psychoanalytic intervention is full of snares, and whatever hesitancy we may have in speaking of the form of the analyst's speech, we are on surer ground when we conclude with Lagache that the spirit of analytical interpretations is interrogative.

The third general trait of dialectic, that it is controversial, also fits analytic interpretation. Again, Lagache is quite explicit: ' . . . en esprit sinon à la lettre, elle [interprétation] est une argumentation logique, étayée sur des données de fait et rétablissant une continuité dans le parcours analytique' (1964, p. 1045; see also p. 1054). Although dialectics and interpretation are both argumentative, there is the obvious difference that the one is more a cognitive abstract exercise whereas the other gives meaning to a situation fraught with transferential intensity; accordingly dilemma and contradiction, the dialectician's delight, take on a profounder role in psychoanalysis as precious indicators of areas of dynamic conflict. It is on a similar plane that Lévi-Valensi (1956) writes:

> Platon va des mots aux idées et l'analyste de ce qui est dit à ce qui est caché. Tous deux recherchent derrière le phénomène ce qui le provoque en tant que tel—ce pour quoi et par quoi il apparaît . . . [on the other hand, the analyst] ne dit pas 'dites la vérité,' mais 'dites tout.' La vérité est bien plus sûrement contenue dans 'tout' que dans ce que l'analysé croit être la vérité [pp. 266–267].

And yet there are striking parallels between the argumentative procedures of the dialectician and analyst. Surely the analyst is akin to Socrates who 'voulait prouver le plus souvent que l'attribution du prédicat au sujet par le partenaire du dialogue était illégitime' (de Pater, 1965, p. 17). And when the patient is carefully led to understand the general import and repetition compulsion of his individual acts, surely the analyst is akin to Socrates who, as the innovator of epagogic arguments in dialectic, led the interlocutor to a generalization by having him acknowledge the truth of particular cases (cf. Hall, 1967).[23] Then, too, Aristotle's advice to the dialectician has some bearing, however essentially modified, on psychoanalytical procedure: ' . . . you should not state the conclusions, but establish them by reasoning all at the same time at a later stage . . . you would keep the answers as far as possible from the original proposition' (*Topica*, VIII, 156a). Finally, there are some curious resemblances between the analyst's proceeding along the path of derivatives and the dialectician's procedure by coordinates.[24]

The fourth trait of dialectic, interminability, certainly holds true for psychoanalysis as well. We have only to think titularly of Freud's late treatise 'Analysis Terminable and Interminable' (1937). Although conflicts may be resolved no cure is absolute, and the insights Kris (1956) describes are always relative ones:

> Interpretation naturally does not lead to insight; much or most of analytic interpretation is carried out in darkness, with here and

there a flash of insight to lighten the path. A connection has been established, but before insight has reached awareness (or, if it does, only for flickering moments), new areas of anxiety and conflict emerge, new material comes, and the process drives on . . . [p. 452].

In that process the analyst's gradual unfolding of his understanding, if effectively adjusted to the patient's receptivity and particular organization of drives and defences at a given moment, recurrently testifies to the insight of cybernetics and information theory that the less expected or probable a message is, the more information it carries (cf. Wiener, 1948). Yet the concrete psychoanalytical situation in the long run eludes any exact definability. The localized quasi-definitude of certain interventions is to be understood within a process governing all analyses, which are open-ended, dialectical, interminable. Although realizing the hazards of grammatical generalization, I have thought for some time that the grammatical form which adequately characterizes both the analytical process and interventions is not the finite verb (do, be, etc.) but the infinite (*to do, to* be). Typical useful interventions as 'It seems that' or 'I wonder if' pale in theoretical exactitude when compared with the infinitive whose essential unendingness is commensurate with the interminability of the semantics of desire.[25]

With a mixture of humor and seriousness Mortimer Adler (1927) suggested that 'The technique of psychoanalysis is, like dialectic, an affair of conversation. The pun that psychoanalysis is conversation *ad libido* is not entirely unworthy' (p. 116).[26] Of course, there is the immediate difference that dialectical discourse in analysis is asymmetrical, thereby departing from the reciprocity and symmetrical give-and-take typifying classical dialectic. The factor of silence in psychoanalysis stands as another eminent distinguishing trait. Jacob Arlow shrewdly observed that the power of the analyst's silence is its ambiguity. With this in mind we may rightly conclude that when the patient's silence issues from certain kinds of resistance, the analytical setting constitutes a play-off between a rhetoric of silence and a dialectic of silence.

In retrospect, I am driven to re-emphasize the uniqueness of psychoanalytic treatment in the history of discourse. In psychoanalysis, then, each of the four primary discourses undergoes a change and acquires new traits, which set it apart from its appearance elsewhere. Truly, one cannot exaggerate the singularity of the psychoanalytic situation which, whatever the patient's initial concerns, becomes itself, through the transference, the central subject of all four discourses. To describe the interaction between the patient's free associations and the analyst's interpretations in another way: there is a calling into play of the intrapsychic, interpsychic and interpersonal and their attendant media, ranging from symptoms to signals to verbalization itself, all of which set the psychoanalytic enterprise apart from preceding kinds of designed human utterance.

Now we have scrutinized the general verbal nature of psychoanalytic treatment, the time has now come to grapple with the text of the dream. As an object of central attention in classical psychoanalysis, the dream continues to be both problematic and fascinating. The dream is a mixed text distinguishable by its internal visual and verbal media, and the complexity of this did not escape Freud's alertness.

Notes

★ First published in *Psychoanalysis and Contemporary Thought* (1979), 2: 77–111.

1 The theory of aesthetic, rhetorical and referential discourse has a long history extending as far back as Aristotle—see Giovannini (1953) and Kinneavy (1971, *passim*). For the fourth kind of discourse—the expressive—there is no long tradition with schools of opinion as Kinneavy points out; he does, however, give a short but perceptive sketch of its exegetical history (1971, pp. 393–396).

2 For the semiology of communication, see Eric Bussens (1966), Luis Prieto (1966), and Georges Mounin (1970, esp. pp. 7–8, 11–15, 89, 91, 101, 170, 190, 194, 209, 233). An acute attack on these positions and a defense of Roland Barthes's semiology of meaning is found in Jean-Pierre Roy's 'Sur l'objet de la sémiologie' (1972). Roy correctly asserts that the sign is not just a product but a means of production (p. 11) and that we must bypass an idealist semiology which crystallizes the sign-product. By contrast, 'Une sémiologie matérialiste part du processus de significance, les seuls réels, au lieu de ne considérer que la traduction figée de ces processus dans la sphère de la circulation des signes' (p. 15).

3 For purposes of fluent readability, I have translated the original Latin text somewhat loosely:

> Qua in fabula eleganter describuntur ingenia et mores hominum, qui variis et indomitis cupiditatibus agitantur, lucri, libidinis, vindictae; qui tamen quamdiu aures praebent praeceptis et suasionibus religionis, legum, magistrorum, in libris, sermonibus, et concionibus eloquenter et suaviter modulantibus, tamdiu pacem colunt et societatem; sin ista sileant aut seditiones et tumultus obstrepant, omnia dissiliunt et in

anarchiam atque confusionem relabuntur' [*The Works of Francis Bacon*, ed. James Spedding *et al.*, 1: 470–471].

4 Letter written by Keats, dated Dec. 22, 1817; in *Letters*, Number 32, p. 71. Cf. Freud's letter to Fliess, Number 58: 'Incidentally theory has receded into the distance. I am postponing all attempts to obtain understanding.'

5 The objection that a patient's intellectual resistance does not fit into this schema may be easily discarded. The fact-laden objective reportage typifying some obsessionals functions within a larger rhetorical design. At any rate, all conscious counter-communication has a rhetorical orientation; unconscious counter-communication, of course, pervades all forms of discourse.

6 There's a strong expressive element in *Beyond the Pleasure Principle*. While writing it 'Freud had no audience in mind beyond himself; it was written in the hope of clarifying some problems that had long puzzled him. It is somewhat discursively written, almost as if by free associations, and there are therefore occasional gaps in the reasoning' (Jones, 1953–1957, 3: 266).

7 But in a footnote written in 1925, Freud held that the essence of dreaming is the dream-work and not the dream-thoughts (*S.E.*, 5: 506–507).

8 I have purposely avoided treating the Aristotelean notion of catharsis in drama. Entralgo (1970) expatiates on the subject at great length and relates it to persuasion and psychotherapy (pp. 183–239). The reasons for my avoidance are twofold: as Freud developed he abandoned cathartic cure as such, and at any rate, catharsis is still a problematic concept in Aristotle and may even be interpreted as applying to the actors rather than to the spectators (see Else, 1957).

9 For the references to ancient therapy, I am generally indebted to the study by Dr. Entralgo (1970), presently professor of the history of medicine at the University of Madrid. Prefacing Entralgo's text are two highly valuable essays, written individually by Walter Ong and the translator L.J. Rather.

10 The Greek words for 'persuasion' and 'belief', *peithô* and *pistis*, are etymologically related. Eng (1973, p. 570) points out that the Greek deity Peithô was at first a goddess of marriage and only later on the goddess of rhetorical persuasion, a historical evolution which is incidentally mirrored in the thematic order of Plato's *Phaedrus*, eros preceding rhetoric. This rejoins the Freud citation that prefaces my essay: in the beginning was the deed and the word came later.

11 I use the word 'selected' with much intent. Entralgo places Galen squarely in the tradition of somatic medicine. True enough, Galen as practitioner of the 'mute art' had the greater influence on Western medicine, yet in actual fact he announced an extraordinary therapeutic

program in his treatise *On the Passions and Errors of the Soul*. W. Reise (Galen, 1963), a modern commentator on the treatise, writes:

> Galen's treatise on the passions can be called a treatise on ethics from which Galen emerges almost as a modern; indeed, it is the mastery of the passions through reason which appears as the basic theme of the treatise and the ultimate goal of his treatment of the passions. Conscious verbalization, which is unquestionably the main carrier of the more systematic and coherent psychotherapeutical devices of our time, is the continuous thread which appears, then fades, but always reappears throughout Galen's treatise [p. 112].

12 This provocative statement is somewhat inaccurate. In his comprehensive history Ellenberger (1970) has demonstrated at length that contrary to common assumption, Modern Dynamic Psychiatry (1983–) is continuous with the First Dynamic Psychiatry (1775–1900) and that the main ideas of Freud's and Jung's systems are traceable to Romantic psychiatry. In a personal communication Ellenberger added: 'Je pense que les deux ordres de traitement [somatic and verbal] ont existé côte à côte depuis 25 siècles . . . les systèmes en usage chez les Pytagoriciens, Stöiciens, Epicuriens, etc. étaient des équivalents de psychothérapie rationnelle, ainsi que l'usage plus ou moins codifié des "consolations," "exhortations" et "administrations."'

In the pages that follow, I hope that Entralgo's overstress on the subsequent influence of Hellenic suggestion and rhetoric will be placed in better perspective. Specific attention must be given to the difference between rhetoric and dialectic; when Freud left hypnotic and suggestive therapy, he abandoned the stance of a rhetorical therapist to give the patient the openness of dialectical freedom.

13 Freud (1917) personally rejected the eristic kind of dialectics: 'I have never been able to convince myself of the truth of the maxim that strife is the father of all things. I believe it is derived from the Greek sophists and is at fault, like them, through overvaluing dialectics' (*S.E.* 16: 244–245).

14 It is worth mentioning that just as there are aesthetic aspects in dialectic discourse (e.g. mimetic elements) there are dialectical aspects in imaginative discourse—a relationship too often neglected in modern literary criticism, which has turned its attention to the links between rhetoric and poetic, rhetoric and fiction. Dialectically considered, the imaginative writer offers a view to the reader to be *entertained* by him, and the reader may respond by surrendering his set position, by suspending disbelief as Coleridge said.

15 There is a similarity between this dialectical freedom and the liberating element that Freud (1927) associates with humor. In humor there is

79

elevation and grandeur, the grandeur lying 'in the triumph of narcissism, the victorious assertion of the ego's vulnerability.' In a way, Freud continues, humor allows a person to treat himself as a child and simultaneously to entertain a superior adult attitude toward that child. If ordinarily the superego acts cruelly toward the ego, in the case of humor the superego comforts the intimidated ego.

16 Grimaldi (1972) neatly distinguishes the logical argument in Aristotelean dialectics and scientific reasoning (p. 106):

> As a general guide it can be said that enthymemes developed from *eikota* [probabilities] and *semeia anonyma* [fallible signs, such as analogies, or in forensic law, circumstantial evidence] represent the kind of reasoning which can be found in Aristotelean dialectics, while those from *tekmeria* [infallible signs, or indices in Peircean semiotics] present more the character of scientific reasoning as found in his *Analytics*.

17 Thinking within a strictly Aristotelean framework, McKeon (1965), pp. 221–222) finds that rhetoric and dialectic

> differ from each other less in the details of the devices which both use for proof and persuasion than in the generality of the opinions to which they appeal: dialectic on opinions which are thought to be universal, or common, or expert, or preferable in some other sense, while rhetoric consults the pecularities of particular men, or groups, or circumstances.

My own stand as elaborated above is not the same as McKeon's. On the other hand, the nuance proposed by Bitzer (1959) seems quite useful: the dialectician takes his premise from the other participant in the discussion; the scientist takes his from empirical observation and deduction; the rhetorician supplies the premises which he judges will gratify the audience.

18 See B. Simon's excellent comments in the *Journal of the History of the Behavioral Sciences* (1973a, esp. pp. 6–7), and in the *Psycho-analytic Quarterly* (1973b, esp. pp. 108–111).

19 My focus is on the nature of analytic interventions in general. A complete study of the various individual types of interventions and their traits does not exist. Rosen's article (1975) offers some suggestive remarks accompanying a proposed schema of nine kinds of interventions. The long panel study 'Aspects of Psycho-analytic Intervention' (reported by Allan Compton [1975]) is full of practical matters bearing the stamp of the main contributor, R. Loewenstein. It is Devereux's essay (1951, pp. 19–20), however, which defines confrontation most clearly:

> confrontation is a device whereby the patient's attention is directed to the bare factual content of his actions or statements, or to a

coincidence which he has perceived, but has not, or professes not to have registered . . . in confrontation the analyst utilizes primarily his secondary thought processes . . . confrontation is a rather superficial manipulation of cathexes, i.e. of attention.

20 'Whether,' incidentally, is a choice word for introducing a question in traditional dialectics (*Topica*, I, 4). Cf. also Aristotle's counsel against dialectical conclusions in question form (*Topica*, VIII, 158a) versus Kris's suggestion (1956) that 'when the analyst interprets, sometimes all he needs to say can be put into a question.'

21 Thus Kelman and Vollmerhausen (1967) spell out their rationale:

> what is implicit, indirect, open-ended, and in the form of a question is a better form of interpreting. . . . What we want is to allow the patient's 'self-propelled feeling process' to move him in the direction of what is being pointed at. The more implicit and open-ended the pointer, the more loosely the field remains organized, with that many more open spaces to be filled and with a wider spectrum of creative possibilites. . . . All our questions have the form of process, ask about processes, and are aimed at the stimulating of processes (p. 416).

22 On a broader stylistic basis, it is generally agreed that the analyst's glossary should be simple, concrete, and like the patient's. Balint extends this technique of lexical regression into syntax: since propositional speech develops relatively late in one's life and since correctly structured sentences may therefore be defensive elaborations, he prefers frequent use of short poignant sentences instead of well-formulated ones spaced at long intervals (Edelheit, 1970, pp. 238–239). On the opposite end of this scale is Reider's (1972) recourse to metaphor as a fundamental interpretative tool; among the justifications for his use of metaphor, Reider says that it is founded on unconscious fantasy. See, however, Rubenstein's (1972) painstaking linguistic study of metaphor, in which he concludes that metaphor need not be unconsciously determined, and hence may in some cases be a product of secondary process.

23 In actual fact, however, the dialectician works chiefly by deduction. Hence the authority on Aristotelean dialectic, Jacques Brunschwig (Aristotle, 1967), states:

> Dans la pratique dialectique, l'induction joue un rôle auxiliaire, soit que le dialecticien l'utilise lorsqu'il se trouve en face d'un partenaire peu exercé . . . soit qu'il ait besoin d'elle pour établir une règle générale qui manque d'évidence propre . . . Il est donc indispensable au dialecticien d'être capable d'argumenter inductivement . . . mais l'essentiel de son pouvoir n'est pas là [p. xxxii].

Cf. Loewald (1960), Shapiro (1970) and Stone (1961) who maintain that a psychoanalytical interpretation is more of a synthetic than an analytic event (Rosen, 1975, p. 195).

24 Hence Aristotle suggests to dialecticians:

> You should also, whenever possible, establish the universal premiss in the form of a definition relating not to the actual terms in question but to co-ordinates of them; for people let themselves be deceived when a definition is established dealing with a co-ordinate, imagining that they are not making the admission universally. This would happen, for example, if it were necessary to establish that the angry man is desirous of a revenge for a fancied slight, and it were to be established that anger is a desire for revenge for a fancied slight; for, obviously, if this were established, we should have the universal admission which we require. On the other hand, it often happens, when people make propositions dealing with the actual term, that the answerer refuses his assent, because he objects more readily when the actual term is used, saying, for example, that the angry man is not desirous of revenge [*Topica*, VIII, 156a].

25 It is literally only after I typed the last word of this sentence that I suddenly established a connection between my idea and a course I took twenty years ago from that famous drama critic and historian, Francis Fergusson. Defining dramatic action in the sense of motive, Fergusson had his students summarize every dramatic scene into an infinitive, every act into an infinitive englobing the infinitives of the composite scenes, and in the same manner, we had to translate the whole play into one comprehensive infinitive. The relevance of this to the drama of analytic treatment is most obvious. To put it somewhat differently, the optative mood, the wish like the infinitive, is incomplete. Dream thoughts are in the optative mood and achieve fulfillment *by being rendered* in the present indicative in the dream content (*S.E.* 5: 534–535, 647–648). Maintaining the parallel between dreams and free associations, we may go on to say that clarification and confrontation would often have more to do with the present indicative, and interpretations, with the optative.

26 Cf. also: 'Psychoanalysis . . . is a dialectic of the neurotic personality, a dialectic of the soul which has been split into two universes of discourse, and which must be reunited by the establishment of translation between them' (Adler, 1927, p. 116).

References

Adler, M. (1927) *Dialectic*. New York: Harcourt, Brace.
Argelander, H. (1968) Der psychoanalytische Dialog. *Psyche*, 22: 325–329.

Aristotle (1954) *The Rhetoric and Poetics*, ed. F. Solmsen and tr. W. Roberts and I. Bywater. New York: Random House.

—— (1960) *Topica*, ed. E.S. Forster. Cambridge, Mass.: Harvard University Press.

—— (1967) *Topique*, vol. 1, ed. J. Brunschwig. Paris: Société d'Editions.

Aubenque, P. (1962) *Le problème de l'être chez Aristote*. Paris: Presses Universitaires de France.

Bacon, F. (1623) *De Dignitate et Augmentis Scientiarum*. In: *The Works of Francis Bacon*, vol. 1, ed. J. Spedding *et al*. London: D.C. Heath, 1858.

Barthes, R. (1970) L'ancienne rhétorique: aide-mémoire. *Communications*, 16: 172–229.

Benveniste, E. (1956) Remarques sur la fonction du langage dans la découverte freudienne. *Psychanalyse*, 1: 3–16.

Bird, O. (1955) Dialectic in philosophical inquiry. *Dialectic*, 9: 287–304.

Bitzer, L. (1959) Aristotle's enthymeme revisited. *Quarterly Journal of Speech*, 45: 399–408.

Booth, W. (1961) *The Rhetoric of Fiction*. Chicago: Chicago University Press.

Bussens, E. (1966) *La communication et l'articulation linguistique*. Paris: Presses Universitaires de France.

Compton, A. (1975) Aspects of psychoanalytic intervention [Kris Study Group of the New York Psychoanalytic Institute, Monogr. VI], ed. B. Fine and H. Waldhorn. New York: International Universities Press, pp. 23–97.

Devereux, G. (1951) Some criteria for the timing of confrontations and interpretations. *International Journal of Psycho-Analysis*, 32: 19–24.

Edelheit, H. (1970) Panel report: Language and psychoanalysis. *International Journal of Psycho-Analysis*, 51: 237–243.

Eissler, K. (1953) Effect of the structure of the ego on psycho-analytic technique. *Journal of the American Psychoanalytic Association*, 1: 104–143.

Ellenberger, H. (1970) *The Discovery of the Unconscious: the History and Evolution of Dynamic Psychiatry*. New York: Basic Books.

—— Private communication.

Else, G. (1957) *Aristotle's Poetics: the Argument*. Cambridge, Mass.: Harvard University Press.

Eng, E. (1973) The significance of the rhetorical tradition for the self-understanding of psychotherapy. *The Human Context*, 5: 569–576.

—— (1974) Modern psychotherapy and ancient rhetoric. *Psychotherapy and Psychosomatics*, 24: 493–496.

Entralgo, L. (1970) *The Therapy of the Word in Classical Antiquity*. New Haven: Yale University Press.

Ferenczi, S. (1926) *Further Contributions to the Theory and Technique of Psycho-analysis*. London: Hogarth Press.

83

Fónagy, I. (1970–1971) Les bases pulsionnelles de la phonation, *Revue Française de Psychanalyse*, 34 et 35: 100–136, 543–591.

—— (1971) The functions of vocal style, In: S. Chatman (ed.), *Literary Style: A Symposium*. London: Oxford University Press, pp. 159–174.

Freud, S. (1900) The interpretation of dreams. *Standard Edition*, 4 and 5. London: Hogarth Press, 1953.

—— (1905) Fragment of an analysis of a case of hysteria. *Standard Edition*, 7: 3–123. London: Hogarth Press, 1953.

—— (1909) Notes upon a case of obsessional neurosis. *Standard Edition*, 10: 153–318. London: Hogarth Press, 1955.

—— (1912) The dynamics of transference. *Standard Edition*, 12: 97–108. London: Hogarth Press, 1958.

—— (1915–1917) Introductory lectures on psychoanalysis. *Standard Edition*, 15 and 16. London: Hogarth Press, 1961–1963.

—— (1926) The question of lay analysis. *Standard Edition*, 20: 3–74. London: Hogarth Press, 1959.

—— (1927a) The future of an illusion. *Standard Edition*, 21: 3–56. London: Hogarth Press, 1961.

—— (1927b) Humour. *Standard Edition*, 21: 159–166. London: Hogarth Press, 1961.

—— (1937) Analysis terminable and interminable. *Standard Edition*, 23: 211–253. London: Hogarth Press, 1964.

—— (1940) *The Origins of Psychoanalysis*, ed. M. Bonaparte *et al.*, tr. E. Mosbacher and J. Strachey. London: Imago.

Frye, N. (1963) *The Well-Tempered Critic*. Bloomington: Indiana University Press.

Galen, (1963) *On the Passions and Errors of the Soul*, tr. P. Haskins and introd. W. Reise. Athens, Ohio: Ohio University Press.

Giovannini, G. (1953) Four forms of composition. In: J. Shipley (ed.), *The Dictionary of World Literature*. New York: Philosophical Library, pp. 73–74.

Greenson, R. (1967) *The Technique and Practice of Psychoanalysis*. New York: International Universities Press.

Grimaldi, W. (1972) *Studies in the Philosophy of Aristotle's Rhetoric*. Wiesbaden: Franz Steiner Verlag.

Hall, R. (1967) Dialectic. In: *The Encyclopedia of Philosophy*. New York: Macmillan, 1: 385–389.

Howarth, W. (1974) Some principles of autobiography. *New Literary History*, 5: 413–425.

Jakobson, R. (1960) Linguistics and poetics. In: T. Sebeok (ed.), *Style in Language*. Cambridge, Mass.: M.I.T. Press.

—— and Halle, M. (1956) *Fundamentals of Language*. The Hague: Mouton.

Jones, E. (1913) *Papers on Psycho-Analysis*. New York: William Wood.

—— (1953–1957) *The Life and Work of Sigmund Freud*, 3 vols. New York: Basic Books.

Jung, C. (1906) Psychoanalysis and association experiments. In: *The Collected Works of C.G. Jung*. Princeton: Princeton University Press, 1973, 2: 288–317.

Keats, J. (1952) *Letters of John Keats*, ed. M. Forman. Oxford: Clarendon Press, 4th edition.

Kelman, H. and Vollermerhausen, J. (1967) On Horney's psychoanalytical techniques: developments and perspectives. In: B. Wolman (ed.) *Psychoanalytical Techniques*. New York: Basic Books, pp. 379–423.

Kinneavy, J. (1971) *A Theory of Discourse*. Englewood-Cliffs, N.J.: Prentice-Hall.

Kris, E. (1956) On some vicissitudes of insight in psycho-analysis. *International Journal of Psycho-Analysis*, 37: 445–455.

Kubie, L. (1950) *Practical and Theoretical Aspects of Psychoanalysis*. New York: International Universities Press.

Lacan, J. (1966) *Ecrits*. Paris: Editions du Seuil.

LaDrière, C. (1948) Rhetoric and 'merely verbal art.' In: *English Institute Essays*. New York: Columbia University Press, pp. 123–152.

Lagache, D. (1964) La méthode psychanalytique. In: L. Michaux *et al.*, *Psychiatrie*. Paris: Vrin, pp. 1036–1066.

Lévi-Valensi, E. (1956) Vérité et langage du dialogue platonicien au dialogue psychanalytique. *La Psychanalyse*, 1: 257–274.

Loewald, H. (1960) On the therapeutic action of psychoanalysis. *International Journal of Psycho-Analysis*, 41: 16–33.

Loewenstein, R. (1956) Some remarks on the role of speech in psychoanalytic technique. *International Journal of Psycho-Analysis*, 37: 460–468.

McKeon, R. (1965) Rhetoric and poetic in the philosophy of Aristotle. In: E. Olson (ed.), *Aristotle's Poetics in English Literature*. Toronto: Toronto University Press, pp. 201–236.

Mahony, P. (1974) Freud in the light of classical rhetoric. *Journal of the History of the Behavioral Sciences*, 10: 413–425.

Mehlman, J. (1970) Entre psychanalyse et psychocritique. *Poétique*, 1: 366–385.

Mounin, G. (1970) *Introduction à la sémiologie*. Paris: Editions de Minuit.

Olinick, S. (1954) Some considerations of the use of questioning as a psychoanalytical technique. *Journal of the American Psychoanalytic Association*, 2: 57–66.

Pater, W.A. de (1965) *Les topiques d'Aristote et la dialectique platonicienne*. Fribourg: Editions de St. Paul.

Prieto, L. (1966) *Messages et signaux*. Paris: Presses Universitaires de Frances.

Rado, S. (1958) Psychotherapy: a problem of controlled communication.

In: P. Hoch and J. Zubin (eds.), *Psychopathology of Communication*. New York: Grune & Stratton, pp. 214–226.

Reider, N. (1972) Metaphor as interpretation. *International Journal of Psycho-Analysis*, 53: 463–469.

Ricoeur, P. (1965) *De l'interprétation: essai sur Freud*. Paris: Editions du Seuil.

—— (1969) *Le conflit des interprétations*. Paris: Editions du Seuil.

—— (1970) *Freud and Philosophy*, tr. Denis Savage. New Haven: Yale University Press.

Rosen, V. (1960) Some aspects of the role of imagination in the psycho-analytic process. *Journal of the American Psychoanalytic Association*, 8: 229–251.

—— (1967) Disorders of communication in psychoanalysis. *Journal of the American Psychoanalytic Association*, 15: 467–490.

—— (1975) The nature of verbal intervention in psycho-analysis. In: *Psychoanalysis and Contemporary Science*, vol. 3. New York: International Universities Press, pp. 189–209.

Roy, J.-P. (1972) Sur l'objet de la sémiologie. *Stratégie*, 1: 4–18.

Rubinstein, B. (1972) On metaphor and related phenomena. In: *Psychoanalysis and Contemporary Science*, vol. 1. New York: Macmillan, pp. 70–108.

Saussure, F. de (1916) *Cours de linguistique générale*, ed. T. de Mauro. Paris: Payot, 1974.

Seidenberg, H. (1971) Panel report: The basic rule: free association—a reconsideration. *Journal of the American Psychoanalytic Association*, 19: 98–109.

Shapiro, T. (1970) Interpretation and naming. *Journal of the American Psychoanalytic Association*, 18: 399–421.

Simon, B. (1972) Models of mind and mental illness in ancient Greece: II. The Platonic model. *Journal of the History of the Behavioral Sciences*, 8: 389–404.

—— (1973a) Models of mind and mental illness in ancient Greece: II. The Platonic model (Section 2). *Journal of the History of the Behavioral Sciences*, 9: 3–17.

—— (1973b) Plato and Freud: the mind in conflict and the mind in dialogue. *Psycho-analytic Quarterly*, 42: 91–122.

Stone, L. (1961) *The Psychoanalytical Situation*. New York: International Universities Press.

Viderman, S. (1972) Comme en un miroir, obscurément . . . *Nouvelle Revue de Psychanalyse*, 5: 131–152.

—— (1974) Interpretation in the analytical space. *International Review of Psycho-Analysis*, 1: 467–480.

Weigert, E. (1955) Special problems in connection with the termination of training analyses. *Journal of the American Psychoanalytic Association*, 3: 630–640.

Wiener, N. (1948) *Cybernetics or Control and Communication in the Animal and the Machine*. Cambridge, Mass.: M.I.T. Press.

Winnicott, D. (1971) *Playing and Reality*. New York: Basic Books.

Yates, F. (1966) *The Art of Memory*. Chicago: Chicago University Press.

4

Freud's interpretation of dreams, semiology, and Chomskian linguistics *

Seen within a semiological and linguistic context, Freud's theoretical treatment of dreams assumes even greater value. In elaborating this point, we shall make convenient, critical reference to the veritably pioneering monograph of Marshall Edelson (1973), who rightly pictures Freud the dream theorist as the forerunner of modern semiology.[1] Accordingly, Edelson specifies that when 'Freud describes the dream as a kind of rebus, he is clearly concerned, and perhaps the first semiologist to state the problem so explicitly, with the translation of the symbolic forms of one symbolic system into those of another symbolic system' (p. 252), i.e. the translation of the verbal latent dream into the predominant visuality of the manifest dream. Edelson's own guiding interest is to harmonize Freudian and Chomskian tenets, to establish an isomorphism between linguistic deep and surface structures and the dual structure of oneiric activity itself. Hence, 'the semantically interpreted deep structures underlying dreams are identical with those underlying linguistic forms generated in waking consciousness' (p. 234). All in all, Edelson's own text merits close attention insofar as it makes a daring attempt in semiological innovation, incorporates a sensitive reading of *The Interpretation of Dreams*, and recurrently offers stimulating questions for further speculation and research.

Granted the merits of Edelson's efforts, however, three major objections, each of which will be taken up in detail in separate sections, may be brought against his approach. First and ironically enough, in spite of Edelson's very enchantment with semiology, he neglects to explore the area in dream analysis where Freud made his most striking semiological observations! Second, the identifications posited between Chomskian and Freudian concepts are, unwittingly, metaphorical and analogical mentations on Edelson's part. Third, his semiological penchant wrongly induces him to challenge the essential existence of censorship, whose function would putatively be subsumed by the factor of representability.

Guided by the law of parsimony, let us now turn to the richness of Freud's ideas that await us. One could semiologically describe some of his efforts in dream theory as an attempt to establish a comparative grammar of interior media. Semiology of course is used somewhat loosely here as a word, for in the strict sense semiology cannot be extended to mental operations since codes exist only for external phenomena and there are no codes for our thoughts. Nevertheless, for example, what may be called the interior visual media of fantasies may be to some extent considered in relation with external media of a visual nature, such as cinema and television. With admirable effort, Freud strove to trace the translation of the syntactic laws of the latent dream or verbosymbolic mode into the manifest dream or pre-dominantly visual mode. Necessarily, however, as Emile Benveniste (1969) suggested about external communicative systems, there is an inevitable relative distortion of a message put in different media: 'There is no "synonymy" between semiotic systems; one cannot "say the same thing" in words and in music. . . . Man does not dispose of several distinct systems for the same relation of meaning' (p. 9).

Thus the individuating features of a medium, sensorial and otherwise, change that which is communicated. Now if we bear in mind that fantasies, somatic symptoms, and latent dreams are intrapsychic phenomena or media with visual, kinesthetic, and verbal bases, the 'same message' should be somewhat altered in each of the three systems. It follows that a modification of this kind occurs in dreams. The verbosymbolic latent dream is rooted in a wish, or grammatically, in the optative mood; yet sheer visuality (and hence the manifest dream) can directly express only the indicative. The hallucinatory dramatization of that indicative mood is ipso facto enacted in the present tense, and defined by it. In this sense Freud (1916/17) declares:

> a dream does not simply give expression to a thought, but represents the wish fulfilled as a hallucinatory experience. '*I should like to go on the lake*' is the wish that instigates the dream. The content of the dream itself is: '*I am going on the lake.*' Thus even in these simple children's dreams a difference remains between the latent and the manifest dream, there is a distortion of the latent dream-thought: *the transformation of a thought into an experience.* In

89

the process of interpreting a dream this alteration must first be undone. If this turns out to be the most universal characteristic of dreams, the fragment of dream which I reported to you earlier 'I saw my brother in a box' is not to be translated 'my brother is restricting himself' but 'I should like my brother to restrict himself: *my brother must restrict himself*' [p. 129].[2]

Freud went on to spell out in some detail the grammar of articulation between the latent and manifest dream; as he insisted, one must discover the 'characters and syntactic laws' of the manifest dream by comparing it with the original (1900, p. 277). The semiological value of this grammar is undeniable, as it directly grapples with the problem of representability, of translating elusive points of lexicality and verbal syntax into oneiric pictures. In this way—one not examined by Edelson—Freud anticipated the contemporary semiological challenge of translating the literary form of, say, a novel into the cinematic medium, or par excellence a short story into a silent movie. Laboring under the same difficulties as the plastic arts of painting and sculpture, dreams generally disregard all conjunctions and the relations between the subject matter of dream thoughts (1900, p. 313). Yet dreams do represent logical relationship, which is revealed mainly in their form.[3] Specifically, it is the dream-work which does 'succeed in expressing some of the content of the latent dream-thoughts by peculiarities in the *form* of the manifest dream—by its clarity or obscurity, by its division into several pieces, and so on. . . . Thus the form of dreams is far from being without significance and itself calls for interpretation' (1916/17, p. 177).

In actuality, then, the form of a manifest dream has a dual importance, thereby going beyond the telling syntax of the latent dream. Perceptively, the varying clarity of either whole dreams or their sections may be highly revelatory. Given the fact that '*The form of a dream or the form in which it is dreamt is used with quite surprising frequency for representing its concealed subject-matter*' (1900, p. 332), a hazy dream, for example, may express the female dreamer's confusion about the father of her child, or a dream of absolute clarity might represent the sleeper's wish that a theoretical problem be flawlessly solveld. And in another case, a great part of the impression of a dream's absurdity 'was brought about by running together sentences from different parts of the dream-thoughts without any transition' (1900, p. 437).

Syntactically as well, Freud's various oneiric translations are worthy of the closest semiological attention:

Either—Or. Though in the great majority of cases, this double conjunction does not succeed in being expressed, occasionally the idea of mutual exclusion is represented in a dream by two equal parts (1900, p. 316 ff.).

If. Sometimes *if* in a dependent conditional clause is represented by a minor dream episode interrupting the main dream scene which has persisted for some time; this minor scene seems describable in these words: 'But then it was as though at the same time it was another place, and there such and such a thing happened.' This spectacular case incorporates a multiple translation: the *if* of the latent dream becoming a sequent visual scene; the sequentiality nevertheless is *verbally* describable as *when, at the same time*, which in turn is to be verbally translated as *if* (1900, p. 335).

Because. Though in the preponderant number of instances causality is lost, it may be expressed by the transformation of an image of a person or thing into another, before our very eyes, or by the division of the dream itself into two unequal parts; extra caution is needed here, for the two unequal parts may otherwise indicate two different points of view (1900, p. 315 f.). Concerning the transformation of one image into another, and its semiological applications to cinema, a passage from Jakobson's essay on the two types of aphasia is especially pertinent:

> Ever since the productions of D.W. Griffith, the art of the cinema, with its highly developed capacity for changing the angle, perspective and focus of 'shots', has broken with the tradition of the theater and ranged an unprecedented variety of synecdochic 'close-ups' and metonymic 'set-ups' in general. In such pictures as those of Charlie Chaplin and Eisenstein these devices in turn were overlayed by a novel, metaphoric 'montage' with its 'lap dissolves'— the filmic similes [1971, p. 256].

A promising area of fruitful semiological investigation lies in the evaluation of Freud's and Jakobson's divergent positions. For Freud, the transformation of one image into another may mean causality, which in itself expresses a metonymy, a syntagmatic relationship between two events. Jakobson on the other hand sees image transformation as metaphorical and paradigmatic, thus contrasting with a cinematic metonymic style.

Elsewhere Freud (1905, p. 172) summarily asserts that dreams replace internal associations (similarity, causality) by external associations (simultaneity in time, contiguity in space, similarity in sound), the very components of infantile causality. In this regard, it is by means of scattered remarks in *Totem and Taboo* (1913, pp. 5 f., 27, 61, 81 ff., 85, 87 f.) that we may construct the most insightful synthesis.

Contact is the most comprehensive term for the two essential ways of association: similarity or metaphorical contact (characterizing imitative or homeopathic magic, where a similarity exists between the act performed and the result expected) and contiguity or literal contact (characterizing contagious magic, in which the contiguity may be spatial or imagined). One may note here, however, a terminological difficulty insofar as imagined contiguity is not easily differentiated from similarity or metaphorical contact. At any event, parallel to the two kinds of contact postulated by Freud, there are two types of displacement: the displacement operative in obsessional neurosis, where prohibitions glide from one object to another, and displacement operative in the taboo-infected individual, who contaminates those coming in contact with him; hence, perhaps since obsessional neurotics displace, they follow the laws of similarity, substitution, and imitation.

Just As. This is the only logical relation that is highly favored by visuality itself, through the dream mechanism of condensation. More precisely, two entities linked by a common element may be represented by a composite reality, or merely by either of the two entities (1900, p. 319 f.).

Logical Connection. Such connections are reproduced by simultaneity in time, like Raphael who in his School of Athens established a conceptual unity between all the poets and philosophers by assembling them all at one time in the same place. For details, dreams express connections by juxtaposing or collocating scenes (1900, p. 314), i.e. by propinquity in time (p. 247).

Independent and Dependent Clauses. With respect to this larger grammatical framework, Freud's suggestions are most provoking:

> The number of part–dreams into which a dream is divided usually corresponds to the number of main topics or groups of thoughts in the latent dream. A short introductory dream will often stand in the relation of a prelude to a following, more detailed, main dream or may give the motive for it; a subordinate clause in the dream-thoughts will be replaced by the interpolation of a change of scene into the manifest dream, and so on [1916/17, p. 177].

By contrast, in the more localized and specific area of syntactical expression, exemplified in at least three instances, Freudian hermeneutics are too readily venturesome:

1. A dependent temporal clause is represented by an introductory or terminal minor dream, the more extensive part of a dream always corresponding to a principal clause (1900, p. 314 f.).

92

2. 'A short introductory dream and a longer main dream following it often stand in the relation of protasis and apodosis [conditional and consequential clauses]' (1933, p. 26). Freud, on the other hand, cites one instance of a screen character adequately representing a conditional sentence. In one of his dreams the substitution of his father for Meynert did not lie in any analogy between them but rather translated 'a conditional sentence in the dream-thoughts, which ran in full: "If only I had been the second generation, the son of a professor or Hofrat, I should certainly have *got on faster*"' (1900, p. 438).
3. 'A dream which is described by the dreamer as "somehow interpolated" will actually correspond to a dependent clause in the dream-thought' (1933, p. 26 f.). Similarly, secondary elaborations, not being especially vivid, are frequently introduced by an 'as though' in postoneiric description (1900, p. 489). At any event, to this postulated correspondence between dream segments and grammatical dependence or independence, one may offer two caveats. First, grammar does not necessarily conform to logic. As the linguist Francis Christensen discovered, contemporary American expository prose is characterized by the most important matter being found in *dependent* grammatical structures; likewise, Baroque prose in seventeenth-century England often had the same trait (see Rooney, 1962). Secondly, just as dream condensation and censorship operate on a semantic basis, they may also do syntactically and, for purposes of disguise and screening, devote the longer oneiric scene to a minor issue.

In sum, the formal traits of a dream that Freud hermeneutically invokes include the length of its parts, the placement of a shorter dream episode (either initially, terminally, or as a medial interpolation), juxtaposition, condensation, metamorphosis of one element into another, and obscurity or distinctness of whole or sections of dreams. Or in other words, the form of a dream ranges from its sheerly external aspects (length) to internal ones (haziness and transformation).

With reference to these findings, much more research must be devoted to the formal aspects of the manifest dream, the results of which should be particularly promising for dream interpretation. There is a pressing need for a comparative syntax of the sensorial dream. How does a tactile imagination, for example, represent syntax? On another score, Robert Blank (1958) reported that 'The congenitally blind do not have visual dreams.'[4] Blank also finds that in the congenitally blind, hearing is the foremost sensory dream element; tactile or kinesthetic next, whereas the gustatory and olfactory are rare. Certainly, the analysis of a dream's form is rendered very difficult by its ephemeral nature. Nevertheless a phenomenological reflection on the nature of dreams—and one is absolutely necessary—should be guided by two essential principles of semiological investigation: the specification of the basic units of a system, and the rules of their combination. To this end, one might explore some of the semiological criteria applied by René Passeron (1962) to painting and by Marcel Martin (1968) and Christian Metz (1968, 1971) to the cinema. Cinematic semiology could be directed to the field of psychoanalytic symbolism, the Wolf Man's primal scene, for example. Though the scene occurred when he was 1½ years old and was only later put into words, it was singled out among other visual incidents; though preverbal, it was given a *signifié*, a signified. Could it be that such traumatic visual phenomena (fantasied or real) might be displaced and deformed into various configurational patterns, much as heavily charged words are both phonologically and orthographically? These configurational patterns may be assigned, then, to objects or shapes far different from those proper to the primal scene. Thus, on a markedly *visual* basis, some object very dissimilar in shape from a breast could be a symbol for it. It remains to determine the practicality and practicability of determining the symbolic vicissitudes of a transformed visuality. On a simple plane, a straight line may be transformed into a circle, a crooked line, etc. It may be that the plethora of metamorphic possibilities discards any practical application. Yet the retention of the viability of such a concept in mind may afford a correcting alternative to restricting symbolism solely to archetypal, verbal, and other considerations.[5]

A second great need in what may be called comparative oneirics is a study of mass media's influence on the form of dreams. Hence one may ask, Is the form of a dream different in an oral-history society as opposed to a literary and print-oriented society? Does the transformation of one dream image into another take place predominantly in a 'movie' culture? To what degree do mass media, each of which has its own syntax, influence the form of the manifest dream? Alongside the very express messages of symbols, the Oedipus complex, infantile wishes, etc., syntax itself in dreams is meaning, message. To this extent one may posit some relevance of McLuhan's theories to dreams.

Thirdly, if hypotaxis[6] is to some degree in the formal nature of the manifest dream, to that degree the dreams of people whose language is marked by hypotactic structure should be different from those whose language (and basis of their latent dreams) is paratactic. Thus the Whorfian hypothesis concerning language as a determinant of culture could be either somewhat shaken or confirmed by dream evidence.

Next on our path is the applicability of Chomsky's theories to Freud's understanding of the dream. This subject has been courageously taken up by Edelson in his work which is full of engaging proposals. Since he is apparently interested in developing an explicit, generative theory of 'dream language' (a cover term we shall use to designate the terminal units in which dreams are represented and various kinds of rules that must necessarily relate these units in a determinable way), some of our comments will necessarily be concerned with his understanding of the generative theory of language, deliberately chosen by him as his model. His larger aim of contributing something to a general theory of what he calls 'symbolic function' will also be taken up.

Edelson is interested in developing propositions about 'the relation between dreams and language,' the outlines of a possible generative theory of dream language, and in examining 'the possible status' of the generative theories of language and dream language in relation to a 'more general theory of semiology or symbolic function.' More specifically, he is concerned with 'the determinacy of the meaning of dreams—what aspects of their mode of construction make their meaning determinable' and with 'the value of using the linguistic distinction between deep and surface structures for appreciating the consequences of the operations of the dreamwork' (1973, p. 209 f.).

Edelson's attempt to provide plausible outlines of a possible generative theory of dream language constitutes a major effort since it could, if it is not devoid of empirical content, have some far-reaching consequences. Chiefly, if his preliminary demonstration succeeds, it would show that there are indeed domains of symbolic function other than language that are characterized by a richness and complexity that most generative grammarians believe is restricted to human language.

Since the parameters of the context within which Edelson's proposals must be examined are overwhelming, it may not be entirely out of place to identify some of them rather clearly. Edelson's hopes provide an optimistic counterpoint to Chomsky's pessimism regarding the problem of 'extending concepts of linguistic structure to other cognitive systems,' which, to Chomsky (1972), does not seem to be in 'too promising a state' (p. 75). The study of other language-like structures has not turned up with anything 'even roughly comparable to language in these domains' (p. 74). Chomsky adds:

> Are there other areas of human competence where one might hope to develop a fruitful theory, analogous to generative theory? Although this is a very important question, there is very little that can be said about it today. One might, for example, consider the problem of how a person comes to acquire a certain concept of three-dimensional space, or an implicit theory of 'human action' in similar terms. Such a study would begin with the attempt to characterize the implicit theory that underlies actual performance and would then turn to the question how this theory develops under the given conditions of time and access to data—that is, in what way the resulting system of beliefs is determined by the interplay of available data, 'heuristic procedures,' and the innate mechanism that restricts and conditions the form of the acquired system [1972, p. 73 f.].

It is important to note the reasons for Chomsky's pessimism. He believes that although various systems have been shown to be rich and complex, their richness and complexity have never been shown to be of that specific kind that generative grammarians attribute to language systems. He believes that there is 'not the slightest reason to believe' that there are other symbolic systems that have specific properties of generative grammars of human languages—say 'the distinction of deep and surface structure, the specific properties of grammatical transformations and phonological rules, the principles of rule ordering, and so on' (1972, p. 175). There is 'little useful analogy between the schema of universal grammar [generative theory of human language] that we must, I believe, assign to the mind as an innate character, and any other known system of mental organization' (p. 90).[7]

If any other system of mental organization can be shown to have the specific properties of generative grammars, Chomsky would be willing to give up his pessimism. It is, he admits, 'quite possible that the lack of analogy testifies to our ignorance of other aspects of mental function, rather than to the absolute uniqueness of linguistic structure' (1972, p. 90). Such a demonstration would also provide an answer to the larger question regarding the number of faculties of the mind. If the theories of the various domains of symbolic functioning were shown to have the specific properties of generative grammars, we would have reason to believe that there is, as Edelson apparently thinks, just one faculty, 'the symbolic function,' of the mind, and not, as advocated by Putnam (1967), for example, several.

Edelson has, thus, undertaken a major challenge. As a serious proposal, it must be understood as an attempt not only to construct a generative theory of 'dream language' but also to answer some of the serious, philosophical questions regarding the nature of the human mind.

Impressed with the generative theory of language and Freud's explicit concern with 'meaning,' Edelson starts out with a catalogue of similarities between Chomsky and Freud, two pioneering theorists dealing with symbolic systems controlled by humans. His ritual citation of similarities between the methodologies pursued by two of the greatest intellects of our age is, however, nothing more than a result of the temptation to 'which we so often succumb in our journals' (Edelson, 1973, p. 222).

Vagueness surrounds his ideas concerning the use of the linguistic distinction between deep and surface structure, one of the specific properties of grammar singled out by Chomsky for 'appreciating the consequences of the operations of the dreamwork' (Edelson, 1973, p. 208). 'Deep structures [he says] are those abstract, syntactic patterns that underlie the simplest, base, or kernel sentences of the language (exemplified, although this is an oversimplification, by simple— noncompound and noncomplex—sentences, which are active, de- clarative, and in the present tense)' (p. 216). The concept of 'kernel sentence' has been shown to be invalid; and 'deep structures' are not simple, active declarative sentences in the present tense. The sentences *John is here* and *Is John here*, for example, are distinguished in the deep structure. The latter contains a marker not present in the former. Though there is some disagreement regarding the precise nature of this marker, its systematic presence is not questioned. Similarly, the sentence *John is here* is different from the sentence *John is not here* because the latter derives from a deep structure that contains the abstract marker *Neg*, which triggers off various transformations that modify the relevant deep structure in appropriate ways. These questions are discussed in Katz and Postal (1964), a source cited in Edelson's bibliography. Edelson uses the term 'deep structure' only metaphorically. He seems to believe that *any* gap between the 'appearance' and the 'reality' of things can justify the postulation of 'deep structure.' Deep structure in generative grammar, however, is a theoretical construct that has to be semantically justified and syntactically motivated. What specific, empirical evidence is there to justify the postulation of an intermediate, theoretical construct like 'deep structure' in a system like 'dream language,' where, as Edelson himself points out (1973, p. 200), the symbolism seems to be nonarbitrarily motivated. As a matter of fact, the evidence that such a hypothetical construct is needed even in grammar has increasingly vanished (Fillmore, 1968; Lakoff, 1970).

Although Edelson recognizes that any generative theory of dream language would have to be based on the assumption that a dream 'yields its meanings only to one who knows its possible "histories" and "actual history"' (1973, p. 215), he does nothing to give empirical content to the various processes of combination, rearrangement, and deletion—his putative transformations—which he talks about. Although he seems to be aware of the fact that a sufficiently powerful theory would be needed to account for his chosen domain, he does not seem to be concerned with the fact that any such theory would need to be constrained in various ways to account for *only* the structures that fall within that domain. Since he gives no instances of the putative transformations within his realm of concern, it is difficult to imagine what some of these constraints might be. In the absence of clearly defined rules and constraints his proposal is bound to appear trivial. It remains only a metaphor.

Metaphor, as a matter of fact, is his chief problem. An example is Edelson's use of the word *generate*: 'Thus, Freud claims that, even though no one has ever dreamed or will ever dream a single one of his dreams, he shares with mankind the process by which dreams are generated. Similarly, Chomsky claims that, even though each of the sentences he may devise is novel, he shares with mankind the process by which these sentences are generated' (1973, p. 210 f.). In the trivial sense, the observation is, of course, true: both Chomsky and Freud belong to the same species. The point is that Chomsky is talking about the calculus called grammar by generative grammarians that assigns structural descriptions to all and only the sentences of a language, and Freud is not. Chomsky uses the word *generate* to mean *enumerate* (to assign structural descriptions to). The grammar, the calculus proposed by grammarians, assigns structural descriptions to the structures it generates. Clearly, Freud is not implying any such enumeration.

While some of Edelson's suggestions sound initially attractive, they rarely rise above the level of vague analogies. Accepting an out-of-date and demonstrably false definition of deep structure, he suggests, for example, that 'wishes' are perhaps analogues to 'that part of the syntactic component the rules of which generate such ['kernel'] structures' (1973, p. 216). The part of the syntactic component he is referring to is called 'the phrase structure component' in generative theory. The phrase structure rules of a grammar generate the structures to which lexical items are, if they meet certain conditions, attached. There are certain ordering relationships in the prelexical nodes that appear in these rules (Chomsky, 1965) and what they generate is assigned hierarchical structure. Hence it is difficult to see precisely what Edelson is claiming. If he is claiming similarity between phrase structure rules and 'wishes,' he does not give any examples of possible constituent structure of 'wishes' and possible hierarchical relationships among them.

Sometimes, unfortunately, Edelson's analogies are not even attractive. He points out that the dream-work, which he considers to be the transformational part of the system dreaming, is constrained by considerations of representability, just as transformational rules are constrained by considerations of phonological representability. We fail to understand the statement because there is no convincing available evidence which would adequately show that phonological constraints restrict transformational rules in any way. Since transformations apply—and Edelson seems to be aware of the fact—after lexical insertion, questions of phonological representability could not possibly constrain their application.

Talking about the filtering function of transformations (Chomsky, 1965), Edelson suggests that 'defense mechanisms and the proscriptions that motivate their use, operating to control access to conscious representation, [are] the transformational processes of another semiological system' (1973, p. 219). What evidence is there to suggest that defense mechanisms are transformational processes of another semiological system? The notion of 'surface structure constraints,' for which there is considerable evidence in Perlmutter (1970), seems far more applicable here. This ultimate filtering mechanism disallows certain structures that cannot be filtered out by the transformational rules. 'Surface structure constraints' (also called 'output conditions') are set up to account systematically for the fact that the blocking or filtering function of obligatory transformations is not enough to rule out certain strings regarded as ungrammatical in natural languages. An example of this is provided by Spanish, where the object pronouns in sentences quite regularly generated by the transformational component must appear in a certain order. If they do not appear in the specified order, the sentence is ungrammatical. This sort of global filtering can be accounted for only in terms of final output conditions. There are, in other words, well-formed deep structures that have no corresponding well-formed surface structures. Perlmutter shows the necessity of such constraints in the grammars of Spanish and French. The difference between transformations and output conditions is that while an obligatory transformation must be applied if its structural description is met, there is no requirement that its structural description must be met;

output conditions, however, have to be met (1970, p. 246).

Edelson's undercutting of the status of censorship is based on his rejection of censorship as a motive for using dream-work; the upshot of such a contention is that, with censorship eliminated, dream distortion and disguise stem solely from the dream-work (1973, p. 245); in line with this process, of course, indifferent elements may be chosen in a dream because of their visual representability and allusiveness to multiple latent dream thoughts. Ultimately, Edelson's rejection of censorship as a necessary component in dream construction rests on two propositions, one based on textual interpretation and the other related to the law of parsimony. In the first instance, Edelson writes: 'My reading of Freud's words is that he tended to give increasing priority as time went on to the intrinsic consequences of choosing a certain way of representing thoughts for determining the form of a dream, and felt less need to postulate the tendentious operation of censorship during a state of sleep as a major contribution to the construction of such a symbolic entity as a dream' (1973, p. 269). But it seems clear to us that the later Freud unequivocally insisted on the centrality of censorship in dreams. Thus in a 1909 addition to his own preferred work Freud declared, 'I may say that the kernel of my theory of dreams lies in my derivation of dream-distortion from the censorship' (1900, p. 308, n. 2); further additions in 1911 and 1919 (pp. 234, 142 f.) explicitly testify to Freud's strong belief in the importance of dream censorship. Since *The Interpretation of Dreams* underwent considerable emendation as well as elaboration, Freud would certainly (if Edelson were right) have expunged or modified at least some of its many references to dream censorship. Furthermore, in 'Revision of Dream-Theory,' the last of Freud's major reflections on dreams published during his lifetime, Freud in six instances stresses the value of censorship in dreams (1933, pp. 15, 18–21, 28). In light of this evidence, then, it seems hazardous to maintain that Freud gave increasingly less importance to censorship in dream formation. What change Edelson could have indicated, however, is that by 1938 Freud reassigned the operations of censorship in dream formation from the superego to the ego, although it must be said that Freud himself did not elaborate on this point (1940, chap. 4).

Edelson's second reason for rejecting censorship in dreams is predicated on the law of parsimony: condensation and figurability suffice in themselves to account for dream distortion (1973, p. 268); collaterally, displacement almost inevitably results from condensation rather than from a motive to disguise (p. 257). Such a position, one may counter, is objectionable for several reasons:

1. Concentrating on dream ideas and thereby attempting to show the superfluity of censorship from a semiological point of view, Edelson neglects the domain of affects and the function of censorship toward them. As Freud (1900) maintained, censorship obviates anxiety and painful affects (p. 267). And again: '*The inhibition of affect, accordingly, must be considered as the second consequence of the censorship of dreams, just as dream-distortion is its first consequence*' (p. 468). One should also bear in mind Freud's explanation of nightmare as a breaking out of affect subsequent to a possible relaxation of censorship.

2. But even remaining in the area of dream ideas, one must state, along with Freud and contrary to Edelson, that at least for three reasons the dynamics of representability do not totally account for the distortion from the latent to the manifest dream:

   (a) Children's dreams are often undistorted, for they lack censorship (1900, pp. 551, 553 f.). If the phenomena of representability necessitated distortion and could entirely account for it, children's dreams should therefore be constantly distorted.

   (b) Pictorial representability is by its very nature absent in imageless dreams, which nevertheless are modified by censorship. As Freud (1900) declares quite clearly: 'It might have been supposed that condensation and the formation of compromises is only carried out for the sake of facilitating regression, that is, when it is a question of transforming thoughts into images. But the analysis—and still more the synthesis—of dreams which include no such regression to images, e.g. the dream of 'Autodidasker', exhibits the same processes of displacement and condensation as the 'rest' (p. 597)—such dreams testify to the existence of censorship, however lowered (see p. 542).

   (c) The selection of both recent and indifferent material in dreams as substitutes for infantile thoughts can be sufficiently elucidated only in a strictly Freudian sense. Such material has 'the least to fear from censorship imposed by resistance . . . the indifferent ones because they have given no occasion for the formation of many ties, and the recent ones because they have not yet had time to form them' (1900, p. 563 fn.).

3. Edelson overlooks a symbolic factor which Freud adequately answers, namely, that dreams make use of unconscious symbols both because of their use of representability and because they generally escape censorship (1973, p. 349).

101

4. Freud found that the dreams of healthy people often contain much more characteristic and simpler symbolism than those of neurotics, in whom a more powerful censorship increases dream distortion (1900, p. 374). Strangely enough, Freud's empirical judgements go unmentioned in Edelson's 'empirical' hypotheses that would bypass censorship.

To sum up: while leaving Freud's understanding of dream censorship intact, a careful examination of Freud's *Interpretation of Dreams* reveals the extent of its extraordinary attempt to lay down a comparative grammar of internal media. We are now equipped to enter more deeply into Freud's masterpiece and analyze its core dream, and in doing so, reconsider the very accuracy of the term 'manifest dream' which we have used up to this point.

Notes

★ Written in collaboration with Rajendra Singh and first published in *The Psychoanalytic Study of the Child* (1975), 30: 221–241.
1 In this new vast field dealing specifically with semiology, three other works deserve special mention: Ernesto Liendo (1967) applies a semiology inspired by Luis Prieto to a noticeably Kleinian conception of object relations; the other two are by David Liberman (1970) and Eugen Bär (1975).
2 See also Freud (1905): 'The dream-work . . . submits the thought-material, which is brought forward in the optative mood, to a most strange revision' (p. 162) and 'Thus dreams make use of the present tense in the same manner and by the same right as day-dreams. The present tense is the one in which wishes are represented as fulfilled' (1900, p. 535).
3 In effect, visual expression cannot directly contain relations, which characterize thoughts. Both phylogenetically and ontogenetically it is older than thinking in words and is in some ways even nearer to unconscious processes (Freud, 1923, p. 21).
4 Blank (1958) says that his finding 'will surprise only those who believe in a racial unconsciousness, hereditary transmission of memories, or other Lamarckian concepts' (p. 159). He adds that if a person is blinded before seven years, there is little chance of his having visual memories or dreams later on, for the period between five and seven is critical for cerebral structural maturation, the development of the visual center, and the completion of early ego growth.
5 At any rate, there would be a great use for a grammar of visual deformation and displacement that could do on a visual basis what Jones

(1916), for example, did with Punchinello as a verbal symbol, tracing its contaminations and so on. Moreover, such a grammar would help to undercut Jones's contention that 'linguistic connections between the symbol and the idea symbolised' (p. 140) are one of the six aspects of true symbolism. The manifold nature of childhood symbolism is even further complicated by the cross-sensory and intermodal possibilities underlined by Howard Gardner (1973). Recent studies indicate more and more that the child, seizing on the modal properties of behavior, may well open his mouth as a response to seeing an open hand. Gardner concludes: 'The sensitivity to modal/vectoral properties (which cut across sensory modalities and are manifest in both perceptual and the motoric realm) is, I would suggest further, a necessary antecedent for the use and comprehension of symbols, and remains fundamental to our cognition in the adult years (1973, p. 206 f.).

6 I.e. sentence structure characterized by subordinate structure and hierarchical organization, exemplified par excellence by the Ciceronian periodic sentence. On the other hand, in parataxis there are no conjunctions (as in a telegram), or if subordinating and coordinating conjunctions be present, they tend to be deprived of their logical force (as in biblical style).

7 Cf. Chomsky (1972) on Lévi-Strauss: 'No one, to my knowledge, has devoted more thought to this problem than Lévi-Strauss. For example, his recent book on the categories of primitive mentality is a serious and thoughtful attempt to come to grips with this problem. Nevertheless, I do not see what conclusions can be reached from a study of his materials beyond the fact that the savage mind attempts to impose some organization on the physical world—that humans classify, if they perform any mental acts at all. Specifically, *Lévi-Strauss's well-known critique of totemism seems to reduce to little more than this conclusion*' (p. 74; italics ours).

References

Bär, E. (1975) *Semiotic Approaches to Psychotherapy*. Bloomington, Indiana: Indiana University Press.

Benveniste, E. (1969) Sémiologie de la langue (1). *Semiotica*, 1: 1–12.

Blank, R.H. (1958) Dreams of the blind. *Psychoanalytic Quarterly*, 27: 158–174.

Chomsky, N. (1965) *Aspects of the Theory of Syntax*. Cambridge, Mass.: M.I.T. Press.

—— (1972) *Language and Mind*. New York: Harcourt Brace & Jovanovich.

Edelson, M. (1973) Language and dreams. *This Annual*, 27: 203–282.

Fillmore, C. (1968) The case for case. In: E. Bach and R. Harms (eds.) *Universals in Linguistics Theory*. New York: Holt, Rinehart & Winston.

Freud, S. (1900). The interpretation of dreams. *Standard Edition*, 4 and 5. London: Hogarth Press, 1953.

—— (1905). Jokes and their relation to the unconscious. *Standard Edition*, 8. London: Hogarth Press, 1960.

—— (1913). Totem and taboo. *Standard Edition*, 13: 1–161. London: Hogarth Press, 1953.

—— (1915–1917). Introductory lectures on psychoanalysis. *Standard Edition*, 15 and 16. London: Hogarth Press, 1961.

—— (1923). The ego and the id. *Standard Edition*, 19: 3–66. London: Hogarth Press, 1961.

—— (1933). New introductory lectures on psychoanalysis. *Standard Edition*, 22; 3–182. London: Hogarth Press, 1964.

—— (1940). An outline of psychoanalysis. *Standard Edition*, 23: 141–207. London: Hogarth Press, 1964.

Gardner, H. (1973) *The Quest for Mind*. New York: Knopf.

Jakobson, R. (1971) Two aspects of language and two types of aphasic disturbances. *Selected Writings*, 2: 239–259. The Hague: Mouton.

Jones, E. (1916) The theory of symbolism. *Papers on Psycho-Analysis*. London: Baillière, 5th edition, 1948, pp. 87–144.

Katz, J. and Postal, P. (1964) *An Integrated Theory of Linguistic Descriptions*. Cambridge, Mass.: M.I.T. Press.

Lakoff, G. (1970) Linguistics and natural logic. *Synthèse*, 22: 151–271.

Liberman, D. (1970) *Lingüística, interracción, communicativa y proceso psico-analítica*. Buenos Aires: Editorial Galerna.

Liendo, E. (1967) Las relaciones objectales y lo simbolización de la angustia. *Rev. Psicoanál*, 24: 839–897.

Martin, M. (1968) *Le Langage cinématographique*. Paris: Seuil.

Metz, C. (1968), *Essais sur la signification du cinéma*. Paris: Klinsksieck.

—— (1971) *Langue et cinéma*. Paris: Larousse.

Passeron, R. (1962) *L'Oeuvre picturale et les fonctions de l'apparence*. Paris: Vrin.

Perlmutter, D. (1970) Surface structure constraints in syntax. *Linguistic Inquiry*, 1: 187–256.

Putnam, H. (1967) The innateness hypothesis and explanatory models in linguistics. *Synthèse*, 17: 2–28.

Rooney, W. (1962) John Donne's second prebend sermon: a stylistic analysis. *Texas Studies in Language and Literature*, 4: 24–34.

5

Towards a formalist approach to Freud's central dream*

In 1923 Freud strove to make a distinction between two kinds of dreams, those 'from above' and those 'from below':

> Dreams from below are those which are provoked by the strength of an unconscious (repressed) wish which has found a means of being represented in some of the day's residues. They may be regarded as inroads of the repressed into waking life. Dreams from above correspond to thoughts or intentions of the day before which have contrived during the night to obtain reinforcement from repressed material that is debarred from the ego [Freud, 1923a, p. 111].

Six years later Freud (1929) specified the nature of 'dreams from above' more elaborately: 'they are formulations of ideas which could have been created just as well in a waking state as during the state of sleep, and which have derived their content only in certain parts from mental states at a comparatively deep level.' And finally, in 1940 Freud concluded, 'In short, dreams may arise either from the id or from the ego' (p. 166).

I should like to caution against a hasty classification of any dream as an ego dream, as one 'from above'—and perhaps even this genetic category itself might be reconsidered at least for some instances. In this light any thorough dream analysis must take account also of a formalist, stylistic approach (dealing with the grammar, figurative language, semantic patterns and the like)—an approach quite in harmony with psychoanalysis. That is to say, whereas the cornerstone of modern Saussurean linguistics is that the connexion between the signifier and signified is arbitrary, the cornerstone of modern

105

stylistics is that the connexion is motivated, non-arbitrary; and in that sense, formalism is close to psychoanalysis and its study of the non-arbitrariness of human behaviour and psychic activity. A formalist approach could demonstrate that Freud's (1900) Irma dream, although immediately dealing with the ego's concerns with professional responsibilities, is saturated with id elements on the manifest level and is an id dream. A formalist analysis, moreover, is liable to uncover covert as well as overt aspects of the so-called manifest dream. Bearing this in mind along with the fact that at least much of the day residue in the latent dream is quite on the surface, if this chapter means anything at all, it means that 'latent' and 'manifest' cannot be used as primary terms for dream classifications; they do, however, stand as valuable secondary terms. The underlying belief throughout my essay is that more precision is gained by first of all categorizing dream events from a neutral, chronological perspective, and then by paying careful attention to the modalities of dream reportage. These various elements, chronological and modal, are represented in the following outline:

1. The proto-dream or the dream activity up to the staged dream. The components of the proto-dream are latent as well as manifest (the day residues).
2. The staged dream or, so to speak, 'the dream dreamt.' To the extent that the staged dream is pictorial, it is known to the non-dreamer only by inference.
3. The reported dream and modalities affecting it:
   (a) Its manifest and latent levels.
   (b) To whom is it told (see Ferenczi, 1913) and, in certain cases, retold? This second possibility is particularly relevant for published dreams, as it may involve a change in several lexical items.
   (c) Is the report given orally or in writing? Volume, tone, suprasegmental phenomena (pitch, stress, juncture), and the like are elaborations specific to an oral dream report. If, however, the dreamer writes down his dream, a whole new list of elaborations proper to the written medium comes into play: spelling, capitalization, punctuation, paragraphing, and the like. It follows then that an analyst's transcription of an orally reported dream necessitates elaborations which are the analyst's own, and not the patient's.

   For all these reasons and others which I shall demonstrate, it is thoroughly misleading to designate the staged dream and reported dream by one term.

4. The dreamer's commentary. It is not quite accurate to label everything in the dreamer's commentary as an association. When Freud subsequently comments that the hosts in the Irma dream were himself and his wife, he is not associating; he is mindful of his addressees and is furnishing a clarification.

In the exposition that follows, I shall use a predominantly formalist approach to study Freud's Irma dream; particular but not exclusive attention will be given to it apart from Freud's associations. Since the Irma dream is a written report, it has certain features of oneiric elaboration that are peculiar to the written medium and by that very fact brings forth another dimension suitable to formalist analysis.

The Irma dream

Freud's Irma dream is the most famous of all in the history of psychoanalysis. It is the first as well as the most elaborately analyzed dream in *The Interpretation of Dreams* (Freud, 1900) and attendantly it has received 'the greatest study in the psycho-analytic literature' (Grinstein, 1968). Furthermore, as Freud (1950a, p. 322) averred in a memorable letter to Fliess some five years later, the Irma dream revealed to him the very mystery about dreams in general. And as Schur (1966) maintains, although Freud had previously analyzed some of his own dreams and had already been aware of their wish-fulfilment nature, '*What Freud may have been attempting for the first time with the Irma dream was the systematic application of free association to every single element of the manifest dream, after which he connected these associations until a meaningful trend emerged.*' As generally sound as this statement is, it is my contrasting belief that there are many very subtle elements in the reported dream which Freud could hardly have noticed.

My analysis of the dream will proceed in the order of the following headings: translation, patterns of semantic oppositions, grammar, punctuation, the key term 'trimethylamin' in all its dimensions extending from the typographical to the semantic and, finally, desire and defence. An exacting investigation of these topics reveals in the Irma dream some elements of sexuality and socio-sexuality that have hitherto been either overlooked or ignored. In the course of uncovering these aspects of the Irma dream, I hope to have contributed to shedding light on Freud's psychic life at the time and,

107

equally, to have brought into focus some new methods of dream analysis.

In a note appended in 1911 to his self-avowed masterpiece, Freud affirmed: 'It is impossible as a rule to translate a dream into a foreign language and this is equally true, I fancy, of a book such as the present one' (1900, p. 99). This affirmation can specifically apply to any possible English translation of the Irma dream. But beyond that, in a general way Strachey has inexplicably distorted the Irma dream and indeed every dream reported by Freud in 'The Interpretation of Dreams'; but what is more serious is that this distortion flies in the face of Freudian dream theory. That is to say, Strachey translated Freud's dreams into the past tense, whereas in the original German they are reported in the present tense; nor does Strachey's translation give the dramatic sense of Freud's commentaries to his dreams, most of which are befittingly in the present tense since they are part of the dreams. Now in 'The Interpretation of Dreams', in the monograph on Jokes (Freud, 1905, p. 162) and in the 'Introductory Lectures' (Freud, 1916–17, p. 129), Freud clearly revealed a basis for the grammar of dreams. The latent dream is in the optative mood and the dream work changes this thought-material into the present indicative: Freud even mentions the Irma dream in this regard and concludes, 'The present tense is the one in which wishes are represented as fulfilled' (1900, pp. 534–535). Nowhere did Freud designate a rationale for such a conception, but one may speculate that there was a twofold reason: first, he semiologically thought of fantasies as not only syntactically limited (as opposed to verbal media) but also chronologically limited, their enactment being rooted in the present; secondly, the present tense is the one *par excellence* that approximates the timelessness of the unconscious. Collaterally, it is relevant to think of the Hebraic conceptions of the timelessness of God: *Yahweh* (Gen. 4), which is usually translated by the impersonal present 'He is'; and *Ehyéh asher éhyéh* (Exod. 3) is usually given as 'I am Who am.' Be as it may, Strachey's use of the past tense is unjustified, departs from the German original and violates conditions of appropriateness; A.A. Brill's translation (see Freud, 1938), by the way, rightly shows the present tense.

Although Strachey's translation is laudable as for detail, I shall supply a new translation which hopefully will more accurately render the complex meaning of the German text.[1] I shall also furnish alternate meanings of key words:

1. *Eine grosse Halle—viele Gäste, die wir empfangen.—Unter ihnen Irma,*

empfangen:	'conceive' (Erikson, 1954)
	'receive'
Fang:	'claw'
	'fang'
unter:	'under'

A large hall—many guests, whom we receive.—Among them Irma,

2. *die ich sofort beiseite nehme, um gleichsam ihren Brief zu beantworten,*
   Seite   'side'
   whom I immediately take aside, as if to answer her letter,

3. *ihr Vorwürfe zu machen, dass sie die 'Lösung' noch nicht akzeptiert.*
   Wurf: 'brood, litter, a throw'
   Lösung: 'liquid solution' (Erikson, 1954)
            'firing (of guns)'
   and to reproach her that she doesn't accept the 'solution' yet.

4. *Ich sage ihr: Wenn du noch Schmerzen hast, so ist es wirklich*
   I say to her: 'If you still have pains, it is really

5. *nur deine Schuld.—Sie antwortet: Wenn du wüsstest, was*
   only your fault.'—She answers: 'If you knew what

6. *ich für Schmerzen jetzt habe im Hals, Magen und Leib,*
   pains I have now in my throat, stomach and abdomen,

7. *es schnürt mich zusammen.—Ich erschrecke und sehe sie an.*
   Schnur: 'string'
            'daughter-in-law' (biblical)
   Same(n)   'sperm'
   it's tightening me up.'—I am startled and look at her.

8. *Sie sieht bleich und gedunsen aus; ich denke, am Ende übersehe ich da doch*
   She looks pallid and puffy; I think, after all I am overlooking

9. *etwas Organisches. Ich nehme sie zum Fenster und schaue ihr in*
   something organic. I take her to the window and look into

10. *den Hals. Dabei zeigt sie etwas Sträuben wie die Frauen,*
    strauben: 'bristle up, resist'
    her throat. With that she shows some resistance, like women

11. *die ein künstliches Gebiss tragen. Ich denke mir,* who wear a denture.
    I think to myself,

12. *sie hat es doch nicht nötig.—Der Mund geht dann auch gut auf,*
    she doesn't need to do that.—Her mouth then opens properly,

13. *und ich finde rechts einen grossen weissen Fleck, und anderwärts*
    Warze: 'wart; nipple'
    and I find on the right a large white spot, and elsewhere

14. *sehe ich an merkwürdigen krausen Gebilden, die offenbar*
    bar: 'naked, nude'

I see on remarkable curled structures which evidently

15. *den Nasenmuscheln nachgebildet sind, ausgedehnte*
    are patterned on the nasal turbinal bones, extensive

16. *weissgraue Schorfe.—Ich rufe schnell Dr. M. hinzu, der*
       grauen: 'shudder'; 'be afraid'
    white-grey scabs.—I quickly call Dr M., who

17. *die Untersuchung wierderholt und bestätigt . . .*
       unter: 'under'
    repeats and confirms the examination . . .

18. *Dr. M. sieht ganz anders aus als sonst; er ist sehr bleich, hinkt,*
    Dr. M. looks entirely different from usual; he is very pallid, limps,

19. *ist am Kinn bartlos . . . Mein Freund Otto*
    is beardless on the chin . . . My friend Otto

20. *steht jetzt auch neben ihr, und Freund Leopold perkutiert sie*
    now also stands next to her, and my friend Leopold percusses her

21. *über dem Leibchen und sagt: Sie hat eine Dämpfung links unten,*
    over the bodice and says: 'She has a dullness below on the left,'

22. *weist auch eine infiltrierte Hautpartie an der linken*
    points also to an infiltrated portion of the skin on the left

23. *Schulter hin (was ich trotz des Kleides wie er spüre) . . .*
    shoulder (which I, in spite of the dress, just as he, feel) . . .

24. *M. sagt: Kein Zweifel, es ist eine Infektion, aber es macht nichts;*
    M. says: 'Without a doubt, it's an infection, but it doesn't matter;

25. *es wird noch Dysenterie hinzukommen und das Gift sich ausscheiden. . .*
       Scheide: 'vagina'
    dysentery will follow and the poison will be eliminated . . .

26. *Wir wissen auch unmittelbar, woher die Infektion rührt.*
       Mittel: 'remedy, medicine'
       Ruhr: 'dysentery'
       bar: 'naked'
    We also directly know where the infection comes from.

27. *Freund Otto hat ihr unlängst, als sie sich unwohl fühlte,*
    Recently my friend Otto, when she was not feeling well,

28. *eine Injektion gegeben mit einem Propylpräparat, Propylen . . .*
       *(Propylon—*Latin, *vestibulum,*
       arch. and anat. term: Erikson, 1954)
    gave her an injection of a preparation of propyl, propyls . . .

29. *Propionsäure . . . Trimethylamin (dessen Formel ich*
       Propion: suggests 'priapic, phallic' (Erikson, 1954)
       lahm: 'crippled, lame'

110

'impotent'

Ammen: 'wet-nurses'

'Amen'

propionic acid . . . trimethylamin (whose formula I

30. *fettgedruckt vor mir sehe*) . . . *Man macht solche Injektionen nicht so*

fett: 'oily, greasy'

see in heavy type before me) . . . one doesn't give such injections

31. *leichtfertig* . . . *Wahrscheinlich war auch die Spritze nicht rein.*

leichtfertig: 'wanton, loose'

Spritze: 'squirter' (Erikson, 1954)

Schein: 'light, shine'

rein: 'chaste'

'kosher'

so lightly . . . Probably, too, the syringe wasn't clean.

Such a translation, revelatory of the extraordinary polysemy of the Irma dream, gives rise to two observations: the dream is drenched in somatic references and subtly involves a number of sexual and familial allusions. First of all, there is the anticipation in *empfangen* ('conceive'; 'claw') of the vagina dentata of Irma's mouth-vagina and its artificial dentures. Then Freud takes Irma aside and as a second reading indicates, by the side (*Seite*). 'Throwing' the blame on the hysterical widow, a bereft daughter-in-law (*Schnur*), suggests her sexually affected history. Freud's solution, in a liquid sense, is phallically overdetermined in the alternate meaning of *Lösung*, i.e. 'the firing (of guns), a volley.' Alongside the professional solution there is a spermatic one, alluded to in trimethylamin. In contrast to '*my* solution,' where *my* is too proximate and personal, 'the' is both imperiously definitive and defensively distancing. To Irma's complaint that she is choked and indeed overcome with *Samen* ('sperm') we should bear in mind Freud's subsequent interpretation of *Gleijisamen*, the Rat Man's magical charm. The word was partially an anagram of his beloved's name, Gisela; and in effect, through the formula, the Rat Man put his *Samen* ('semen') in contiguity with his girlfriend and thereby masturbated with her image (Freud, 1909, pp. 225, 281). Now then, a precursor of Irma is Freud's own childhood maid ('Kinderfrau'), his first seductress, on whom he also inaccurately projected the identity of wet-nurse or *Amme* (see Grigg, 1973, p. 112; Schur, 1972, p. 124). Following Freud's logic in the Rat Man case, we may say that, phonemically, he is in spermatic contact not only with Irma but also with the world of *Ammen* ('wet-nurses' or 'seductresses'). In any event, the German prefix *zusammen* is not

111

necessary for the verb *schnüren*, ('choke') but merely acts as an intensifier. Bearing in mind that language has the properties of self-reference as well as extralinguistic reference, we may anticipate Freud's criticism of Irma and apply it to him; 'He doesn't need to do that—that's to say, use *zusammen*.' For purposes of clarity it should be mentioned that between *Samen* and *zusammen* and between other lexical pairs pertinent to the dream, there is phonological and orthographical similarity, not identity; such divergence, especially when slight, of course does not obviate textual relevance.

According to Freud's interpretation, Irma's opening her mouth properly means also, in another register, that she speaks with less resistance. This openness is further overdetermined, for in the same sentence we read that when her mouth opens, it makes mouth—genitalia resemblances *openly* demonstrable. As opposed to an alternate and less resonant adverb such as *clearly* (*deutlich*), *offenbar* has a suffix (*bar*) which means 'naked' and is quite to the point. One may also observe that the locution Freud uses ('her mouth opens,' instead of 'she opens her mouth') is one which is indicative of the mechanical. It is as if Freud, threatened by Irma's sexual cooperation, dissociates the mouth-vagina from the rest of her body. Incidentally, Erikson's (1954) translation of this phrase ('Sie hat es doch nicht') as 'She doesn't have to put on such airs' (pp. 12, 25) is totally pejorative and discards Freud's first association to it, namely, a compliment (1900, p. 109). At this point of the oneiric drama, the male dreamer mechanizes Irma, whether she be uncooperative (as if she wears a denture) or cooperative (her mouth opening properly). Plainly enough, there is only one simile in the dream, and it is somewhat detrimental to women at that—they furthermore are the only personages that wear something artificial. Another inferiorization is seen in the sense that, conforming to psychoanalytical theory that the juxtaposition of events may indicate causality, Freud's reflexion about Irma's uncooperation is immediately followed by her co-operation—another instance of the domination and magicality of male thought that marks the dream. Then again, the word for her bodice is *Leibchen* which in the most literal sense means 'little body' and is slightly pejorative.

Appropriate to the male identifications that Freud assigns her, Irma can not only resist but stiffen up (*Sträuben*)—a bisexual, a phallicized woman. Freud's male outlook may be seen in the fact that Irma's *active* resistance is rendered by a phallic reference (stiffening). Apart from infantile wishes, this dream also presents a latent body schema rooted in polymorphous infantile sexuality. In line with this, not only are there nipples ('ander*wärts*) in the interior of her mouth,

112

but it also resembles the nose. Fliess (1893) had pointed out resemblances between the nose and the male and female genitalia (significantly, Freud in this matter mentions only the female organs!—p. 117). Propylon as an entrance, anatomically speaking, may be considered with reference to the vagina (*ausscheiden*); but also, by extension, the mouth is a propylon to the throat. Finally, if the syringe is not clean (*rein*), it must be understood that neither is the squirter chaste (*rein*); he is *leichtfertig* ('wanton, loose')—*fett* as 'oily, greasy,' fits into the context here. As a dirty squirter, this would be another reason for Freud's wanting Otto to get married. Marriage would equally solve Irma's problems (pp. 116–117) and we must remember too that Fliess was a kind of foster-parent, says Freud, of 'all my writings during their period of gestation' (p. 116).

Coinciding with the somatic density of the dream, the voyeuristic element is quite pronounced. Accordingly, the very opening lines of Freud's analysis must be underscored: his summer house was called 'Bellevue,' right near Kahlenberg, or translated, a 'beautiful view' right near 'bald mountain.' The visuality keynoting the geographical setting of the dream is strongly repeated in the dream itself: I look at her, she looks, I overlook, I look into, I see, Dr. M. looks different, I see before me. The German word for *probably*, moreover, pivots around a visual meaning ('wahr*schein*lich'; 'light, shine'). But it is in terms of vertical references that the voyeuristic element is most nuanced. The medical examination in effect is a real *Untersuchung*, an 'under-searching' which can uncover a dullness *down below*, something which Freud had *over*looked. Significantly, from a choice of prepositions Freud opts for *unter* to indicate that Irma is 'among' the guests. This importance of the above/under opposition is clearly brought out by the dreamer's remark that both he and Leopold perceive the infection on Irma's shoulder in spite of the dress. It is as if the 'position over' urgently gives place to 'position under', i.e. mediation is discarded. This notion is further brought out by the fact that the four doctors know immediately (without mediation) the source of Irma's infection. Now the main component of *unmittelbar* ('immediately') is *Mittel* ('remedy, medicine')—which 'punfully' encapsulates the dream's somatic/psychic, above/under dichotomy and as well comments ironically on Breuer's prognosis for he postulates dysentery as a remedy, a means, to eliminate the toxin.

Revolving around the word dysentery is the dream's extraordinary manipulation of the temporal antithesis 'before/after' which parallels the undercutting of the 'above/under' antinomy. The infection is to be subsequently eliminated by dysentery, for which a German synonym is *Ruhr*; concomitantly the doctors all know where the infection comes from (*rührt*). Accordingly the German synonymy between the *cause* of infection and the agent *effecting* the purge testifies in a spectacular fashion to the dream's use of primary process and to the absence of contradiction in the unconscious. In a way, the lexical complexity of the term *rühr(t)*, in which different notes of cause and effect coexist, symbolizes the reversibility of the dream's total structure. Specifically, the dream is an interesting instance of those dreams that yield meaning if read backwards (Freud, 1900, p. 328), hence: the dirty syringe, Otto's injection, common knowledge of that injection, the examination, group intercourse, physical symptoms, the large hall or pregnancy.

A third prepositional antinomy is 'outer/inner.' The dichotomy between the inner, private life of Freud and his public professional life is rendered conflictual by Irma, a family friend, who introduces a 'mixed relationship' (1900, p. 106) in the therapy; her particular case also activates Freud's professional struggling quest for the origin of neuroses, somatic or psychological. Physically Irma is portrayed both in a surface and inner sense (e.g. her stomach pains); mentally she is portrayed only in terms of surface phenomena—what she says. This schema is reversed for the males. Physically they are depicted only on the surface level; mentally, however, they are described in terms of their *inner* thoughts and perceptions as well as what they express. In sum, the exclusive attention given to Irma's inner physicality contrasts with the exclusive attention given to the males' non-surfaced mentation to which the male Freud is naturally akin. This split, then, sheds light on Freud's own body ego, especially when we bear in mind his statement that just as the conscious ego is 'first and foremost a body-ego', similarly the deepest and most unknown unconscious aspects of the ego are based on the body (Freud, 1923b, 26–27). It follows that Freud's concern with the body ego goes definitely beyond surface appearances. This nuance is very apparent when Irma complains about pains *in* her throat, stomach and abdomen, a nuance absent in such an alternate German rendition as 'I have pains at (*am*) . . .'

On an overall basis, the dream may be seen as a transition from an outer to an inner scene. In the outer framework, there is the projection of the setting and the external actions and dialogue of the protagonists; the closing scene comprises Freud's inner reflexions, his verbal associations and the perception of a formula. Spanning the two scenes are Freud's communicative gestures which are outer and inner directed: he says to another, he thinks to himself; he looks *at* Irma; he looks *into* her mouth. Then again, the initial reception (taking in) is echoed by the lexical item *in*jection, and even more

114

convincingly, by *infection* and *infiltrated* for which Freud could have chosen other convenient synonyms. Opposed to this, Freud's reproaches (*Vorwürfe*: 'a throwing forward', or literally in Latin: 'a projection'), venting his ill-feelings, match the elimination of the poison in Irma's body. This elimination or *ex*pelling of what has been *in*troduced into the body reverses the dominant exterior to interior movement in the dream, from Irma's conception to Freud's 'conceptions', from Irma's interior to Freud's interiorizations. There is yet another 'projection'—the dreamer who interiorizes, who sees *before* (*vor*) his eyes. The preposition is capital, for it signifies a reactive distancing to trimethylamin, a product of sexual metabolism. Though the image is in Freud's mind, he may at least optically project it outside: the very word itself is close to being a bad object.

Also to be considered is the motif of circulation in the dream, notable in various manifestations ranging from personages to phonemics. Irma herself has circulated among four doctors. There is a sexual symbolism that circulates among various parts of Irma's body and binds them together: mouth, nose, throat, stomach, abdomen and genitalia. In Irma's body there is the circulating disease itself, which Freud specifically stresses four times (1900, pp. 113, 117) is metastatic in nature (incidentally, to some degree metastasis is the medical counterpart of metonymy, the rhetorical term for displacement). There is the circulation of Irma's identity among Freud, Fliess and seventeen others, as indicated by Freud himself. A peculiar phonemic circulation is even prominent in the dream. Aggressively Freud attributed to Irma a severe disease, *Diphtherie*, which, he declared, sounds like *Dysenterie*. Both words, moreover, have the same terminal double rhyme as *Hysterie*. But even more imposing than that, Otto stands for Oskar *Rie*, the culprit of the dream. Hence, *Dysenterie* represents a positive 'dissent' from the 'Rie' complex: *Hysterie, Diphtherie*, Oskar Rie. Seen in another way, there is a counterpoint between circulating activity and elimination or segregation. In keeping with this, the initially receptive Freud is all alone at the dream's end.

To summarize at this point, a study of the various motifs—above/under, before/after, outer/inner, and circularity—affords a unique insight into the intense activity of Freud's unconscious. These motifs are traceable in the polysemy of central words, in overdetermined prepositions, and in the beginnings and endings of words. Attention to these defensive displacements and condensations permits us to appreciate further Freud's extraordinary preoccupation and curiosity concerning the body image and human sexuality. In other words,

115

careful studies which heed all detail are promising ways to explore symbol formation and the body image.

A strictly grammatical analysis extracts even more meaning from the dream, going from a subtle indication of Freud's character and then his dominating attitude to women, to raising issues about the activity of censorship if adverbs are omitted in the reported dream, to finally appreciating punctuation as a possibly most important element in oneiric elaboration. The dream opens abruptly with a telegraphic style, with neither copula nor existential modifiers ('there is, there are'). It is a sort of camera sweep whose rapidity already demonstrates to us the impulsive, precipitous nature of Freud who, in the next setting, *immediately* takes Irma aside and who *quickly* calls in Breuer. In a strictly relative sense, the most complicated syntax occurs with the observation of the mouth: the circuitous syntax is somewhat mimetic of the curly nasal structures as well as Freud's devious anatomical associations to them. (I use *mimetic* here in the sense of indicating a homology between grammatical structure and semantic content). The second half of the dream, more condensed and less syntactically elaborated, is marked by a striking set of grammatical shifts. The defensive projection of guilt characterizes Freud's wandering interiorizations and self-justifications: the primary process and elliptical groping for the chemical agent yields to a moralistic declarative sentence that actually is a submerged imperative, which in turn is followed by a speculative rumination in the past tense. The sole diptych piece in the dream, the exchange of dialogue between Freud and Irma, is precious for its apparent symmetry. The tit-for-tat and the superficial egalitarianism of its grammatical structure and meaning have a deeper lopsided level, tilted in favour of male domination. The parallel structure of the confrontation conveniently lends itself to the following division:

(a) I say to her: 'If you still get pains. . .'
   She replies: 'If you only knew what pains I've got. . . .'
(b) Freud: 'it's really only your fault.'
   Irma: 'it's choking me.'

In the first part of the dialogue, the two 'if's' are diametrically opposed in meaning. Freud's 'if,' which expresses the grammatical presupposition of factivity, can be paraphrased as 'given the fact that'; in other words, it is a pseudo-supposition. Irma's 'if' is truly conditional and, instead of fact, expresses desire; it could be reworded 'would that you knew.' Freud's second clause is a true apodosis or consequential clause and is accusatory in nature, whereas Irma's second clause is in no sense a logical consequent but rather changes subject in mid-stream (rhetorically, an anacoluthon) and is plaintive and self-referential in nature. Briefly, Freud has the facts so to speak, Irma has the desires; Freud is sadistically aggressive, Irma is masochistically grieving. It is worth mentioning, by the way, that Freud and Irma use the familiar form (*du*) in their dialogue. But such a potential marker of egalitarian interchange should be ranked with the illusory identity of the two 'if's,' for the dreamer clings to a superior stance.

In fact, Freud's grammatical domination of Irma is, broadly speaking, a grammatical domination of women in the dream. Freud's wife, the hostess giving her own birthday party, appears but once in the dream but she is not given independent pronominal status; she is pronominally absorbed into the initial 'We' and then completely disappears. In line with this, we may note that Leopold's diagnosis is addressed to the doctors; Irma is merely referred to in the third person. And even at that, she is only once referred to by her proper name; afterwards she is no longer granted this identity but is consistently dwindled to a pronominal reference. By contrast Breuer, the foremost personage in Freud's circle, is thrice given the initial M. and only once is referred to pronominally. The value of pronouns in the dream to signify covert depreciation cannot be insisted upon enough—a fact which is borne out by other material. Breuer is twice given the title Dr. but significantly loses it when he utters a ridiculous prognosis.

What is so striking, too, is the paucity of adverbs of manner in the reported dream. To take one example, how were the guests received? Joyfully? Hurriedly? The presence of the pictorial equivalent of some such qualifier must necessarily be postulated for the staged dream. There is an obvious resemblance between a staged dream and a commonday discourse, which tends to have more adverbs of manner than a factual discourse. In the dream at hand, though, Freud's professional competence is at stake, and he overcompensates on the grammatical level. The few adverbs of manner—'directly,' 'probably'—are cognitive or judgmental in nature. Freud only once attributes emotion to himself, and that is in the verb 'am startled.' Yet, even then most of the verbs are general rather than specific. For instance, were the various statements whispers? cautionings? growlings? Were the various lookings a peering? a scrutinizing? a scanning? When Freud became startled, we can assert that he must have stared, for however long (and not just looked) at Irma. An interesting parallel may be made here between Freud's tendency to use generalizing verbs and the development of classical Greek from concrete language to the later acquisition of abstract and generalizing terms. In Homer and the pre-Socratic philosophers, 'There is not an abstract term for "to see" or for "vision" . . . but rather a classification of visual activity along concrete lines, with verbs denoting "to peer," "to notice," "to stare," "to glare," and so forth' (Simon, 1972).

The upshot of this perspective is that whereas Freud considered the representability of the verbal aspects of the latent dream, he hardly treated the presentational imperatives of the staged dream itself. Which is to say that in a dream involving action, the manifest pictorial quality contains many qualitative characteristics that are not necessarily in the proto-dream. The immediate critical question to be asked is whether the omission of those qualifying characteristics in the reported dream is due to another censorship.

With respect to punctuation—which is an added elaboration in the reported dream—Leopold's cited diagnosis is very revelatory. The German text precedes Leopold's quotation with a colon and follows it with a comma, and then continues the sentence material from before the colon:

Leopold says: 'She also has a dullness on the left,' points also to . . .

By the nature of this punctuation—a dream elaboration reflecting Freud's preoccupation—he blends expression (an outer-ing) of oneself and a retained observation; he collapses the outer/inner dichotomy of the dream; the punctuation serves to present an immediacy, a non-mediation like *unmittelbar*.

Freud's use of parentheses on two occasions recalls their use by certain Renaissance masters of prose parody, who tactically set off the most important matter of the sentence in that manner. In the Irma dream, however, the practice may stem from the censor's extraordinary manipulation of anxiogenic material. The two instances when Freud utilizes parentheses deal with perception in an uncommon sense: an empathetic sensation and an exacting internalized visualization. The latter represents the greatest condensation in the dream. With reference to the first instance and the context around it, there is much to be said. In a defensive minimization, Freud calls this parenthetical remark 'only an insertion' ('nur eine Einschaltung') and he balks at commentary. Here the German text, when translated as literally as fluency will permit, is quite suggestive: 'To speak *openly*, any further distance is dark to me: I have no *inclination* to let myself *in* here more *deeply*' (my italics). ('Das Weitere ist mir dunkel, ich habe, offen gesagt, keine Neigung, mich hier tiefer einzulassen'); *Neigung* ('inclination'), it is worth underscoring, comes from *Neige* ('slope, decline'). Said otherwise, Freud is willing to insert only his parenthesis, but nothing more, nothing deeper. Three other elements merit attention at this point:

1. Freud identified Irma's infiltrated shoulder with the rheumatism in his own shoulder which was invariably active when he stayed up late at night (1900, p. 113). The evening before the dream Freud wrote out a long self-justification of Irma's treatment to Breuer. Since the writing lasted 'far into the night' (p. 108) evidently his very self-defence caused him pain in the left shoulder. Since *Schulter* ('shoulder') phonologically incorporates *Schuld* (pronounced *Schult*, 'guilt'), an apt figurative translation for Freud's accusation ('it's really only your fault') would be 'You alone must shoulder the guilt' and indeed 'my guilt as well.'
2. The sentence 'My friend Leopold was percussing her over the bodice' is the one remarkable instance of detail in the dream that Freud disregarded in his analysis. The following reason may be suggested: the dream satirizes Breuer and Otto but not Leopold who, reserved and prudent by nature, resembles Freud. In the dream Freud is largely voyeuristic, as he touches Irma only on the side; and yet his identification with Leopold moves him defensively to avoid any commentary on the percussing as such.
3. The verbal account of Irma's malady is the dream's impressive example of a switch in lexical register, from a properly scientific nomenclature ('a left upper posterior infiltration') to a more familiar description ('a portion of the skin on the left shoulder was infiltrated'). Thus, as a defence reaction against such intimacy, Freud relegates to sheer subordinate parenthesized interpolation both his and Leopold's voyeuristically disrobing powers.

My final commentary about punctuation deals with Freud's use of dashes and ellipses in the written dream. Here I am somewhat puzzled and what I have to say is entirely tentative and speculative. One thing for sure, Freud uses the dash consistently in the first half of the dream—up to the entrance of Breuer on the scene; and after that dashes no longer appear but give way to ellipses. Typographically, are the dashes suggestive of the phallic, a mark of punctuation which Freud defensively removes from the second half of the dream where three other males are protagonists? Another lead for us may come from the German for 'dash', namely *Gedankenstrich*, literally a 'thoughts-dash'. In comparison with the dream's first part where the dashes are, the second part stands out for its specious reasoning and even more remarkable condensation and primary process. It is possible that there is a significant pictorial quality which is present in

119

Freud's reported dream and absent in the staged dream, i.e. the punctuation itself may be a pictorial rebus!

The most overdetermined part of the dream concerns trimethylamin, the one word which Freud sees in another coded language. It is the dream's most concentrated dynamic representation of both axes of language, paradigmatic and syntagmatic, as formulated by de Saussure. Concurrently, it has many significant dimensions, familial, anatomical, sexual, professional, satirical, phonological and orthographical—multiple dimensions that we must study with all the analytical tools at our disposal. Apart from the triangular relations outlined by Anzieu (1959) the *tri* equally refers to the three turbinal-like structures that Freud saw in Irma's throat (1900, p. 117). The *lam* ('impotent, crippled') directly relates to the satirized and limping Dr. M. as well as to those defectives who, following Fliess's opinion, need trimethylamin as a solution to their sexual problems. The terminal *amin* refers to *Ammen* ('wet-nurses'), which occurred previously in 'zusammen'. The centrality of this mother surrogate for the first two and a half years of Freud's life is well known. It was she who was the 'primary originator' of his neurosis, who told him about God and hell, who gave him 'the means to live and go on living.' Appropriately enough, *Amme* puns on the 'Amen' in prayers and thereby underscores the Catholicism of his nursemaid. In addition, Grigg (1973, p. 112) points out the remarkable assonance between *Amme* and Amalie, the name of Freud's mother. In effect, it was she that played the capital part in Freud's early approach to the Oedipal complex; by contrast the later Freud increasingly connects the mother with the child's sexuality and now names her as the first seductress (Swann, 1974, pp. 1, 16–19). At any rate, the phonological assimilation of *Amme* and Amalie, 'wet-nurse' and mother, further testifies to their fusion in the Irma dream.

Anzieu (1959) spells out the chemical formula seen by Freud and develops some remarkable observations springing from it: $N(CH_3)_3$. But much more remains to be said. First, the trimethylamin (which is seen as a bracketed formula) is indeed a 'solution,' the one word in the dream set off by quotation marks. The solution may be seen, on one level as spermatic, and *amin* is a partial echo of 'es schnürt mich zu*sammen*' ('it's tightening me up'). Furthermore, there is a most fascinating and reinforcing link with the German word for N or Nitrogen, namely *Stickstoff* ('choking matter')! A further consideration of this formula, I contend, reveals some of the deepest parts of the dream and its fascinating overdetermined associations. In the organic molecule that Freud considers, the N atom is the hetero-atom; moreover, as written out linearly, it is extrapolated and saliently affects the rest of the formula. The questions arise, why, after finding the term trimethylamin, did Freud make such a strenuous effort in the dream to visualize its formula? And one wonders why this formula is exceptionally visualized in print that is heavy (*fett*, literally, 'oily, greasy')—in 1895, in a partial report of the dream in the 'Project,' Freud (1950a, p. 342) does not use *fett* but *lebhaft* ('vivid, full of life'). Freud tells us that the formula is visualized 'because of quite a special importance.' In continuing this line of thought I further propose that the prime importance is to be assigned to the atom N, a typographical symbol which binds anatomy, sexuality and personal histories into one. The very letter orthographically represents a nasal, like *m*, which serves to unite in the most intriguing way various personages and themes in the dream. First, we may listen to Freud (1900) and his *idée fixe*, a nasal obsession:[2]

> I [see] the chemical formula . . . in my dream, which bears witness to a great effort on the part of my memory. Moreover, the formula [is] printed in heavy type, as though there were a desire to lay emphasis on some part of the context as being of quite special importance [p. 116].

> I [begin] to guess why the formula for trimethylamin [was] so prominent in the dream. So many important subjects [converge] upon that one word. Trimethylamin [is] an allusion not only to the immensely powerful factor of sexuality, but also to a person whose agreement I [recall] with satisfaction whenever [I feel] isolated in my opinions. Surely this friend who [plays] so large a part in my life must appear again elsewhere in these trains of thought. Yes. For he [has] a special knowledge of the consequences of affections of the nose and its accessory cavities; . . . I [have] Irma examined by him to see whether her gastric pains [may] be of nasal origin. But he [suffers] himself from suppurative rhinitis, which [causes] me anxiety [p. 117].

A careful reading of Schur's (1966, 1972) two pertinent monographs and Fliess's address in 1893 adduces other crucial evidence about the significance of nasality for the dream:

1. Fliess, a rhinolaryngologist, postulated a comprehensive 'nasal reflex neurosis' whose symptoms ranged from migraines to gastrointestinal disorders to sexual dysfunctions to pathology in the shoulder (cf. Irma). Such symptoms, he believed, could be relieved by applying cocaine to the mucous membranes and operating on the turbinate bone and nasal sinuses.
2. Freud's letters about his patient Emma furnish some of the

121

background for the dream. Early in 1895 Freud requested Fliess to come to Vienna and determine whether there was a nasal origin to Emma's somatic symptoms; Fliess decided to operate on her nose. In a way, parallel to that was Freud's own phonemic 'operation' on the name Emma. He extracted the first syllable, which can be totally represented by the nasal M, and replaced it by the phoneme Ir (similar in pronunciation to *irr*, 'in error, wrong, delirious, insane').

3. At the time Freud himself had nasal and gastrointestinal symptoms. However, his greatest illness then was cardiac, yet even for that Fliess proposed a nasal cause.
4. In February 1895 Fliess applied cocaine to Freud's nose and also cauterized it.
5. In the summer of 1894 and again in the spring of 1895 Fliess himself underwent nasal operations.
6. Most significantly of all, on 24 July 1895, the day that Freud avowedly discovered the secret of dreams, he wrote to Fliess: 'What's happening with the nose, menstruation, labour pains, neuroses, your dear wife and the budding little one?' (Schur, 1972, pp. 87–88). Freud then went on to mention his own ill health, undoubtedly having in mind his nasal pains, for in effect his ethmoidal bone was operated on by Fliess during their next meeting in September.
7. The initiator of the chemical series ending in trimethylamin was actually a gift from Otto to Freud, a bottle of liqueur which was offensive to Freud's nose. Furthermore, the bottle bore the name of A*na*nas, which, Freud pointed out, resembled Irma's family name. In short, there is a continuum from a purely olfactory sensation to orthography and typography.
8. The reception in the dream was a birthday celebration for Freud's wife, pregnant with her sixth child, who could be named A*nn*a if a girl and Wilhel*m* if a boy. Acting as a symbolic link, the nasal letters figure also in:

Ir*ma*/E*mma*/A*na*nas
Sig*m*und
M. (Breuer, 'the leading figure in our circle')
*M*ethyl/a*m*yl,/tri*m*ethyla*m*in/A*m*alie.

In summary, the N, the hetero-atom that Freud reflected on orthographically, olfactorily, medically and symbolically establishes crucial links, extending from Fliess the rhinologist and his all-embracing theories about the nose, to the nasal operations of Emma, Freud and Fliess, to the smelly bottle of liqueur. Or, said somewhat differently, the letter N, the chemical sign for nitrogen, which also orthographically represents the first consonant of the word *Nase* ('nose'), significantly enough represents a sound the linguistic decoding of which inevitably constitutes a kinesthetically nasal performance. A further point: given the spectacular condensation of trimethylamin, it is most revealing that Freud never *wrote out* the formula that he *saw* in the staged dream. Since he had visualized that formula, it presents no problem with representability and so stands alone among all the elements in the staged dream. This extraordinary allusiveness of the reported dream is equally an elusiveness and an indication of strong censorship. And so we have all the more reason to avoid calling the visualized and reported dream by the same qualifying term—whether it be *manifest* or whatsoever.

When explaining the dream as wish-fulfilment, Freud deals solely with the professional level: he is not responsible for Irma's persisting pains. Responsibility for her illness is rather to be found in four causes, which are not listed close together but rather scattered throughout the dream. Whereas, however, the reported dream links the causes by 'and's', these 'and's' are to be retranslated as 'either/or's' in the proto-dream (see Freud, 1900, pp. 316–317; 1905, p. 205). Thus, contends Freud in the dream, responsibility stems from either her recalcitrancy to his solution, or the organic rather than hysterical aetiology of her pains, or from Otto's contaminated injection needle, or from her unfavourable sex life (the latter cause, by the way, is the *only* one given in the short account of the dream in 1895) (Freud, 1950b, pp. 341–342).

But this tetrad of justifications alone does not satisfy the guilt-laden Freud. The proto-dream clearly shows the number of instances he collects to demonstrate his conscientiousness and, counter to those, there is a whole series of incidents, from illness to fatality, which inculpate Freud. In his intense aggressive drives he does not stop at one example; there must be many. Freud writes (1900, pp. 294–295; see fn. 2): 'All through the dream, indeed, I [keep] on turning from someone who [annoys] me to someone else who [can] be agreeably contrasted with him; point by point, I [call] up a friend against an opponent.' The sadistic aspect of the aggression is best seen in Freud's giving such a severe malady as diphtheria to Irma merely to exonerate himself.

One may point out, however, that the wish-fulfilment in a dream may itself be a defence against a pre-oneiric wish. That is to say, Freud's self-exculpation is a defensive displacement of a pre-oneiric desire to exculpate Fliess for his deficient treatment of Irma. Schur (1966, pp. 84–85) specifically confirms the hypothesis that 'day

123

residues' may have an origin much earlier than the day preceding the dream; and in the case at hand these residues point back more than three months prior. Early in 1895, at Freud's request, Fliess went to Vienna to determine if the somatic symptoms had a nasal aetiology. He stayed to operate on her, and left more than a half-meter of iodoform gauze in her nose. Emma's state was deplorable: within a week after, she had painful swellings which made treatment by morphine indispensable; she hemorrhaged greatly and a penny-sized bone chip broke loose—with the result that Freud had to call in another specialist. And two weeks after Fliess's departure Freud was forced to enlist a third specialist, and it was he who accidentally discovered the fetid gauze. Upon the extraction of this putridly smelling gauze, incidentally, Freud became sick and fled to the next room where a 'Frau Doktor' attended him with cognac. Somewhat shaken still, Freud returned to the operating room where the ever-awake Emma greeted him with the 'condescending' comment: 'This is the strong sex.' Freud's dream, too, is a pronounced male reaction against this abasement.

Nevertheless, the need to exonerate Fliess from unsatisfactory treatment of Emma's nearly fatal condition 'was probably the strongest (immediate) motive for the constellation' of the Irma dream (Schur, 1966, p. 70). We must not forget that at this time Fliess was not only friend, confidant, intellectual companion, but also the personal physician of Freud, and had even treated his severe cardiac illness for the two previous years. Accordingly, as Schur establishes in his fine biography, the criticism launched against Otto is a displacement of hostile feelings against Fliess that had become implanted in Freud's unconscious. Hence, 'What Freud had not yet realized was the transference of the dream, especially the negative transference and the defences against it which operate in dream formation' (Schur, 1972, p. 89). In this respect we may now outline the series of defences culminating in the Irma dream: it is Freud's self-defense, which is in turn a defense against his positive transference onto Fliess, which in turn is partially a defense against the ever-growing animosity in Freud's unconscious directed towards Fliess.

If Oedipal references are in the dream, they exist not as a resolution of the Oedipal complex but as a defense against it. In this regard it might be well not to conceive automatically of the term progression always within the framework of Darwinian evolution, but rather to see that progression, like regression, may be a defense. That is to say, progression may be a defense not in a normative sense but in a dynamic phenomenal one. As such, progression may be ego-syntonic (flight into health) or ego-dystonic (e.g. Oedipal fantasies as a defence against more basic conflicts). In this connection, Freud (1900) repeatedly gave the title 'the dream of Irma's injection' (pp. 163, 165, 173, 180, 292, 316) to a dream in which there are many more issues besides symbolized intercourse. Could not Waelder's concept of multiple function be applied to Oedipal fantasies, especially those of a marked Oedipal conflict, with the conclusion that the fantasies are not only a 'progressive' wish but also a defense against early symbiosis? The fantasmagoric diffusion of references to inner/outer, above/below come from a Freud bewildered by his bisexuality and even more bewildered by the covertness of female sexuality. Freud's oneiric drama testifies to fusional anxiety—what are the *in*sides of a woman and what has been his relation to them? Alongside this, the dream contains orality, anality and also phallicity without felicity. Voyeurism, prudishness, envy, sadistic castration, pejoration of intercourse—these are the characteristics of the dreamer's intimate attitude to eroticism.

The many partial identifications assigned to Irma include both Freud and Fliess, who in turn figure elsewhere in the dream. Even apart from that, a whirligig of fused representations dominate the picture. Irma's mouth is a mouth-vagina-penis-nose. Falling into Freud's early sexual theories, she is neurasthenic because of her lack of libidinal discharge. Freud is attracted to this mother-wife figure, and at three points Freud even explicitly identifies her with his wife. Implied in this identification is Freud's conflictual attraction to Irma. Unfulfilled sexuality, such as marked the widow Irma, was held to be an aetiological factor in hysteria; at the same time, Freud's own wife was in her sixth pregnancy, a situation which caused the economically harassed Freud to express acute interest in Fliess's 'solution' for birth control in 1895 (see Freud, 1950a, p. 120). All this bears on the dream episode in which Freud takes her on one *side* as if to berate her for not accepting the 'solution'. It is obliquely indicated that her mouth is full of sperm (*Samen*) and wet-nurse milk (*Ammen*): fellatio and breastfeeding are blended. Concurrently, the mouth is nippled and resembles a penis: a schema of bisexuality along with a fusion of container/contained is established. On top of all this, writes Freud, Fliess fostered all his writings in gestation and, one may add, even the analysis of this very dream. Freud's assertion is capital, for if we extend it to its logical conclusion, it bypasses an idealist semiology which crystallizes the sign-product and it constitutes discourse as a dynamic production of signs. In this light the dream does not interrupt but rather generates other discourse. Such an idea is to some degree to be found in secondary elaboration, reaching into the transcription of the dream itself. For example, the parentheses, one of the most *visible* marks of punctuation, are used in the reported dream to underscore two voyeuristic elements in the staged dream.

One may conjecture that the dream's basic fusional anxiety is, through deferred action, inadequately worked out on the phallic level. In other words, it is as if Freud, reacting to primary dependence and passivity on a maternal figure, vengefully works out Emma's remark about females as the strong sex and he fabricates a dream of male domination. Both as patient and woman Irma is anything but highly esteemed; she is as a second-class citizen grammatically and thematically. When Freud berates her about *not yet* having accepted the solution and her having pains *yet*, he asserts his superiority obliquely through these 'mere workaday' adverbs, the implied statement being that the future holds out a cure for her if she submits to him. She is unjustly criticized, she receives unscrupulous medical treatment, but no male or representative of the power structure asks her pardon or defends her. She is likewise excluded from the male doctors' intuitive knowledge, even when that knowledge deals with her very own body. Looked at from another point of view, Freud's union with Irma is in terms of body and guilt (his guilt or *Schuld* is even phonologically incorporated in her body, synecdochically figured in her *Schulter*); his union with the male protagonists is in terms of body and knowledge. Males can confirm Freud's examination; they can intuit together and feel together—all this in contrast to Freud's reaction to Irma. She must *first* tell him she has pains, which *then* causes him, *after* he has already been speaking, indeed, accusing her, to look at her and notice her pallid condition.

It could be contended that Freud variously identifies with and reacts to each of the three doctors' physical treatment of Irma. But Freud's primary identification is to be found in terms of his own activities, which are voyeuristic and pregenital in nature. Freud strongly defends against an Oedipal culmination with the mother-wife-Irma figure; he merely looks at her or into her mouth. With reference to the other doctors, Leopold is given an honoured position in sharing secret knowledge with Freud about Irma's infected body. In effect, after Irma draws Freud's attention to her physical condition, knowledge undergoes several different exclusivities, which can be outlined in this way:

(a) Knowledge of the source of the infection—restricted to the four doctors.
(b) Perception of the infiltrated shoulder—restricted to Freud and Leopold.

(c) The mnemic image of trimethylamin—restricted to Freud.

Be that as it may, the reserved Leopold, who merely percusses, is the only doctor who is spared criticism from Freud. Otto, the most sexually active, the one who stands by (erectile), is denounced as a 'dirty squirter'; he is the one who with a venereal disease infects Irma's mouth-vagina, who causes scabs there that are 'white-grey', 'white *fearing*' (*weissgraue*) detected by the *startled* Freud. Otto is also a dirty squirter because he inseminated Irma when she felt unwell ('sie sich unwohl fühlte'), the German euphemism for a menstruating women. There is also a hint of distrust here towards Oskar Rie, the paediatrician for Freud's then pregnant wife. But, for other reasons, Freud takes out vengeance on Breuer who, after all, only repeats the visual, non-tactile examination that Freud himself made. We can conclude that after submitting to a figure of authority and paternal domination, Freud in retaliation castrates him, makes him limp, takes away his beard as a sign of social distinction and finally drops his honorific title of doctor. The incidence of his physical description in the dream-narrative and its comparison with Irma's is revelatory here. Both persons, one may note, are 'pallid'; like Breuer, her power has been undercut since her mouth-vagina, her vagina dentata, has only an artificial bite; they both are devalued, genitally and socially. Yet since their delineations are not juxtaposed, they can constitute only a quasi-diptych. At any rate, it takes a complaint from Irma to elicit Freud's somewhat sympathetic physical description; it takes but Breuer's confirmation of Freud's findings to elicit a retaliatory ridiculing portrait. Incidentally, the fact that Breuer limps (*hinkt*) can in German be taken in a figurative sense to mean 'reasons faultily', thus anticipating Breuer's subsequent nonsensical diagnosis. That Freud attributes physical traits of his beloved half-brother Emmanuel to Breuer is a compromise formation—the father figure wins some respect and yet is kept distant in being but 'half' of Freud's blood. Succinctly, Freud's aggression flails out in all directions: against the mother figure, against the authority figure and against Otto's genitality. With the renunciation of the father figure who is split off into authoritarian and 'dirty' sexual figures, we are left with a puritanically emasculating voyeurism.

On two occasions Freud partially identifies himself with Irma, and significantly both times deals with parts of the body, namely the mouth and shoulder. Freud depicts Irma as protesting, self-protective, but not aggressive in an other-directed manner. In fact, as a recipient of whatsoever, be it an erroneous diagnosis, group examination, or an unsuitable injection, she represents Freud's passive self that homosexually submits to male inspection. This is an aspect of his nature that Freud hesitates to admit; as Swann (1974) maintains, Freud is readier in his commentary to acknowledge his aggressive side rather than passive and dependent one (pp. 25, 27). We may go further and conclude that Irma stirs up sexual conflict and censorship in Freud on account of her being a multiple feminine figure and also her being a compromise identity-formation, screening Freud's homosexual attraction to Fliess. In the light of Irma's double role we can see that Freud's voyeurism is not satisfied with surface appearances. The motifs of above/below and outer/inner manifest Freud's anxious quest for identity. No wonder, as even the grammar shows, he has traits of impulsiveness, and yet he attempts to contain that in a dream which, by virtue of its paucity of qualitative adverbs, takes on some semblance of factual discourse.

On first appearance, the Irma dream is an ego dream, dealing with the exigencies of professional life. But a closer look at the dream in its semantic and formal aspects reveals a dream drenched in id content. In the final account, the full analysis of a dream must deal with all elements of its specificity, including the formal: its polysemous nature even down to the prefixes, suffixes and preposi-tions; its grammar and its revelatory use of pronouns, proper names and titles; punctuation, typography, phonology, orthography, style and the place and function of detail in the narrative. As I said previously, one should be aware too of the larger parameters modifying a staged dream. Is it recited or written? And not only should we bear in mind to whom it is addressed, but also to whom it may be readdressed. Such considerations are capital if a lexical distributional analysis were to be made of several people's dreams. Typography and punctuation apart, Freud's Irma dream would be verbally different if recited on the couch, starting from the very beginning with its telegraphic ellipses. Moreover, patients character-istically narrate their dreams in the past tense: 'I dreamt that there was . . .' And again, apart from the use of pseudonyms, the qualifiers 'my friend' for both Otto and Leopold demonstrate that the dream is being readdressed to a reading audience not acquainted with Freud's intimate circle. To this degree, alongside the difference between the proto and staged dream should be set the difference between the staged and the reported dream. But on the other hand, *to the extent of its being verbal in nature, the reported dream is not as close to the staged dream as to the proto-dream.*

The Irma dream bears the marks of special influence; it is a middle-class dream. Since my approach in this long essay has greatly emphasized the verbal, I might start here by making a few comments about one aspect of the sociolinguistic background of the dream. For a period of over a millennium, from the sixth to the sixteenth century, a great part of the West moved increasingly towards a linguistic male chauvinism (see especially Ong, 1959). Latin was a sexed language. Those who spoke it, besides the vernacular mother tongue, were nearly exclusively men; women were mostly unilingual. Only those who could first of all read it could speak it; the chronological opposite happens with a mother tongue. Learning Latin had all the semblances of a puberty rite, a 'rite de passage'. In order to learn it, the boy had to leave home; the teaching of Latin in schools, which gave linguistic access to abstract tribal lore, was accompanied by discipline and beating. The acquisition of that language served as a preparation for extrafamilial activity, a passport into the adult professional world, the world of law, medicine, diplomacy, and so on. From the seventeenth to the nineteenth century, although Latin lost its place as an oral instrument, it enjoyed a dominant position in the humanist tradition. It is only in the twentieth century, concurrently with the advent of women into higher education, that classical literature has fully yielded its imperial place in the curriculum to vernacular literatures, the literatures of the 'mother tongue'. So at the end of the nineteenth century, those who knew any Greek or Latin were mostly those of the ruling class, namely male society. Doctors, and they were mostly males like Freud, wrote prescriptions of course in Latin. The very epigraph to 'The Interpretation of Dreams' is a quotation in Latin from Virgil. And to be sure, its treatment of the Oedipus complex is titularly indebted to Greek classical drama. Again, the associations to the Irma dream involve the classical Propylaea in Athens. Not least of all, the word *classical* comes from the Latin *classicus* ('of the *aristocratic* class')!

Now we may recall that beyond the Irma dream is the touching episode of the hysterical Emma. To repeat, it was she who said condescendingly to Freud: 'This is the strong sex'. And to repeat, just hours before the dream, Freud wrote a self-justificatory case to the authority figure, Breuer. The outcome of all this is that, both as a patient and woman, Irma is *unter* the male doctors, which is spectacularly evidenced even in the way that Freud grammatically slights her. Her hysterical symptoms, moreover, are also due to her self-frustrating acceptance of sexual mores dictated by the contemporary society. Curiously enough, parallel to this is the societal influence on dream–theorizing itself. So when Pontalis (1974) asserts that dream interpretation is paternal since it *penetrates* the dream, is he not, through a submerged metaphor, assimilating

129

analysis with the term 'penetration'? In which case the tail is wagging the dog, and the phallus straightway gives rise to the—fallacy, the restriction of analyzing to a male activity.

To conclude, I should like to consider the dream in another light: that is, as a maternal object, in the sense of Erikson (1954, pp. 45–46) and Pontalis (1974, pp. 127–128). Freud himself asserted that there is one point, or more precisely *ein Nabel* ('a navel') in every dream that is undecipherable. Like the dream in the dreamer, the fetus is one with the mother. The uterine existence involves, in the most physical sense, both similarity and contiguity. Similarity and contiguity equally are the basic principles of metaphor and metonymy respectively and they are also the bases of the laws of association. The most extraordinary consequences, linguistic as well as physiological, are occasioned by the act of birth. Birth rips apart uterine contiguity and similarity—it is the ontogenetic Tower of Babel. By dreaming we incorporate a maternal object and to some degree free ourselves from the separation between contiguity and similarity. There is the pregnant fact that about 2350 B.C. during the reign of Urukagina of Lagesh 'freedom' (*amargi*) as a word appears for the first time in recorded history (Kramer, 1963). And literally *amargi* means 'return to the mother'.

Notes

* First published in the *International Review of Psycho-Analysis* (1977), 4: 83–98.
1 For various points in the translation I am indebted to Dr. Henri Ellenberger; Dr. Kurt Eissler; Professor Hans Galinsky; Professor Walter Moser; Dr. James Naiman and Dr. Eric Wittkower.
   The German text of the Irma dream is taken entirely from the *Gesammelte Werke* (see Freud, 1942). Incidentally, I did compare it with the first and seventh German editions of *Die Traumdeutung* and discovered, between the three texts, a couple of dozen textual variants occurring in the Irma dream alone! The most significant difference concerns the ellipsis, which varies from two to four periods in the first and seventh editions and is uniformly three in the *Gesammelte Werke*. The obliteration of that variation is unfortunate, in terms of revealing elaboration. The *Gesammelte Werke* does not list textual variants and I suspect it is a 'cleaned up' edition. Such evidence demonstrates that we lack a German edition of Freud that will compare to the scientific bibliographical standards required in other disciplines, such as literary and biblical scholarship.

2 The square brackets in the quotation indicate where, in accordance with the German text, I have revised Strachey's verb tenses.

References

Anzieu, D. (1959 *L'Auto-analyse*. Paris: Presses Universitaires de France.

Erikson, E. (1954) The dream specimen of psychoanalysis. *Journal of the American Psychoanalytic Association*, 2: 5–56.

Ferenczi, S. (1913) To whom does one relate one's dreams? In *Further Contributions to the Theory of Psychoanalysis*. London: Hogarth Press, 1950.

Freud, S. (1900). The interpretation of dreams. *Standard Edition*, 4 and 5. London: Hogarth Press, 1953. [*G.W.* 2/3. Frankfurt a.M.: Fischer, 1942].

—— (1905). Jokes and their relation to the unconscious. *Standard Edition*, 8. London: Hogarth Press, 1960.

—— (1916–1917). Introductory lectures on psychoanalysis. *Standard Edition*, 15 and 16. London: Hogarth Press, 1961.

—— (1923a). Remarks on the theory and practice of dream-interpretation. *Standard Edition*, 19: 109–121. London: Hogarth Press, 1961.

—— (1923b). The ego and the id. *Standard Edition*, 19: 3–66. London: Hogarth Press, 1961.

—— (1929). Some dreams of Descartes': a letter to Maxime Leroy. *Standard Edition*, 21: 199–204. London: Hogarth Press, 1961.

—— (1938). *The Basic Writings of Sigmund Freud*, tr. A.A. Brill. New York: Random House.

—— (1940). An outline of psychoanalysis. *Standard Edition*, 23: 141–207. London: Hogarth Press, 1964.

—— (1950a). *The Origins of Psychoanalysis*, eds. M. Bonaparte, A. Freud and E. Kris. London: Imago.

—— (1950b). Project for a scientific psychology. *Standard Edition* 1. London: Hogarth Press, 1966.

Grigg, K. (1973) 'All roads lead to Rome': the role of the nursemaid in Freud's dreams. *Journal of the American Psychoanalytic Association*, 21, 108–126.

Grinstein, A. (1968) *On Sigmund Freud's Dream*. Detroit: Wayne State University Press.

Kramer, S. (1963) *The Sumerians: Their History, Culture and Character*. Chicago: University of Chicago Press.

Mahony, P. and Singh, R. (1975) *The Interpretation of Dreams*, semiology, and Chomskian linguistics: a radical critique. *Psychoanalytic Study of the Child*, 30.

Ong, W. (1959) Latin language study as a Renaissance puberty rite. *Studies in Philology*, 56: 103–124.

Pontalis, J.-B. (1974) Dream as an object. *International Review of Psycho-Analysis*, 1: 125–133.

Schur, M. (1966) Some additional 'day residues' of 'the specimen dream of psycho-analysis.' In: R.M. Loewenstein *et al.* (eds.), *Psychoanalysis: A General Psychology*. New York: International Universities Press.

—— (1972) *Freud: Living and Dying*. New York: International Universities Press.

Simon, B. (1972) Models of mind and mental illness in Ancient Greece: II. The Platonic mode. *Journal of the History of Behavioral Science*, 8: 389–404.

Swann, J. (1974) *Mater* and Nannie: Freud's two mothers and the discovery of the Oedipus complex. *American Imago*, 31: 1–64.

Imitative elaboration in the oral reporting of dreams: another formal feature of dream interpretation*

It must be stressed that the Irma dream was communicated in writing and that such formal features as orthography and punctuation were Freud's own elaboration of the dream. In our own clinical practice, most dreams of course are conveyed not in writing but *viva voce*. In dealing with these orally delivered dreams, we sometimes come unexpectedly upon a peculiar type of dream elaboration that has hitherto escaped focused consideration and which I have judged significant enough to disclose for its implications and its future applicability. At the outset, however, we find in our path a major terminological difficulty and we shall facilitate our progress if we first clear it up.

Basing himself on a thorough collection of references to dream elaboration in the Freudian canon, Breznitz (1971) shows that Freud was inconsistent in chronologically situating secondary revision during dream-work, after the dream-work proper, and after awakening. To these three moments Breznitz assigns three different labels, viz. primary, secondary, and tertiary revision (PR, SR, TR) respectively. He concludes (p. 412) that PR is chiefly a primary-process operation; TR is conceivable 'mainly' as secondary process (though on p. 411 he states that TR is using 'only' secondary-process type of thought): and SR is a mixture of primary and secondary process. By contrast Silber's study (1973) concentrates on the dream elaboration after awakening, and more specifically, on the patient's reporting of the dream itself, a phase marked by the synthetic functions of the ego and the mechanisms of the secondary process. While retaining though further distinguishing Freud's own terminology, Silber posits a dual aspect to this ulterior phase of dream

133

construction: secondary revision, which disguises the dream to the dreamer himself; and secondary elaboration, which obscures the dream's meaning to the person to whom the dream is reported. As an example of the latter, Silber refers to a patient's state of confusion woven into the 'content' of the dream report (1973, p. 164).

My own position is that the part of the dream elaboration which extends into the very recitation of the dream may have an importance in terms of its form, i.e. that the form may be imitative or mimetic of the content. As such, this mimetic elaboration is influenced by primary process and would reveal as only partially accurate Freud's conception of the effect of intrapsychic elaboration on the dream's form. For Freud, the formal significance of that elaboration is twofold: it can make a vague dream more vivid and give it plastic intensity (1900, p. 500), and secondly, it fills in gaps and contributes coherence to the dream (1900, p. 490). Thus it is in keeping with 'an intellectual function in us which demands unity, connection and intelligibility from any material,' and so it follows that the purpose of oneiric elaboration 'is evidently to get rid of the disconnectedness and unintelligibility produced by the dream-work' (1913, p. 95). Freud in effect conceives of such elaboration as introducing a logical or intellectual coherence into the fragmentary dream material. I intend to show, however, that in the patient's very recital of his dreams, there may occur an elaboration with its own kind of imitative coherence. In these instances, the logical coherence of the oneiric matter (Breznitz's secondary revision) is supplanted by an imitative, symbolic coherence (applicable to Silber's secondary elaboration *and* revision). The inadvertent analyst reporting such dreams would unfortunately be apt to undo the imitative coherence and thereby distortingly revert to the logical secondary elaboration as the patient's final reconstruction of the dreams. To exemplify my position I turn to dream material from a patient whom we shall call Ms. B.

In this female patient's obsessional and phobic character, anal material of the most explicit kind dominated a number of sessions. She anguishingly described her two earliest sexual and traumatic experiences: at the age of three, she had a stick inserted into her anus by an older playmate; and about three years later, she thrust a safety pin into a cat's rectum. These incidents formed the basis of her associating the word *back* with (1) the past; (2) her back; (3) her buttocks, and (4) me as analyst, the persecutory superego, behind her. She went on to describe her phobia of a particularly ambivalent reaction formation. As a foreigner in Canada, she complained of native motorists honking behind her to indicate that she should drive faster—a disguised spatial and critical reference to me. Along the same lines, she lamented a brewing anti-American sentiment in Canada and accordingly claimed that as an immigrant she discovered that 'something was going behind our Yankee backs.' Finally she related her horror upon seeing her daughter's buttocks being fondly caressed by her grandmother, an incident triggering a deep fear of perversion and launching her, eighteen months previously, into her ongoing depression.

During this same period, the patient came forth with several dreams which are notable for the distinctive nature of their imitative elaboration. More specifically, I want to call attention to the crucial difference between the dream dreamt and the dream recited, in terms of form rather than content. Ms. B. narrated one dream in the following way:

> I was in your office sitting up. Three other women were also in your office. I said to myself, 'I'm the only sane one.' Then my son Tommy walked in from the waiting room and asked me to scratch his back. I took him back to the waiting room and scratched his back and then I came back to your office.
>
> Oh, but that was the second part of the dream. Before coming to your office, I was over at my girlfriend Betty's house that was being remodeled. She had a list in her hand of things I borrowed. She told me, 'You owe me this and this.' I said to myself, 'How peculiar she is.' Then we went into her car and her dog and I were in the back seat. The dog was very nice to me, and I asked Betty what I could give him so that he'd always be nice to me, and she said, 'Cracker-jacks.' Then Betty drove me nearby your office.

Strikingly enough, alongside the varying grammatical occurrences (substantival, adjectival, and adverbial) of *back*, the form of the dream narrated is backwards, reversed. By this we readily perceive that the recitation of the dream distorts a prior chronological arrangement and imposes a mimetic coherence on the dream. The reversed form of the dream, as well, imitates Ms. B.'s dynamic association of her genitalia and anus, her front and rear.

A week later, the patient reported two more dreams:

> I was in a big room. There were lots of people there. And you were there, and you were talking to me over the heads of some people. Then I said, 'Do we have to have this session here with all these people looking?' And then I stood up, I zipped up the back of my formal, and the towel around my wet hair fell off.

That was my second dream, and in the first dream I was in a car, but I don't remember anything more.

Once more there is reversal, but this time not in the organization internal to one dream, only rather in the order of the dreams dreamt as a whole. Again, the elaboration is imitative of the 'backwards' theme and serves as a gloss on a transference dream, told in a straightforward manner, in which my front lawn and balcony were transposed to the back of my house; Ms. B. was relaxing on the lawn and simultaneously listening to an analytical session that I was conducting above on the back balcony.

Then in a subsequent session came this remarkable account of a dream:

My hair was cut, all on one side, the left. It was like in a classroom, everybody sitting at desks, waiting to have their pictures taken. I didn't want my picture taken, I had to have my picture taken. I had to first fill in an application. I was the first. I had a big pencil; it was dull or too big to fill in the little boxes in the application—there wasn't enough room. I messed up the sheet; I needed another sheet. I suggested to the lady teacher that she give out forms to several people instead of just to one at a time so things would go faster. Then she gave me another form sheet and another pencil and also to five other people. It was easier to fill out, and I brought up the form to the teacher but she told me, 'You can't have your picture taken, your PAP test is no good.' I said to myself, 'There was sperm in my vagina—it was dirty.'

That was the middle of the dream. There was a beginning and an end, but I can't remember them . . . oh yes, in the beginning I was someplace with people; then I was going someplace with someone.

My vagina was dirty, I remember—that must have been the end of the dream.

The night before, my husband and I had intercourse, but I was too tired and after it happened, I stayed in bed and didn't get up to wash myself. That was the end—I didn't have my picture taken. I didn't feel there was an end because I didn't have my picture taken. The other night we used no rubber. We do this during the safe times of the month. We were both tired, there were no preliminaries . . . it's not worth for what you get in the end.

In the case at hand, the patient's opening hesitation about the front and terminal parts of the dream constitutes the way in which imitative elaboration enacts her dynamic association of the anus and genitalia. Although in one sense both the genitalia and the anus are centrally located in the body, the common designation of the anus as the *behind* or *rear-end* makes it very suitable for discourse in its linguistic nature as a linearity and verbal string to refer imitatively to the anus at the end of an utterance. In a way, the dream as initially remembered by Ms. B. imitates the intercourse she had had the previous night; the dream's beginning was forgotten—there were no sexual preliminaries; after some doubt, she concluded that the dream's middle was in fact its end—the sperm in her vagina was analyzed, dirty.

Apart from these anal dreams, I think it is worthwhile to concentrate on another specimen which merits attention for qualities of imitative form:

Ann and I were together in a desert. We were not being chased. We were in California, up in the mountains, looking at San Francisco. I was telling her how beautiful the city is, and that's funny, because that's where she comes from (3).

There was another group of people there—the wives of the employees were there. Whether Ann and I were separated and staying away from them or they from us, I don't know (4).

In the dream, we were all trying to get away from something or someone (1).

The rest of the group disappeared, and then I was alone with Ann by a bar (5).

In the beginning, we all ran into a building (2).

The numerals after the dream's five parts indicate the chronological sequence in the dream dreamt. In narrating the dream, however, the patient disrupted their temporal sequence, and thereby she symbolically imitated here her pathological concern about separation in all forms—a concern going to such lengths that when lying down, she keeps the thumb of her left hand touching her side, for if she did not she would feel separated from herself.

In the light of these various dream samples, we must hesitate to endorse Freud's global assertion that secondary revision does not 'present us with anything more than a glaring misunderstanding of the dream-thoughts' (1901, p. 666). In reality, that part of the elaboration that extends into the very recitation of the dream may actually, through the symbolic nature of its imitative sequencing, proceed from a precise though unconscious awareness of the dream's meaning. Given this possibility, clinical caution is called for. Analysts must not carelessly contribute an elaboration of their own and rearrange the patient's narration of the dream when it departs from the logical coherence of the dream dreamt. We might remember in this connection the archeological tenet that the spatial organization and relationship of the artifacts may be just as important as the objects themselves.

There are two matters which remain to be clarified, the first being form. As Freud said, a lack of clarity or a gap in the dream dreamt may be formal representations of undecided paternity or female genitalia respectively. In these instances, then, there is a distinctive homology between the dream's subject-matter and its form, much as the blank dream represents the mother's breast (Lewin, 1946, 1948).[1] On the other hand, Freud also thought of dream form being differently judged by the dreamer during his first waking thoughts. Thus upon awakening, though still under the spell of the dream-work and wish-fulfillment, he mistakenly judged that his dream about a long-sought theory of bisexuality was flawless and without gaps in its structure (1900, p. 331). It is within this framework of understanding elaboration that I have been moved to show that semantic content and the narrative form of an orally reported dream may constitute a relationship that is mimetic.

For a moment in this exposition we might profitably dwell on the notion of mimesis or imitation, which can be justly and fully appreciated only if we realize that it is paramount in such psychically relevant events as ideational mimetics, hysterical symptomatology, and defensive reaction. Through ideational mimetics the speaker combines mimetic and verbal representation and hence his thoughts are also manifested in his expressive movements, be it in manual gesturing, voice variation, or even in the size of the eyes commensurate to the size of a described object. Furthermore, somatic innervations indicative of level of attention or abstract thinking are traceable to the basic phenomenon of size, since what is more interesting or more sublime can be considered as modalities of what is larger (Freud, 1905, pp. 193–201). In his comprehensive *The Aesthetics of Freud*, Spector (1972, p. 119) considers Freud's notion of ideational mimetics 'as potentially his most valuable contribution to esthetics, and the best bridge leading from his psychoanalytic views on art to the general field of esthetic appreciation.' Spector then goes on to indicate briefly a fruitful link between ideational mimetics and Silber's functional phenomenon whereby the dreamer's subjective state of mind or mode of functioning rather than the content of his thoughts becomes the subject of the dream.

Briefly, when taken together, ideational mimetics and functional phenomena involve an imitative act expressed in somatic or psychic media, concomitant or subsequent to thinking or proprioceptive activity. With his typical astuteness Freud dealt with this temporal factor in a related imitative area, namely, the symbolic relation between the precipating cause and the pathological phenomenon in hysteria (1893–1895, pp. 176, 178–181). But it is in a brilliant essay by Waelder (1951) that the imitative principle is given an endopsychic significance on a grand scale. More precisely, there is what Waelder calls an isomorphism between defense and subsequent symptom:

> if warded-off instinctual drives make their come-back, the return has the same form as the defence mechanism had; they return, as it were, through the same door through which they were ousted (isomorphism). If the defence mechanism had the form of denial, the return must have the form of an assertion. . . . It may be that further generalizations are possible and that *all* pathological processes, neurotic, psychotic, psychopathic, have the same basic structure, i.e. conflict—defence and countercathexis—return of the warded-off. . . . In this way, the defence mechanism is largely responsible for the form of pathology and the old problem of the choice of neurosis can for the most part be reduced to the problem of the choice of defence mechanism [p. 176].

In summary we realize the psychoanalytic richness of the concept of imitative form as it is manifested in various somatic and psychic phenomena, not the least of which is the orally reported dream. The scope of our reflection is the poorer if we overlook the fact that imitation plays the profoundest role in the functioning and expression of the human psyche: in casual verbal and gestural expression, dreaming, symptomatology and art. Within these activities, the prime object of imitation ranges from somatic innervation, verbal representation to the psyche's functions or its thought-content.

Finally we come to the second matter of theoretical concern: we must attempt to specify the ego functions that are involved with the mimetic phenomenon in oral dream reporting. Silber for instance sees secondary revision and secondary elaboration as manifestations of the synthetic functions of the ego (1973, p. 166). Kavka (1968) speaks of a patient whose dream narration was so fragmented by association that the dream was able to be sorted out only by questioning; for Kavka, this fragmented dream narrative was a defensive process. In my material, the imitative aspect in the dream reportage had nothing at all to do with the logical coherence arising from the secondary process which Freud attributes to dream elaboration. Ms. B.'s imitative elaboration as such did not evince condensation but rather displacement, one of the other elements in primary process dream-work, and can be ascribable to the influence of the defensive function

139

of the ego; and yet obviously, because of the evident organization and integration in the mimetics of dream reporting, elaboration of that kind emanates also from a synthetic ego function. This combining of ego functions in imitative dream reporting highlights further the complexity of psychic activity, a consideration of which never fails to stimulate psychoanalytic researchers in pursuing their demons. Our pursuit continues next outside the literal clinical setting, where the variety and complexity of psychic activity are engaged in discourses no less fascinating.

Notes

* First published in *Contemporary Psycho-analysis* (1981), 17: 350–358.
1 These examples are quite different, however, from those dreams which, whatever their content, are dreamt to be bribes, gifts and the like destined for the analyst (see Altman, 1969, pp. 71, 86); in these cases the dreaming itself, apart from any specific form or content, acquires a new meaning.

References

Altman, L. (1969) *The Dream in Psychoanalysis*. New York: International Universities Press.

Blum, H. (1968) Notes on the written dream. *Journal of the Hillside Hospital*, 17: 67–78.

Breznitz, S. (1971) A critical note on secondary revision. *International Journal of Psycho-Analysis*, 52: 407–412.

Freud, S. (1893–1895) Studies on hysteria. *Standard Edition*, 2: 3–122. London, Hogarth Press, 1955.

—— (1900) The interpretation of dreams. *Standard Edition*, 4, 5. London: Hogarth Press, 1953.

—— (1901) On dreams. *Standard Edition*, 5: 631–686. London: Hogarth Press, 1953.

—— (1905) Jokes and their relation to the unconscious. *Standard Edition*, 8. London: Hogarth Press, 1960.

—— (1913) Totem and taboo. *Standard Edition*, 13: 1–162. London, Hogarth Press, 1953.

—— (1916–1917) Introductory lectures on psychoanalysis. *Standard Edition*, 15, 16. London, Hogarth Press: 1963.

Kavka, J. (1968) The fractionated dream narrative as transference communication. *Bulletin of the Philadelphia Association of Psychoanalysis*, 18: 205–209.

Lewin, B. (1946) Sleep, the mouth and the dream screen. *Psychoanalytic Quarterly*, 15: 419–443.

—— (1948) Inferences from the dream screen. *International Journal of Psycho-Analysis*, 29: 224–241.

Mahony, P. (1977) Towards a formalist approach to dreams. *International Review of Psycho-Analysis*, 4: 83–98.

Silber, A. (1973) Secondary revision, secondary elaboration and ego synthesis. *International Journal of Psycho-Analysis*, 54: 161–168.

Spector, J. (1972) *The Aesthetics of Freud*. New York: Praeger Publishers.

Waelder, R. (1951) The structure of paranoid ideas. *International Journal of Psycho-Analysis*, 32: 167–177.

PART TWO

Non-clinical discourse and psychoanalysis

7

Further thoughts on Freud and his writing*

Freud, of all contemporaries, is the one with the greatest cultural influence on the twentieth century. As psychoanalysts, we are both tremendously privileged and burdened that the founder of our discipline was such a towering figure—privileged, because if he were a lesser spirit, psychoanalysis would hardly be so widespread as it is today, and many of us would not have had the freeing experience of being analyzed; burdened because psycho-analytic theory and practice are so peculiarly interdependent that to challenge Freud's tenets 'has usually been responded to with anxiety, as if a sacrilegious outrage were being perpetrated' (Sutherland, 1980, p. 842). Pursuing the same line of thought, we quickly come upon the surprising reflection that among contemporary disciplines 'theology and psychoanalysis are unique . . . in that their specialists constantly have their originator in mind' (Mahony, 1977, p. 57).

Perhaps what I have been groping to explain is that the mystification and overidealization surrounding Freud have been inevitable to some extent. Yet it is my conviction that such overidealization, characterized by endlessly repeated generalizations, has been very stultifying to scholarship on Freud, so that an astonishing amount of research remains to be done, both in correcting old distortions and in discovering new truths, including those about Freud the writer.

A brief look at Freud as a reader might set into relief my proper concern. We can draw large profit from scrutinizing the summaries of texts Freud the reader has given us, since the degree to which those summaries distort original texts tells much about Freud's own

145

tendentiousness. Hence the reader-critic might procure one of Freud's primary sources, simply underlining all the passages not accounted for in Freud's summary, draw up an overall diagnostic picture of those passages, and compare it with Freud's. Such a logical, sure-fire procedure is evident in the remarkable study of Jensen's *Gradiva* by Kofman (1972). Among other things, she pointed up Freud's neglect of the protagonist's castration anxiety and she minutely traced in Freud's resumé the omission of certain revelatory indices, so that Jensen's novel was made to appear more enigmatic than it really was. Another precious indicator of how Freud read is his marginalia and marking in his private books.[1] Finally, there remains the open consideration of Freud as self-reader, and here we would examine how he summarizes his own previous writings (although to distinguish what he reread of himself and what he wrote from his retentive memory is hardly resolvable, save through his explicit avowal).

As we turn more directly to Freud as a writer, several general comments about Strachey's translation are in order. Strachey's written English, like Jones's, is within the tradition of the best Victorian prose. Strachey (1966) acknowledges this: 'The imaginary model which I have always kept before me is of the writings of some English man of science of wide education born in the middle of the nineteenth century' (p. xix). But in spite of its virtues, time and time again he silently embellishes and even tidies up the ideas in the original German—so much so that a psychoanalytic evaluation of Strachey's translation would be highly desirable. Surely Freud can stand on his own, his foibles included; his stature does not require distorting idealizations, even if they be hidden in translation.

Let me now give two concise instances of objectionable editorializing in Strachey's translation of the Wolf Man case (Freud, 1918). Each concerns the word 'more.' The first occurs with the detail that the Wolf Man at eighteen months saw his parents making love precisely three times. To the patient's protest that the detail of three times was not his association, Strachey's Freud tells us: 'It was a spontaneous association . . . in his usual way he passed it off on to me, and by this projection tried to make it seem more trustworthy' (*S.E.* 17: 37 fn. 5). Actually *seem* and *more* are Strachey's own unjustified verbal projections into the text. Only by following the German text do we properly understand the patient's deficient self-esteem and massive transferential dependence in the treatment. Accordingly the Wolf Man, not considering his own statements trustworthy, typically projected them onto Freud in order, the original text reads, to lend them credibility: 'Es war ein spontaner . . . den er nach seiner

Gewohnheit mir zuschob und ihn durch diese Projektion vertrauens-würdig machte' (*G.W.* 12: 64 fn. 3).

If here Strachey wantonly introduced the word 'more,' in another place he suppressed the same word; but behind the two meddlings the overall effect is the same, a doctoring up of the case. In the second instance, Strachey's Freud says that the subject of primal scenes in the Wolf Man case was also taken up in his *Introductory Lectures* 'with no controversial aim in view' (*S.E.* 17: 57). In reality, Freud declared that his discussion of primal scenes in the *Introductory Lectures* was 'no longer with a controversial aim' ('nicht mehr in polemischer Absicht' *G.W.* 12: 86). The definite implication of the text in the *Gesammelte Werke*, effaced in Strachey's rendition, is that the Wolf Man case indeed was polemically written. What Strachey's silent erasure achieves is the suppression of Freud's self-contradiction. Thus, in the very first footnote to the Wolf Man case, Freud (1918, p. 7) contradictorily posits that 'an objective estimation of the analytic material' in the case 'supplements the polemic' and 'personal character' of 'On the History of the Psycho-Analytic Movement' (Freud, 1914). In sum, these two limited samplings from the *Gesammelte Werke* show us highly significant and interrelated implications not present in Strachey's translation: specifically, that the Wolf Man had no confidence in his remarks and that Freud contradictorily calls his case history both polemical and nonpolemical.[2]

Apart from the translation, we may also question the accuracy of Strachey's edition as a bibliographical production. Actually the title *Standard Edition* is the greatest misnomer used in our discipline, for the edition is a standardized one, not a standard one. According to criteria set down by modern bibliographical specialists, Strachey's enterprise, indisputably monumental as it is, nevertheless has serious limitations. Strachey readily admits that, with the exception of the *Project* (Freud, 1895) and a few others, he did not consult any of Freud's manuscripts which, from 1908, were all preserved. An authentic edition, on the other hand, should account for all such manuscripts; besides, it should furnish a thorough bibliographical description of all source texts, identify where they are to be found, reproduce all textual revisions and variants, and justify final textual choices. At the present moment, one of the few well-edited Freud texts is Hawelka's (1974) publication of the complete original notes to the Rat Man case. Editorially, Hawelka's achievement is a classic, with its scrupulous transcription of Freud's spelling, punctuation, crossings-out, and marginalized guide words. For that eventual *Standard Edition* in a future century, editors will look upon Hawelka's accomplishment as a veritable model and supposedly will have access to the voluminous correspondence between Strachey and Jones on textual matters in Freud's writings.[3] That future edition should also include the many first-hand reports and abstracts published in contemporary periodicals of lectures given by Freud in Vienna (see Strachey, 1966, pp. xiii–xxii). A special place in that edition might be accorded to *The Significance of Psychoanalysis for Mental Sciences* (Rank and Sachs, 1916). If we credit Sandor Rado's testimony, Sachs divulged to him that both he and Rank, excellent stenographers, wrote down Freud's series of lectures and published them as their own (see Rado, n.d., pp. 156–157).

I suspect that the future 'complete works' of Freud might be near one hundred volumes, which in large part would consist of his letters. Along this line, Freud is typical of other renowned figures in that those of succeeding ages could read more of their writings than could their contemporaries. Freud was one of the most prolific letter-writers in the history of world literature. To be more specific: Eissler (1980, pp. 104–105) estimated that there are between 10,000 and 15,000 extant letters written by Freud. If we take the higher figure, we arrive at the dumbfounding realization that Freud composed approximately one letter every two days of his eighty-three years. But even if we take the lower figure, Freud would still rank eminently among the world practitioners of the epistolary genre. For instance, the most famous letter-writers in English literature are Lord Chesterfield with approximately 2,600, Horace Walpole with 6,000, and Virginia Woolf with 4,000. No one in Spanish literature comes anywhere near Freud's epistolary production. In French literature Freud is surpassed only by Voltaire with 10,000 extant letters out of a total of 20,000, making him perhaps the supreme literary correspondent. In German literature a unique position is held by Goethe whose 14,000 letters take up some 50 volumes in the *Sophien-Ausgabe*. A full edition of primary sources of Freud's works would be suitably complemented by a comprehensive collection of first-hand accounts of analyses with him. The *pièce de résistance* of such a collection would be the private journal Marie Bonaparte meticulously kept for three months of her analysis, noting down while on the couch everything Freud said, before being ordered to stop. The journal was vividly described as a 'fascinating document' by the sober Heinz Hartmann whose own analysis with Freud was rather long—three years.[4]

As I proceed along in my exposition, I realize more and more that my aim has been to be apocalyptic in the etymological sense of that word: *apo kalyptein*, 'to uncover' (cf. the alternate titles for the last book of the New Testament, the Book of the Apocalypse or Book of

148

Revelation). Relevant here is that the English word 'hell' probably comes from the Old High German *helan*, 'to hide', and in this connection one might recall Freud's picturesque notion of unconscious ideas as resembling demons, afraid of annihilation if they reach the light of day. But without further ado I now direct my attention to the uncovering, discovering the essence of Freud's writing itself.

More than most scientific writers, Freud fashioned a written expression that discloses his own conscious as well as unconscious processes generally. And whereas the preponderant number of psychoanalytic authors merely describe the unconscious, Freud also aimed to let it emerge in his writing so that his texts combine both exposition and enactment. This distinguishing feature we happily encounter in both the early and late Freud. Thus, in sending another chapter of *The Interpretation of Dreams* (Freud, 1900) to Fliess, Freud averred: 'It was all written by the unconscious, on the well-known principle of Itzig, the Sunday horseman. "Itzig, where are you going?" "Don't ask me, ask the horse!" At the beginning of a paragraph I never knew where I should end up' (Freud, 1887–1902, p. 258).

Let us now listen to the later Freud, disclosing once more that he writes from an inner impulse and risks whatever outcome. One such risk was the final shape of *Civilization and Its Discontents* (1930), which Freud exposed to the Vienna Psychoanalytic Society in the following way:

> The book does not deal exhaustively enough with the subject [namely, the discomfort in our culture]. And on top of this rough foundation is put an overdifficult and overcompensating examination of the analytic theory of the feeling of guilt. But one does not make such compositions, they make themselves, and if one resists writing them down as they come, one does not know what the result will be. The analytic insight into the feeling of guilt was supposed to be in a dominant position [Sterba, 1978, p. 184].

Amidst the trace of impulse in Freud's writing we constantly enjoy the vivid immediacy of his active authorial presence. This latter feature contrasts with the dominance of the third person and passive voice characterizing psychiatric and behavioristic writing, which is keynoted by such phrases as 'It is observed that,' 'It is to be concluded that,' and so on to a lifeless *infinitum*. Such writing, too, persists throughout that unfortunate product of American psychoanalysis, the *Abstracts of the Standard Edition of the Complete Psychological Works of Sigmund Freud* (Rothgeb, 1973), which as a widely used handbook has done much to vitiate the understanding of Freud.

149

Guided by an alienating rationale, the authors of the *Abstracts* omit Freud's use of the personal pronoun 'I' and rampantly promote the passive voice (e.g. 'The method of interpreting dreams is presented . . . it is perceived that a dream is the fulfillment of a wish' [p. 31]. In fact we ought to distinguish between two kinds of 'it': the 'it' or *das Es* which pulsates through Freud's writing, and the lifeless 'it' prevalent in psychiatric journals *inter alia*. Although the latter is grammatically an expletive and seemingly functions merely as a dispensable filler, in reality that driveless 'it' is highly subversive, tacitly alluding to the privileged status, impersonality, and infallibility of mechanized calculations.

Freud did not hesitate to acknowledge the profound instinctual undergirdings of his writings. Just about all of them, moreover—even the early ones he surpassed and rejected on scientific grounds—have a perennial validity, for they embody the quintessential psychoanalytic experience of ongoingness or processiveness. Through this processiveness, Freud resembled such masters as Baroque prose as Montaigne, Francis Bacon, and Thomas Browne, that polymathic seventeenth-century doctor who also qualifies as the Shakespeare of English prose. In Browne we detect a 'disdain of revision.' He 'deliberately avoided the processes of mental revision in order to express his idea when it . . . was nearer the point of its origin in his mind.' Browne's mastery 'gives his writing constantly the effect of being, not the result of a meditation, but an actual meditation in process.' His purpose was to present 'not a thought, but a mind thinking, or, in Pascal's words, *la peinture de la pensée* . . . he knew that an idea separated from the act of experiencing it is not the idea that was experienced. The ardor of its conception in the mind is a necessary part of its truth' for Browne.[5]

We must not, however, reduce Freud's prose to a *déjà vu*, for it contains another trait, which is very much its own. I refer to that dynamic quality in Freud's corpus which engages the reader during the very act of reading to participate in the textual ongoingness. Although the readers Freud appeals to appear sometimes to be completely externalized, we detect interlocutory differences between his 'private' letters and his 'public' writing with internalized addresses. Worth considering also is that Freud had the advantage of imagining and enjoying immediate readership; much more strain is put on modern psycho-analysts' imaginations (mine included), due to the impressive time gap between scriptorial inspiration and its appearance in print. Then again, much freshness in Freud's expression is due to the fact that he did not have to contend with a bevy of nameless editors with overready pencils; for *The Interpretation of*

Dreams, Fliess was actually Freud's editor, not anonymous people in the backroom of Deuticke's *Verlag*. And still the truth remains that although Freud's psychoanalytic contemporaries had the same advantages as he as far as immediate readership is concerned, they nevertheless lack that vibrating immediacy in their prose.

When we turn to Freud's case histories, we meet with a peculiar variation in the elements of processiveness and interlocution. Insofar as Freud rarely gives a patient's reaction to an interpretation, his case histories are more end-products than accounts of process. Yet the case histories are eminently processive in that Freud shifts the interactional focus: engaging in a processive involvement with the reader, Freud variously invites him to participate in the scene of the treatment or in its subsequent write-up. In general, the challenge in any attempt to combine processiveness with the patient and the reader in any one account is the standing ambiguity of the little word 'we' which could confusingly refer to the analyst-writer and the patient or reader.

As an artist of Olympian stature and exquisite sensibility, Freud bequeathed us a mosaic patterning of multileveled textuality. His is not a linear style of sheerly cognitive progression. Instead of being fixed at one level of reference, Freud so easily changes course that we might better withdraw our static epithet of 'multileveled' and call his prose polyphonic. Perhaps this explains to some extent why even the early Freud will outlast many current psychoanalytic theorists who expound conceptually deficient hypotheses in a nonprocessive, devitalized language and write themselves into oblivion.

Truly we need a variegated sensibility in order to appreciate Freud's polyphonic prose and its orchestrated strains of cognition, affect, exaggerated statement, hesitation, speculation, dispute, doubt, slowness, rapidity, and modulated authorial distancing; and in order to enjoy his moving effortlessly amongst theoretical perspectives, sharpened with frequent analogies and citations from many quarters —history, literature, folklore, art. Such a prose differs from that of Lacan and some of his followers, who subjugate their own written discourse to the overwhelming influence of primary process and drive derivatives, resulting in unorthodox syntax, unexpected punctuation, neologisms, strained tropes, klang associations, and the like; the aim of those Lacanians is to throw the reader forcefully upon his own unconscious (see Lebovici and Widlöcher, 1980, esp. pp. x–xi). A subsequent age may better judge whether their raw importation of the clinical setting of psychoanalysis into the act of writing arises from unresolved countertransference conflicts. Freud, at any event, while responsive to impulse, authorially accepted the responsibility to be consciously understood, and accordingly he did not omit a communicative appeal to the ego. In short, an authentic comprehension of Freud requires a specifically psychoanalytic reading which includes, though not exclusively, free association and a free-floating attention (see Laplanche, 1976, p. 4). I shall let that hypothesis hover over the rest of my paper.

Upon examination, we may detect subliminal effects in reading Freud as we attend to his lexical choices. In his address to Viennese ophthalmologists entitled 'The Psycho-analytic View of Psychogenic Disturbance of Vision' (1910), he artfully resorts to a series of expository expressions that are visual in nature, e.g.: 'As you see, Gentlemen . . . we have come to see that these separate instincts . . . The light thrown by psychology . . . We should have to see in those conditions.'[6] Hence Freud masterfully unites his theme, addressee, and expository expressions in a soft focus. Proceeding now to the more general perspective on Freud's works as a whole, we notice that the accumulative impact of such interrelated terms as 'expose,' '(un)cover,' 'hide,' 'disclose,' 'reveal,' and 'naked' produces a running intertextual polysemy. For example, the words *hide* and *reveal*, apart from directly describing the psychoanalytic pursuit of truth, variously evoke and interrelate on unconscious, preconscious, and conscious levels the archeological, sexual, and landscape analogies populating Freud's corpus. Significantly, screen memories in German are literally 'cover' memories (*Deckerinnerungen*). Both the early and late Freud applied the term 'coating' (*Umkleidung*) to a variety of psychical phenomena (1905, pp. 83, 84, 99; 1912, p. 248; 1924, p. 165). He also relied on activities of stripping and dressing to describe that a psychical and physical stripping are preparatory to sleep (1917, p. 222) and that sleep in turn involves a preparatory stripping for dreams (1915, p. 286).[7] For another though partial example, I cannot fail to bring Jacques Derrida's (1975) perspicacious commentary on Freud's analysis of the dream about the emperor's uniform (Freud, 1900, pp. 242–244). This dream, based on the equivalence between nudity and clothing (*Kleidung*), prompts Freud to think of a relevant fairy tale, Andersen's *The Emperor's New Clothes*. Freud proposes, in fact, that the tale had originally been a dream which was then given a new 'form'—but Strachey's translation here hides the richness of the German word *Einkleidung*. Actually Freud's analysis is an exegetical disrobing of the fundamental dream about clothing which itself is put in the dress (*Einkleidung*) of a fairy tale. As Derrida says, from both a formal and semantic point of view, Freud's explanation blends into what is explained.

Commentators have not drawn attention to the polysemous verbal choice that frequently occurs at the endings of Freud's monographs. There he is apt to introduce what I call the terminal culminative word or words that nodally resume much of the previous exposition. As an example, I refer to the terms 'troubled' and 'forebearance' in the last sentence of 'A Disturbance of Memory on the Acropolis' (Freud, 1936): 'And now you will no longer wonder that the recollection of this incident on the Acropolis should have troubled me so often since I myself have grown old and stand in need of forebearance and can travel no more' (p. 248). The word 'troubled' in German is *heimsucht* (*G.W.* 16: 257), whose alternate meaning is 'visits' and whose literal meaning is 'seeks home.' The recollection of the Acropolis troubled and visited the old Freud who could no longer physically revisit the Acropolis. Previously in the essay, the incredulity of visiting the Acropolis summons up an analogy about a girl who loves 'secretly' (the German is *heimlich*!). In addition, Freud links his derealization on the Acropolis to past distressing experiences which subsequently have 'fallen' (*anheimgefallen*) to repression. Such experiences, furthermore, relate to 'dissatisfaction with home' (*Unzufriedenheit mit Haus*) and the resultant desire 'to run away from home' (*vom Hause durchzugehen*). Next, although 'forebearance' is the correct modern rendition of *Nachsicht*, we should know that the archaic meaning of that term in German is 'hindsight.' Yet this lexicographically obsolete meaning is pertinently up to date in Freud's essay: imprisoned in his sick obsolete body, Freud exposes his need for forebearance and simultaneously shows much hindsight about his derealization in Athens. What is more, the term 'hindsight' is summative of a whole series of prior references to vision, internal and external. Initially Freud refers to himself as a being who has 'seen better days' and then points to his essay as one which might 'bear witness' (*bezeugen*) to his gratitude. At the Acropolis Freud 'cast [his] eyes around' and to some extent reacted like someone who had 'caught sight' of the Loch Ness monster. In effect, 'seeing something with one's own eyes' differs from a reading or hearsay experience, Freud repeatedly insists. That seeing, moreover, makes a person feel heroic as he first 'catches sight' of some landmark which hitherto was thought to be an unrealizable desire. Such facts lead Freud to an inner perception: 'It seems [*es sieht aus*] as though the essence of success was to have got further than one's father, and as though to excel one's father was still something forbidden' (1936, p. 247).

Moving to a broader expository level, we may further enhance our estimation of Freud's texts when we realize that whether as a speaker or writer he was wont to have a double audience in mind—the interlocutors or hearers at large and the ones he privately addressed;

the latter could be internalized or externalized, as in the case of Freud's private appeal during his addresses to the Vienna Psychoanalytic Society. This reference to the arts of talking and writing prompts me to proclaim again one of Freud's most epochal discoveries: grappling with the boundless elusiveness of the unconscious, he invented a technically novel kind of talking strategy which is indebted to and yet transcends both oral and written traditions and which, not only among therapies but also in the grander history of discourse, stands apart from whatever before has been spoken, written, or read.

As an added consideration we may ask ourselves why Freud did not communicate more about discourse and writing with his followers. His processive style was unlike that of any other psychoanalyst, but why did he not say so? How did Freud silently react to the writings of those around him who explained psychoanalysis in a static language that militated against the very insights of psychoanalysis about the vitality of psychic reality? For so long I have been intrigued by those perplexing questions, and my answers thus far remain partial as well as tentative. I believe that Freud lived to a great degree in solitude all his life and that his 'splendid isolation' was not merely confined to the 1890's. Among his friends he simply had no intellectual equal. I surmise that the rareness of his comments about the inherent relation between his written expression and the psychoanalytic matter being expounded testifies to his large capacity for a certain intellectual loneliness that he lived out amidst his circle. To appreciate Freud's adaptability to the inevitable loneliness that is the fate of all genius, we might ask how this had been earlier prepared for in his marriage. Unfortunately Jones's account does not help us here, for he covers over the lack of a satisfactory exchange between Freud and Martha on psychoanalytic matters: 'She would hardly have been familiar with the details of her husband's work' but did have some knowledge of it, was 'very cultivated' and kept 'abreast with current literature' (Jones, 1955, p. 387). In our efforts to grasp Freud's toleration of isolation we might bring in the differing observation of another contemporary. Laforgue (1956) narrates how Martha asked for his opinion about a tic which a certain little boy had: 'I told her of my astonishment at her addressing herself to me and not to her husband. She replied with her customary frankness, "Do you really think one can employ psychoanalysis with children? I must admit that if I did not realize how seriously my husband takes his treatments, I should think that psychoanalysis is a form of pornography!"' (Laforgue, p. 342).[8] Perhaps now I may return to my original puzzlement and venture another answer. Freud's appreciable ability to derive narcissistic satisfaction in writing compensated for his pains of loneliness. As he said: 'nevertheless we write in the first place for ourselves' (Jones, 1955, p. 397).

By way of conclusion, I reaffirm that in our preoccupations it should be constantly profitable to scrutinize the ever-so nuanced texts of our founder and to use his clinical and theoretical insights as a window from which we might inspect our own findings and expectations regarding his ideas. Whatever our refined options as Freud's pupils or followers, we can scarcely fail to admire his pioneering work as a psychic speleologist exploring by reflection the cave of human minds. Most pertinent here is a little-known statement Freud once proposed as his own memorial: 'When you think of me, think of Rembrandt, a little light and a great deal of darkness' (cited in Bergmann and Hartman, 1976, p. xiv). At times, as psychoanalysts all know, the unconscious inundates us with powerful evidence of its blinding force, and then we might find ourselves awaiting a quieter moment for perspicacious comprehension or for speculating in the coolness of recollection, a kind of jalousie allowing more light than heat. At such moments, a silent gratefulness for the discovery of psychoanalysis and its classical inscription is liable to join our repose. And then, too, we might find that thunderous fiat, 'a little light and a great deal of darkness'—a fit opening for the Book of Neurogenesis.

We should also be aware, however, that at the genesis of psycho-analysis itself, thunder had drowned out the mutual gratefulness among some of its pioneers. It is that story that bids us on to the next chapter. A necessary, historical prologue will gradually clarify the enactive character of Freud's most outstanding anthropological text.

Notes

* First published in *Journal of the American Psycho-Analytic Association.* (1984), 32: 874–864.
1 For example, in my cursory examination of some of Freud's library, now partly resituated in New York, I was intrigued how he could pen bilingual comments mixing Latin and German; how he could be so laconically expressive; and how he modulated emphasis in his notation, from a single vertical to parallel vertical lines in the margin, rarely accompanied by underlining the main text. As an instance of the latter, I cite from Romanes's *Mental Evolution in Man* (1888, pp. 118–119). The sentence that captivated Freud reads: '. . . "to be" as a copula or predicant does not have any place in sign-language.' As a matter of fact, the whole

155

section in Romanes's book on communication by deaf-mutes is heavily marked by Freud. Apart from its general value, the marked book expresses Freud's early interest in intersemiotic translation.

2 See also Ornston (1982). One can find throughout Freud's texts, of course, passages which defy satisfactory translation.

3 At present we have no one piece of Freud's writing that is adequately annotated. The kind of careful lexical study done by Holt (1962) and more globally by Laplanche and Pontalis (1973) must be extended and then redistributed into annotations for separate texts, joined by indications of ambiguities, logical inconsistencies, and the like. As of now, the reader of Freud must engage in hermeneutic reconstructions which are liable to postdictive and retrodictive distortions.

4 See Bertin (1982), especially chap. 7, and the transcribed interviews with Heinz Hartmann and then with Dora Hartmann, deposited at the New York Psychoanalytic Institute.

5 The statements in quotation marks in this paragraph are from Croll's (1929) brilliant essay, 'The Baroque Style in Prose,' pp. 209, 210, 226.

6 Sometimes Strachey's English in this essay has a visual cast that does not exist in the original German. On the other hand, sometimes Strachey's translation overlooks a visual note in the German (*G.W.* 8: 94–102): attempted explanation/*Erklärungsversuches*, angle/*Gesichspunkte*, make easier/*erleichtern*, if we find/*wenn wir sehen*, standpoint/*Gesichtspunkt*.

7 The use of clothing references to portray psychic phenomena has more than just a superficial analogic value: evocative of ego and superego inhibitions, the image of undressing is inherently pertinent to central dynamic factors in the psychoanalytic process. Waelder (1956, p. 367) pertinently describes the transference as conditioned by the patient's unilateral exposure of 'the most intimate aspects of his life—putting him in the position of the child that is nude in the presence of adults.' In the most profound sense we ask the patient to tell the 'naked' truth.

8 See also Theodor Reik's note on his discussion with Martha: 'She said about psychoanalysis for instance: "Oh well, hysteria and so on. We had also our troubles when we were young. But comes the menopause, then it's over." But she said to me that she never understood what is so great about analysis' (Freeman [1971], p. 80; see also the report of Jung's visit to Vienna in 1907 [Billinsky, 1969, p. 42]). Finally, there is Marie Bonaparte's interesting exchange with Freud: 'Mrs. Freud told me how much the work of her husband had surprised her and shocked her in that it treats sexuality so freely. It is almost *on purpose* that she ignored it. *Meine Frau ist sehr bürgerlich* (my wife is very 'bourgeois') said Freud when I told him about it. She would have never, he said, expressed her opinion so forthrightly to him' (Bertin, 1982, p. 289). When all is said and done, however, we must recognize the contradiction between *Frau* Freud's

'customary frankness' and her allegedly being so 'bourgeois.' Indeed, her independence of spirit, which Freud avowedly admired, was a vital complementary factor in their special relationship.

References

Bergmann, M. and Hartman, F. (eds.) (1976) *The Evolution of Psychoanalytic Technique*. New York: Basic Books.

Bertin, C. (1982) *La dernière Bonaparte*. Paris: Librairie Académique Perrin.

Billinsky, J. (1969) Jung and Freud (the end of a romance). *Andover Newton Quarterly*, 10: 39–43.

Croll, M. (1929) The Baroque style in prose. In: J.M. Patrick *et al.*, *Style, Rhetoric, and Rhythm: Essays by Morris W. Croll*. Princeton: Princeton University Press, 1966, pp. 207–233.

Derrida, J. (1975) Le facteur de la vérité. *Poétique*, 21: 96–147.

Eissler, K.R. (1980) Report on the Sigmund Freud Archives, *International Journal of the Psychoanalytic Association*, 61: 104–105.

Freeman, E. (1971) *Insights: Conversations with Theodor Reik*. Englewood Cliffs, N.J.: Prentice-Hall.

Freud, S. (1887–1902) *The Origins of Psychoanalysis*. New York: Basic Books, 1954.

—— (1895) Project for a scientific psychology. *Standard Edition (S.E.)* 1 (1966).

—— (1900) The interpretation of dreams. *S.E.* 4, 5 (1953).

—— (1905) Fragment of an analysis of a case of hysteria. *S.E.* 7: 3–122 (1953).

—— (1907) Delusions and dreams in Jensen's *Gradiva*. *S.E.* 9: 3–95 (1959).

—— (1910) The psychoanalytic view of psychogenic disturbance of vision. *S.E.* 11: 211–218 [*G.W.* 94–102. Frankfurt a.M.: Fischer, 1945].

—— (1912) Contributions to a discussion of masturbation. *S.E.* 12: 239–254 (1958).

—— (1914) On the history of the psychoanalytic movement. *S.E.* 14: 7–66 (1957).

—— (1915) Thoughts on war and death. *S.E.* 14: 273–302 (1957).

—— (1916–1917) Introductory lectures on psychoanalysis. *S.E.* 15, 16 (1961).

—— (1917) A metapsychological supplement to the theory of dreams. *S.E.* 14: 217–236 (1961).

—— (1918) From the history of an infantile neurosis. *S.E.* 17: 3–122 (1955). [*G.W.* 12: 29–157. Frankfurt a.M.: Fischer, 1947].

—— (1924) The economic problem of masochism. *S.E.* 19: 157–172 (1961).

—— (1925) Negation. *S.E.* 19: 157–172 (1961).

—— (1930) Civilization and its discontents. *S.E.* 21: 59–148 (1961).

—— (1936) A disturbance of memory on the Acropolis. *S.E.* 22: 239–250 (1964). [*G.W.* 16: 250–257. Frankfurt a.M.: Fischer, 1950].

Hawelka, E. (ed.) (1974) *L'Homme aux Rats: Journal d'une Analyse par Sigmund Freud.* Paris: Presses Universitaires de France.

Holt, R.R. (1962) A critical examination of Freud's concept of bound vs. free cathexis. *Journal of American Psychoanalytic Association,* 10: 475–525.

Jones, E. (1955) *The Life and Work of Sigmund Freud,* vol. 2. New York: Basic Books.

Kofman, S. (1972) Résumer, interpréter (*Gradiva*). *Critique,* 305: 892–916.

Laforgue, R. (1956) Personal memories of Freud. In: H. Ruitenbeek (ed.) *Freud As We Knew Him.* Detroit: Wayne State University Press, 1973, pp. 341–349.

Laplanche, J. (1976) *Life and Death in Psychoanalysis.* Baltimore: Johns Hopkins University Press.

——and Pontalis, J.-B. (1973) *The Language of Psychoanalysis.* New York: Norton.

Lebovici, S. and Widlöcher, D. (1980) *Psychoanalysis in France.* New York: International Universities Press.

Mahony, P. (1977) Friendship and its discontents. *Contemporary Psychoanalysis,* 15: 55–109.

—— (1979) The place of psychoanalytic treatment in the history of discourse. *Psychoanalysis and Contemporary Thought,* 2: 77–111.

—— (1981) *Freud as a Writer.* New York: International Universities Press.

—— and Singh, R. (1975) *The Interpretation of Dreams,* semiology, and Chomskian linguistics: a radical critique. *The Psychoanalytic Study of the Child,* 30: 221–242.

Ornston, D. (1982) Strachey's influence: a preliminary report. *International Journal of Psycho-analysis,* 63: 409–426.

Rado, S. (n.d.) Transcribed interview, deposed in the Oral History Research Section, Columbia University.

Rank, O. and Sachs, H. (1916) *The Significance of Psychoanalysis for Mental Sciences.* New York: Macmillan.

Romanes, G. (1888) *Mental Evolution in Man.* London: Kegan Paul.

Rothgeb, C.L. (ed.) (1973) *Abstracts of the Standard Edition of the Complete Psychological Works of Sigmund Freud.* New York: Int. Universities Press.

Sterba, R. (1978) Discussions of Sigmund Freud. *Psychoanalytic Quarterly,* 47: 173–191.

Strachey, J. (1966) General preface. In Freud, S., *S.E.* 1.

Sutherland, J. (1980) The British object relations theorists: Balint, Winnicott, Fairbairn, Guntrip. *Journal of the American Psychoanalytic Association,* 28: 829–860.

Waelder, R. (1956) Introduction to the discussion on problems of transference. *International Journal of Psycho-Analysis,* 37: 367–376.

8
The budding International Association of Psychoanalysis and its discontents: a feature of Freud's discourse*

In 'Friendship and Its Discontents' (Mahony, 1979), I traced in elaborate detail the origins of psychoanalysis in the personal life of Freud, his self analysis, and his relationships with his sister-in-law, Minna Bernays, and with Wilhelm Fliess. The period I then focused on, though not exclusively, was from approximately 1887 to 1904, and for principal documents I naturally relied on the Fliess correspondence (Freud, 1887–1902) and *The Interpretation of Dreams*. My present concern is again with origins, this time with the very origins of the psycho-analytic movement in which Jung appears as a protagonist. My primary texts now are collections of Freud's letters, the biographies by Jones (1953, 1955, 1957) and Schur (1972), the *Minutes of the Vienna Psychoanalytic Society* (Nunberg and Federn, 1906–1918), pertinent writings in the *Standard Edition* of Freud's works, and, most particularly, his analysis of primal family phenomena in *Totem and Taboo* (1913a).[1]

Analyzing what might be called the birth and early growth of the psychoanalytic family, I shall concentrate on the period from about 1902 to 1913, with 1910 as a focal point of those four years from 1910 to 1913 when the young psychoanalytic movement was racked with disruption. The reason for these chronological road-signs is very simple: in 1902 a small Viennese group had begun to gather around Freud; by 1910 that modest beginning formally assumed an international character, and *Totem and Taboo* was published in 1912–1913, concurrent with the final period of discord. In my previous study (1979), I pointed out the pivotal importance of the year 1910, and adduced several reasons for it, but much of what occurred then remained basically perplexing to me. I have now acquired considerably more insight into that year, although this has also prompted other unanswered questions. The year 1910 has become simultaneously the sun and the center of darkness, enveloped by the penumbra of the surrounding years.

Central to my thesis is that during this time Freud was especially concerned with such issues as homosexuality, paranoia, the etiology of religion, and father–son relationships, issues deeply personally felt by the father of the psychoanalytic primal horde. His *Totem and Taboo* can, in part, be described as the memoirs of an aging father beleaguered by the interpretation of dreams—his own castrating dreams and those of his sons, their totems and taboos. Indeed, with some justice *Totem and Taboo* could be re-entitled *The Interpretation of Psychoanalysts' Dreams*. With these dreams in mind, we may take a cue from Philip Rieff's stimulating essay on 'The Meaning and History of Religion in Freud's Thought' (1951) and postulate three myths that dominated the budding psychoanalytic movement: the Oedipal myth or parricide; the Cain myth or fratricide, seen in the well-known rivalry among Freud's disciples; and the Abraham myth or filicide. In three partially overlapping sections, I shall first concentrate on *Totem and Taboo* as a historical exposition of the birth of the primal horde in the Freudian circle. I shall then give a short account of the psychoanalytic movement from 1902 to 1913; and finally I shall examine Freud's *Totem and Taboo* and Jung's *Psychology of the Unconscious* (1916) as not just expositions but also enactments of their subject matter.

Family romance in the primal horde

A few remarks drawn from the first essays of *Totem and Taboo* serve as an introduction to the all-important fourth essay. As a rule, a totem is an animal that is regarded by a clan as its common ancestor. Nearly everywhere where there are totems, there are laws of incest taboos demanding that the clan members be exogamous, that is, they must avoid incest by marrying members of another clan or totem. More generally, a taboo is a primitive prohibition, dealing essentially with touching, which is forcibly imposed from the outside and directed against the most powerful longings to which humans are subject.

In the famous fourth essay, Freud combines Darwin's hypothesis about the primal horde and Robertson Smith's hypothesis about the totemic meal to make the following story:

160

[In the primal horde] there is a violent and jealous father who keeps all the females for himself and drives away his sons as they grow up. . . . One day[2] the brothers who had been driven out came together, killed and devoured their father and so made an end of the patriarchal horde. . . . The violent primal father had doubtless been the feared and envied model of each one of the company of brothers:[3] and in the act of devouring him they accomplished their identification with him, and each one of them acquired a portion of his strength. The totem meal, which is perhaps mankind's earliest festival, would thus be a repetition and a commemoration of this memorable and criminal deed, which was the beginning of so many things—of social organization, of moral restrictions and of religion. . . . [Hence, according to what we now call deferred obedience, the sons] revoked their deed by forbidding the killing of the totem, the substitute for their father; and they renounced its fruits by resigning their claim to the women who had now been set free. They thus created out of their filial sense of guilt the two fundamental taboos of totemism, which for that very reason inevitably corresponded to the two repressed wishes of the Oedipus complex [1913a, pp. 141–143].

Onto this complex Freud affixes his own brand of Lamarckism: the inheritance of an acquired character now includes the domain of the psychic, of both ideation and feeling, of both primal parricide and the subsequent guilt. Hence, for Freud, 'the assumption of a collective mind, [of a continuity in the emotional life of man]' (p. 158),[4] makes possible the existence of social psychology. Guided by social psychology, an understanding of the totemic feast rectifies the adage 'One man's meal is another man's poison' into 'One man's poisonous totem is equally his enjoyable taboo.'

Besides being an analysis and a reconstruction of primitive history, *Totem and Taboo* is also a commentary on the early history of the psychoanalytic movement itself, and especially the period between 1910 and 1913, which are respectively the dates of the First International Psychoanalytical Congress and Jung's resignation from the editorship of the main psychoanalytic journal, *Das Jahrbuch für psychoanalytische und psychopathologische Forschungen*. During that very period, 1910 to 1913, Freud completed *Totem and Taboo*.[5]

Various conflicting elements intensified transference and counter-transference relationships and thereby amplified the power of Freud, the primal father of psychoanalysis. In his dealings with others, Freud recognized the paternal streak in his character[6] which, in the light of the domestic atmosphere described by Sachs, could only be expected:

> Friends of the family frequently made fun of the solemn way they spoke of everything concerning their father. For instance it was said that [if] one of the children had been absent for some time and was met by another, the first word from the newcomer was 'Father now drinks his tea from the green cup instead of from the blue one.' Such jokes and jibes always contain a grain, more often than one grain, of truth. The life of the family revolved around the father as his life revolved around his work. These things were never talked about; there was no need for words since the facts were taken for granted [Sachs, 1944, p. 74].

This strongly entrenched paternalism was complemented by the early 'sons' of the Vienna Society, who referred explicitly to Freud's father role and vied for his preferential attention. When, in 1910, Freud offered his resignation as president of the Vienna Society, the reluctant Federn regretfully saw this as the passing of an 'old patriarchal relationship' (*Minutes*, v. 2, p. 466). In addition to his paternal stature, Freud was the scientific pioneer with gigantic intellectual powers and a remarkably forceful personality, characterized by boundless courage. As Nunberg comments, for his pupils, Freud was an unattainable ideal, so much excelling them in theory and technique that he frustrated any full identification (*Minutes*, v. 1, p. xxx). On 3 June 1909, for instance, Freud wrote Jung that he was simultaneously working on eight different paths of research, an aspect of his genius that was ever to make Freud in part solitary and lonely (*FJL*, p. 227). An added isolatory burden was that as father, Freud felt obliged to supply patients to his disciples, which made him complain to Pfister and Jung.[7] Then, too, Freud's position of authority was increased by the fact that he analyzed some of his early colleagues and their intimates, such as Stekel and Jones's companion Loe Kann.[8] As can be imagined, such close relationships were liable to entail numerous difficulties, and certainly those prompted by Stekel would rank among the foremost, for one of his

> unpleasant habits was to illustrate his contentions at the Society's meetings by quoting material from his personal life, especially his early childhood. It was mostly quite invented or else grossly falsified, and he would defiantly glare at Freud, who of course knew the real facts from his analysis, knowing full well he would not contradict him. This sort of thing must have been very irksome, and Freud unburdened his mind by telling me, as a

foreigner, something about the actual analysis [Jones, 1959, p. 220].[9]

A further complication of the father–son imbroglio pertains to Freud's own desire that his adherents literally become his sons-in-law. Thus on Ferenczi's very first visit, Freud secretly wished that he would marry his daughter Mathilde, and he also wanted Rank to marry one of his daughters.[10]

At one time Freud referred to his flock of disciples as 'the wild hunt.'[11] Prominent among them was Rank, who, according to Freud, liquidated his regicidal tendencies by an intellectual interest in the subject and thereby could become such a devoted son. The case was different with Tausk, whose aggressive and fiery independence, disruptive of calm scientific reflection, was ill-supported by Freud.[12] Whether Adler ever was a disciple of Freud's has been subject to dispute (cf. Ansbacher, 1962, 1963; E. Federn, 1963). But we cannot ignore the fact that Stekel (1950) looked on his collaborator and co-rebeller Adler as distinctly one of Freud's 'pupils' (pp. 129, 141). If Adler judged Freud to be an old despot impeding the progress of young men (*FJL*, 25 Nov. 1910, p. 373), for his part Freud could dismiss Adler with one of the most incisive one-sentence statements ever written about paranoia: 'As a paranoiac of course he is right about many things, though wrong about everything' (*FJL*, 15 June 1911, p. 428). Significantly, after seeing a stage presentation of *Oedipus Rex*, Freud avowed that he had become more discontent with Adler (*FJL*, 12 May 1911, p. 422).

Of all the early pupils it was Jung, Fliess's replacant, who was chosen to be Freud's successor. Both Jung's and Freud's initial difficulties with each other were covered up in subsequent letters of praise hiding repressed hostility—a correspondence that reminds us of Freud's earlier repression of deep animosity in his eulogistic letters to Fliess (see Schur, 1966, 1972). Freud admired the imaginative capacities of Fliess and Jung. Both had mystico-religious bents, and it was precisely this mystical flair that wrought havoc in their amity with Freud. Freud's double transference onto Fleiss—paternal and fraternal—comes out in the tone of his letters, suggesting that he was addressing either a social equal or superior.[13] That Jung had partial awareness of the character of that amity is revealed in his reactive plea to Freud: 'your relationship with him [Fliess] impels me to ask you to let me enjoy your friendship not as one between equals but as that of father and son' (*FJL*, 20 Feb. 1908, p. 122). Along this line of thought, comparison ought to be made between Fliess's Freud and Jung's Freud. Long before his friendship with Jung, Freud had discovered the Oedipus complex, a discovery adopted by him on an intellectual level although endopsychically it was never fully resolved (as is recurrently evident in the exchange of letters between Vienna and Zurich). However, a very different situation existed in the late 1890's when Freud's personally and scientifically groping acceptance of bisexuality was enmeshed in his turbulent attitude to Fliess.

Freud's leaning toward Jung and his Swiss countrymen was partially motivated by a geographical factor: Freud associated Vienna with the East, whereas Zurich represented the West.[14] And perhaps this usually overlooked East to West shift was a factor in his liking the Berliner Fliess and in moving the Israelite Moses' birthplace westward to Egypt. But Jung stood for more than just Zurich; he stood for the dominance of Christian political power in the Western world. Not wanting psychoanalysis to die in a war of fratricide between Christians and Jews, Freud chose his successor from the Christian totem alone, so to speak, thereby preventing his founded science from 'becoming a Jewish national affair' which then 'would succumb to anti-Semitism.'[15] Neither must we forget the positive influence of Freud's belief that Jung's great-grandfather was Goethe, whom Freud held in the greatest esteem.[16]

One of the finest comments on the relationship between Freud, his Viennese followers, and Jung comes unexpectedly from an observation made by Freud himself to the tired Jung. Referring to Jung's 'counter-effects' stemming from the great influence he was exerting on his superior Bleuler, Freud trenchantly averred, 'It is not possible to push without being pushed' (*FJL*, 3 May 1908, p. 145). This insight into the ambivalence of the professorial role should especially be applied to any understanding of Freud during those early organizational years.

Though openly acknowledging the paternal traits in his character, Freud could become irritated by the dependent father complexes of his younger colleagues.[17] Jung's transference was massive and bound to cause trouble eventually. He himself characterized it as a kind of religious crush with an erotic element in it, arising from being sexually abused in his youth by someone he idolized. Although Freud was quick to caution him that a religious transference could terminate in an apostasy, Jung continued to refer to his father complex as a fact and something he wanted to preserve.[18] For the while there was no stopping Jung: he went on to call himself the famulus of Freud the human hero and demi-god, even though he found it arduous to work alongside the 'father creator,' a phrase written significantly enough on Christmas day.[19] Another complication was that due to his father complex. Jung was greatly hurt by the break with the older Bleuler; but then, reversing the roles somewhat with respect to his assistant Honegger, Jung cast a new generational picture with himself as the father, now asking Freud for his 'grandfatherly opinion.'[20] Interestingly, too, when Jung became a real father and contentedly said he could now depart in peace, Freud chided him for a premature abandonment of the ideal father role with a few uncanny words: 'The child will find you indispensable as a father for many years, first in a positive, then in a negative sense' (*FJL*, 11 Dec. 1908, p. 186).

Age, succession, and father–son rivalry were subjects dominating the relationship of Jung and Freud from its very beginning to its end and indeed toll like a ceaseless bell throughout their correspondence. But if one were to parcel out diagnoses that actually affected both protagonists, one would have to state that Freud had more of a pathological reaction to aging and Jung to paternal transference. Repeatedly, Freud mentions his succession by Jung, and sometimes in very glowing terms: 'My dear friend and heir'; 'if I am Moses, then you are Joshua'; 'my successor and crown prince'; 'dear son Alexander.'[21] Interweaving through these investitures is the gnawing feeling of old age, and yet Freud could generously hope that any defective ideas would be liquidated by Jung, who would retain the solid theory.[22] 'But,' a critical reader might well object, 'if Freud was so much the jealous and domineering primal father, how was it that he enthusiastically advanced Jung's cause and indeed proposed him as president of the International Psycho-Analytical Association?' The answer is quite simple if we do not permit ourselves to be nominally misled. If Jung were president, then Freud would be arch-president. True enough, Freud could casually submit to Jung, but in fact the correspondence in general amply testifies as to who had the guiding hand.[23] As Jones accurately puts it:

> Freud was too mistrustful of the average mind to adopt the democratic attitude customary in scientific societies, so he wished there to be a prominent 'leader' who should guide the doings of branch societies and their members; moreover he wanted the leader to be in a permanent position, like a monarch. . . . At the time he only withdrew nominally; in fact he retained a tight hold on all matters of policy and his influence was so powerful that the president could not deviate far from it [1959, pp. 214–215].

Although in August 1910 Freud rebuffed his 'dear son and successor' for his faulty four-month start as president of the International Association, by the end of the same year Freud was more convinced than ever that Jung was 'the man of the future,' a conviction that was spelled out several months later to Binswanger: 'When the empire I founded is orphaned, no one but Jung must inherit the whole thing.'[24] In view of the fact that 1911 was a period of stormy personal conflicts, it is rather baffling that as late as 5 March 1912 Freud solemnly described Jung as his unique friend, helper, and heir (*FJL*, p. 493).[25] When the dissolution of their friendship was no longer deniable, Jung did a turnabout in vehemently criticizing their moribund father–son relationship.[26] And yet the process of mourning would be much more taxing for him than for Freud, whose dependence was not as great and who already had been through such an experience with Fliess. Nevertheless, from an overall perspective, Freud was still caught on the tenterhooks of his family romance, rebel that he was, and irked at those who rebelled against him:

> He was indeed a tormented titan. However, Freud's greatest opponent came from within himself—from the beleaguered ego that sought to be free from the same patriarchal superego and, still incompletely analyzed, had to be projected through unconscious sympathy into a counteridentification with his own critics in the society. . . . An inner bond with the rebel against the father and the paternalistic aspects of psychoanalysis seems to have been present [Kanzer, 1971, pp. 38, 44].

At this point I must venture the statement that the son's choice of his father's profession occurs much less frequently in psychoanalysis than in other professions, precisely because of a mixture of hyperawareness and Oedipal counteridentification. Be that as it may, the family romance as the collective fantasy of the embryonic psychoanalytic organization was such that it intensified the concerns with youth and age, identification, rivalry, autonomy, rebellion, death wishes, betrayal, authority, and castration fears; in sum, the Oedipus complex of the psychoanalytic primal horde.

The future of an illusion: a chronicle of its discontent

First of all I shall briefly sketch some relevant background information, a good deal of which is generally known. Though Freud's friendship with Fliess was just about over by 1900, their regular correspondence trickled on until 1902. In that same year, Stekel, who had had eight hours of analysis with Freud, suggested that a group be formed, and so the Psychological Wednesday Society was inaugurated (Stekel, 1950, pp. 107, 115–116). Initially this small group of Stekel, Adler, and two others met weekly in Freud's own residence, thus ending

Freud's eight years of 'splendid isolation,' which more or less started with his break-up with Breuer in 1894.

In the following years, the little group added memorable names to its rolls with remarkable celerity. Joining in 1904, Paul Federn's thirty-five years of collaboration was to be unmatched in Freud's circle.[27] In 1906, the same year that Fliess publicly attacked Freud by publishing, *inter alia*, a short exchange of private correspondence between them, Rank joined the group and continued on as secretary for the *Minutes* until 1918. In 1907, the relative obscurity of psycho-analysis changed suddenly beyond all expectations and attention was attracted from abroad (Freud, 1914, p. 26). Between 1907 and 1908, other notable names came in contact with Freud either as guests or members: Eitingon, Abraham, Jung, Jones, and Ferenczi. Freud had much to be content about, even though in those early years he was often involved in regulating two problems: personal quarrels among the members and disputes about priority in discoveries.[28]

The friendship between Freud and Jung was a curious one in its birth and demise. The very issue bringing them together—the psychic mechanism behind dementia praecox and its connection with libido theory—was the decisive factor that led to their friendship's disruption. Indeed, although he defended Freud's sexual theory for several years, Jung never fully accepted it, and, despite the cross-fertilization of ideas, Freud's major impact on Jung occurred before they met each other. Jung's contributions were both substantial and incidental; concerning the latter, there is good evidence that Jung directed Freud's attention to Schreber's (1903) autobiography—evidence that underscores Jones's reluctance to give any credit to Jung, for Jones asserts that Freud merely 'had come across' the Schreber papers (1955, p. 268).[29]

The first contact between Jung and Freud took place in April 1906, when Jung sent Freud a copy of his *Diagnostic Association Studies*, a text whose experimental design contributed further to Freud's insights into the associative activity of the unconscious. This gift prompted an exchange of letters, and in March 1907, Jung, accompanied by his wife, Emma, and Ludwig Binswanger, visited Freud in Vienna.[30] The encounter between Jung and Freud was electrifying—they met at one in the afternoon and talked nearly non-stop for 13 hours. Though Jung was overwhelmed, even then he had some doubts which were not fully removed, reluctant as he was to agree with Freud's firm emphasis on sexuality and the collateral explanation of art and spirituality as expressions of repressed sexuality. Freud's marked emotional involvement in sexual theory and his abandonment of a typically critical and skeptical reserve when talking about sexual topics also served to estrange Jung (see Jung, 1961, pp. 159–160).

A few days into the visit, Jung was informed by Freud's sister-in-law, Minna, that Freud was in love with her and that they had an intimate relationship; the reaction of the admiring Jung was one of both shock and agony (Billinsky, 1969, p. 43). Also, during his stay, Jung had an unsettling dream which retrospectively we can recognize as portentous. In the dream Jung 'was in a Ghetto, and the place was narrow and twisted, with low ceilings and staircases hanging down. He thought to himself: "How in hell can people live in such a place" ' (Bennet, 1961, p. 34). In another dream, Jung saw Freud walking beside him as a *'very, very frail old man.'* Freud interpreted it as a dream of rivalry, but it was only later that Jung felt the dream was an essentially peaceful dream setting his mind at ease by banishing the dangers of Freud's sexual theories (*FJL*, 2 Nov. 1907, p. 96).

Like the first dreams of a psychoanalytic treatment, the fantasy material already bespoke the eventual course of their friendship; nevertheless, during that same first visit, Jung inspired Freud with so much confidence for the future that Freud realized his own expendability in the psychoanalytic movement and saw his honorable and competent successor in none other than Jung himself (*FJL*, 7 Apr. 1907, p. 27).

The central event of 1908 was the First International Psycho-Analytical Congress, held in April in Salzburg. Abraham and Jung clashed at the Congress, and the Viennese group already looked on the activity of the Zurich contingent as dissident. Within the next several months there was talk about a 'negative fluctuation' in Zurich and Jung's reversion to his former spiritualistic leanings. Freud felt that the suppressed Swiss anti-Semitism deflected onto Abraham was really directed at himself, a deflection which he also later interpreted in attacks on Stekel and Jung.[31] The situation was so bad that in June 1908 Freud himself suggested visiting Jung and finally stayed in Zurich from 18 September to 21 September (*FJL*, pp. 161, 171 n). So wide was the chasm between Freud and Jung that as late as June 1912 Freud could refer to the year of 1908 as a period of 'profounder differences' (*FJL*, p. 510). Meanwhile, in Vienna, Freud's local group selected a new name, the Vienna Psycho-Analytical Society, which instituted a practice of disbanding and re-establishing itself every three years in order to allow disinterested or reluctant members the freedom of resigning quietly.

The year 1909 saw the first marriage of one of Freud's daughters, Mathilde, and also the completion of 'Family Romances' (1909), surely no mere coincidence. It was also the year of the first publication of the *Jahrbuch*, which made the psychoanalytic movement no longer dependent on oral tradition and which permitted Freud a major stylistic change, since he no longer found it necessary to restate primary assumptions and deal with elementary objections in each paper.[32] More to our purpose are the momentous happenings prior to Freud's and Jung's well-received lectures at Clark University in Massachusetts. Freud met Jung and Ferenczi in Bremen on 20 August, the day before their departure. Jung enthusiastically discussed the peat-bog corpses found in northern Europe, his fascination focusing on the effect of the humic acid in the bog water, which consumed the bones of the prehistoric corpses while tanning and preserving the skin. Confusing these peat-bog corpses with mummies of the perfectly preserved Teutons located in the lead vault of Bremen Cathedral, Jung expressed his desire to see them, and several times the irritated Freud challenged Jung's fascination with the topic. During lunch Jung resumed the topic, and thereupon Freud suddenly fainted. Afterward he interpreted Jung's death wish toward him as the latent meaning beneath the subject of the corpses.[33]

The concern in Bremen over death wishes continued during their nine-day boat trip to the States, which was pivotal for the history of psychoanalysis. Freud was excited by the trip and thought that, with the exception of the *Jahrbuch*, it was his greatest thrill in years.[34] We are entitled to surmise that it had an effect on his Indian summer of eroticism, which he disclosed to Jung on the boat trip and whose withering away within six months afterward made Freud resign himself to old age (*FJL*, 2 Feb. 1910, p. 292). During the journey, Jung and Freud analyzed each other and tried to interpret each other's dreams, with two of them proving to be particularly important (Billinsky, 1969, p. 42). Jung had a long dream that was his first inkling of a collective unconscious and that constituted in effect a kind of prelude to his *Psychology of the Unconscious* (1916).[35] With great resistance, he took issue with Freud's self-referential outlook that at the dream's end there had to be a death wish connected with the discovery of a couple of skulls.

On the other hand, Freud had a dream dealing with his wife and sister-in-law, and when Jung asked for associations from his personal life, Freud responded with a curious look, 'But I cannot risk my authority' (Jung, 1961, p. 158). Feeling that Freud placed personal authority above the truth, Jung quipped: 'Analysis is excellent, except for the analyst' (Bennet, 1961, p. 40).[36] Two of Jung's very last letters to Freud bitterly refer to this incident, which was a decisive moment in the friendship and, as Jung at another time said, foreshadowed its end.[37] In any case, the two continued to analyze each other's dreams for the rest of the trip, during their stay in the States, and on the way back.[38] Seeds of future dissension were also present in their conversation when their boat was approaching New York. Musing on their upcoming lectures, Freud exclaimed, 'Won't they get a surprise when they hear what we have to say to them.' When Jung marveled at this ambitiousness, Freud continued, 'I'm the most humble of men, and the only man who isn't ambitious,' to which Jung curtly replied, 'That's a big thing—to be the only one' (Bennet, 1961, pp. 40–41).[39]

In an important letter opening the new year of 1910, Freud expressed two related ideas: that for some time he had been thinking of uniting the psychoanalysts in a closer bond and that religion is ultimately based on 'the infantile helplessness of mankind' (Jones, 1955, pp. 69, 350). These ideas threaded through a series of activities: Freud's preoccupation with Fliess to a degree of renewed intensity, his work on homosexuality and paranoia (Leonardo da Vinci and Schreber), the beginning of his research for *Totem and Taboo*, the increasing rebellion by the Viennese, and the precipitous founding of the International Psycho-Analytical Association, which was the main purpose behind the Second International Congress at Nuremberg.

Jones's description of the Nuremberg Congress falls woefully short of the truth. For purposes of accuracy, I shall quote the beginning of Jones's long account in full:

> Freud had for some time been occupied with the idea of bringing together analysts in a closer bond, and he had charged Ferenczi with the task of making the necessary proposals at the forthcoming Congress. After the scientific program Ferenczi addressed the meeting on the future organization of analysts and their work. There was at once a storm of protest. In his speech he had made some very derogatory remarks about the quality of Viennese analysts and suggested that the center of the future administration could only be Zurich, with Jung as President. Moreover, Ferenczi, with all his personal charm, had a decidedly dictatorial side to him, and some of his proposals went far beyond what is customary in scientific circles. Before the Congress he had already informed Freud that 'the psychoanalytical outlook does not lead to democratic equalizing; there should be an *élite* rather on the lines of Plato's rule of philosophers.' In his reply Freud said he had already had the same idea.
>
> After making the sensible proposal that an international association be formed, with branch societies in various countries,

Ferenczi went on to assert the necessity for all papers written or addresses delivered by any psychoanalyst to be first submitted for approval to the President of the Association, who was thus to have unheard-of censoring powers. It was this attitude of Ferenczi's that was later to cause such trouble between European and American analysts which it took me, in particular, years to compose. The discussion that arose after Ferenczi's paper was so acrimonious that it had to be postponed to the next day. There was, of course, no question of accepting his more extreme suggestions, but the Viennese, especially Adler and Stekel, also angrily opposed the nomination of Swiss analysts to the positions of President and Secretary, their own long and faithful services being ignored. Freud himself perceived the advantage of establishing a broader basis for the work than could be provided by Viennese Jewry, and that it was necessary to convince his Viennese colleagues of this [1955, p. 69].

The upshot of Jones's account is that both he and Freud are moderate and rational and the Viennese are partially blameworthy; in ascribing to Ferenczi alone a dictatorial character, Jones's negative transference to his former analyst comes to the fore. The truth is that Ferenczi's proposals were not all his own, as I have discovered in a letter of 16 October 1910 from Freud to Bleuler; Freud worked together with Ferenczi on his speech.[40] And what were the details of this speech? In *Free Associations* (1959), Jones himself tells us that although he was not at the Nuremberg meeting, he was subsequently told that Wittels's summary was 'substantially correct' (pp. 215–216). But in Wittels's biography of Freud one reads the following discrepant account:

Ferenczi proposed the foundation of an International Psychoanalytical Association. Jung was to be its perpetual president, with absolute power to appoint and depose analysts. All the scientific writings of the members of the Association were to be submitted to him for approval before publication. The responsibility was to be taken out of the hands of Freud, and was to be entrusted to those of Jung.

It can readily be imagined that the unsuspecting Viennese ('We had no anticipation of such an onslaught') were utterly dismayed by these proposals. I doubt if powers so absolute have ever been entrusted to any one except the heads of certain Roman Catholic orders [1923, pp. 138–139].[41]

Even the slightest reflection on this description makes us realize that

Jones was caught up in the perpetuation of an idealized father. He sought to be a preferred son by degrading Ferenczi with suppressive jealousy, and he withheld telling information from his readers, who should be allowed to make their own judgements from adequate historical information. With more good reason than Jones admits, the Viennese revolted against the tyrannical move and, after the first session, held a secret meeting in Stekel's hotel room. Suddenly, Wittels tells us, the uninvited Freud burst into the room and exclaimed:

> 'Most of you are Jews, and therefore you are incompetent to win friends for the new teaching. Jews must be content with the modest role of preparing the ground. It is absolutely essential that I should form ties in the world of general science. I am getting on in years, and am weary of being perpetually attacked. We are all in danger.' Seizing his coat by the lapels, he said: 'They won't even leave me a coat on my back. The Swiss will save us—will save me, and all of you as well' [1923, p. 140].[42]

Finally a compromise was reached. The president would have but a two-year term and no powers of censorship; Freud proposed that Adler replace him as president of the Vienna Society; and a new periodical was founded, the *Zentralblatt für Psychoanalyse* jointly edited by Adler and Stekel, thereby counterbalancing the *Jahrbuch* edited by Jung.

At this point we must ask: Although Freud always retained effective power over the psychoanalytic movement, why did he cede its presidency to Jung? And why did he in the first place found the International Association which, as he later said, was done prematurely? The answers to these questions bring us back to the primal horde theory and his own complex over aging. Freud believed that he was too old to assume formal direction of the Association (1914, p. 43).

Yet he was only fifty-four in 1910. I suggest that the same age complex contributed to his motivation to bypass Bleuler, who was then fifty-three, to settle on the youthful Jung, aged thirty-five. In justifying his founding of the Association to Bleuler, Freud gave reasons with an ego coloring: the Association would refute opponents who believed that psychoanalysis began and ended with the person of Freud; it would officially disseminate authentic information about analysis and would thereby serve to dissuade adherents from reacting unwisely to personal attacks.[43] On the other hand, Freud's subsequent letter about the Congress to Ferenczi is laden with id-content and firmly implanted in his primal horde theory. Here he reveals that one of his principal motivations was to avoid the symbolic death of the primal father and to establish during his lifetime the rule of a fraternal band: 'I had almost got into the painful role of the dissatisfied and unwanted old man. That I certainly don't want, so I prefer to go before I need, but voluntarily. The leaders will all be of the same age and rank; they can then develop freely and come to terms with one another' (Jones, 1955, p. 71).[44] In the light of this, it becomes even more meaningful that at the Nuremberg Congress Freud's lecture was devoted to the topic of countertransference.

Later on that year, the tired Freud traveled extensively in Italy, a trip that had a crucial bearing on his Savonarola dream and a parapraxis. If we compare Freud's Three Fates dream of 1898 with the Savonarola dream of 1910, we can trace the enlargement of his own ego. In the earlier dream, Freud is needy and passive before parental figures, whereas in the later dream he himself is the parental figure who gives something valuable to the younger generation.[45] The parapraxis gives us an invaluable insight into Freud's extreme sensitivity to his own age. Freud and Ferenczi were trying to remember a certain place in Sicily they had recently visited. After a couple of fruitless stabs, Freud declared that he himself had forgotten many of the Sicilian names and hence it would be a suitable time for experiment. Then Freud asked and immediately answered himself: 'What was the name of the place on a hill that was called Enna in antiquity? Oh I know—Castrogiovanni.' At this point Ferenczi correctly supplied the forgotten place name, Castelvetrano. Freud traced his parapraxis to his being hurt by the American neurologist James Putnam, who had innocently described Freud as being 'no longer a young man.' To this, the offended Freud reacted by adding a descriptive note to his translation of Putnam's article, saying that the author 'has left his youth far behind him.' More immediately, Freud attributed his lapsus to the fact that *giovanni* sounds like *giovane* (young; also the translation of the German *jung*) and *vetrano* sounds like *veterano* (old).[46] In an explanation to Jung, Freud wrote of his old-age complex with its erotic basis (*FJL*, 27 Apr. 1911, p. 419). Later on he noted: 'It is the old mythological motif: the old god wants to be sacrificed and rise again rejuvenated in the new one. I hope that you will fare better than I have and not just copy me' (*FJL*, 27 July 1911, p. 436).

Betrayal, rivalry, and secession were more forcefully emerging in the primal horde during the year 1911. In February, Adler and Stekel resigned their respective posts of president and vice-president of the Vienna Society; the last surviving record of Adler's attendance at a meeting is dated 24 May.[47] The same year also saw the publication of

Part One of Jung's *Psychology of the Unconscious*, a mythological study worlds apart from Freud's approach in *Totem and Taboo*.

During 1912, the second half of the *Psychology of the Unconscious* as well as the first two books of *Totem and Taboo* appeared in print, and tension between Freud and Jung had its ups and downs. In March, Jung's temper flared up and ended in a renunciation of any pupil status, a renunciation Freud welcomed. He again declared Jung his heir (*FJL*, pp. 491–493). In a series of missives from April to August, Jung clarified his opposition to the Oedipus complex and the libido theory. Sensing danger, a secret committee, 'a happy band of brothers,' formed around Freud to protect psychoanalytic doctrine from such heresies as those of Adler, Stekel, and Jung (Jones, 1955, p. 164). The discontented Jung took off on a two-month transatlantic trip, which Freud reviled as a sore neglect of presidential duties (*FJL*, 14 Nov. 1912, p. 517).

Then, in November, the same month that Stekel turned in his membership, a conference at Munich was organized. Along with a reconciliation, there was another of Freud's fainting episodes. Before Freud fainted, the discussions included Freud's accusation that the Swiss were not mentioning his name in their psychoanalytic publications and also the dispute over interpreting the actions of the Egyptian king, Amenhotep IV. Freud held that a negative father complex lurked behind the king's removal of his father's name from monuments. For Jung, the meaning was different: other kings too had removed their fathers' names since they believed they were incarnations of the same god; accordingly, the real motive for Amenhotep's action was to inaugurate monotheism and wage a campaign against the god Amon, whose name he had annihilated everywhere. Then Freud fainted, and on coming to, his first words were, 'How sweet it is to die' (Jones, 1953, p. 317).[48] Afterward Freud related this to his reaction as a young child to surviving the death of a baby brother, to the residue of an 'unruly homosexual feeling' from his relationship to Fliess, and to repressed feelings directed against Jung as Fliess's successor (the latter motives not at all incompatible with Jung's feeling that his own vehement objections caused Freud's fainting).[49] At any event, by the next month their relations had broken down forever, leaving cooperation on the most restricted scientific level.

The year 1913 was a strain for both Freud and Jung. Anna Freud remembers that the only time she saw her father depressed was during the month of July in Marienbad where he went for a rest.[50] And it was sometime during the second half of 1913 that Jung's long period of inner uncertainty and state of disorientation began, a good indication that the rebellious Jung was more conflictually implicated than Freud in their relationship (see Jung, 1961, pp. 170–199).

At the Munich Congress in September, despite sizeable opposition, Jung was re-elected president of the International Psycho-Analytical Association. During the Congress he gave a lecture which was the basis of his future *Psychological Types* (1921), a work that Jung often declared was written to understand dissension in Freud's circle.[51] Immediately after the Congress, the last time he saw Jung, Freud visited Italy with Minna, a sequence recalling his last encounter with Fliess in the summer of 1900, after which Freud went on a trip with his wife and Minna and subsequently traveled with Minna alone. Toward the end of 1913, Freud dreamed about a gladiator dressed in a Swiss costume and holding a sword in his hand, but because of his own resistance did not see in it the obvious reference to Jung, his anti-Semitism, and his impending defection.[52] In April 1914, Jung resigned as president. There now remained the arch-president with his secret committee of arch-brothers (the others outside the covenant were just brothers). Yet both inside and outside the covenant, remorseless Fate was silently setting the stage once more for the interflowing myths of Abraham, Oedipus, and Cain.

Acting out and writing in:
the legend of inscriptive enactment

Freud's *Totem and Taboo* (1913a) and Jung's *Psychology of the Unconscious* (1916), both composed in the final years of their amity, are not just scientific expository treatises. They are self-reflexive, auto–symbolic; they not merely say but do, not merely represent but present. Overtly scientific, covertly autobiographical, they are half-disguised rhetorical dramas in their particular brand of psychoanalysis. This autobiographical trace assumes manifold appearances in psycho-therapeutic literature. Succeeding Kraepelin as the world's foremost psychiatrist, Bleuler introduced the concept of ambivalence, and this was due, as Freud pointedly observed, to Bleuler's own personal ambivalence (Jones, 1955, p. 72). But if personal traits can be the source of discovery, they perhaps have even a greater potential for distorting objectivity. Freud said as much in his *The Psychopathology of Everyday Life* (1901) when he posited the customary occurrence of parapraxes in science. Indeed, to imagine a lasting absence of parapraxes throughout science is to indulge in utopianism: 'Only for the rarest and best adjusted mind does it seem possible to preserve the picture of external reality, as it is perceived, against the distortion to which it is normally subjected in its passage through the psychical individuality of the percipient' (Freud, 1901, p. 229). At the end of his essay on Leonardo da Vinci (1910, p. 134) did not Freud admit to the possibility that his own treatise might be just a psychoanalytic novel? Did he not say (1911b, p. 79) that his own analysis of Schreber's psychotic delusions might itself be a delusion?

But I want to call attention to an even more spectacular example, an essay entitled 'Formulations on the Two Principles of Mental Functioning' (1911a) written, incidentally, at the same time as the Schreber case. There are two principles governing mental functioning: the pleasure principle, according to which the instincts strive for immediate discharge, and the reality principle, according to which immediate instinctual satisfaction is postponed for a later and greater satisfaction. Imposing restraint on immediate discharge, the reality principle is indispensable for thinking. Now, what kind of thinking went on in Freud's essay one may ask? And one may ask further, although his writing was governed by thought and therefore the reality principle, to what extent was it influenced by the pleasure principle and therefore immediate discharge? The answer comes from an extraordinary gloss I discovered in one of Freud's letters, which sheds light on the reluctant birth of that essay: 'My mood and atmosphere have prevented me from doing any work here. And I am not capable of enjoying the rest. A number of things, e.g., the paper on the two principles of ψ functioning, are already tormenting me like a blocked bowel movement. (There is a good reason for the metaphor too.)' (*FJL*, 10 Oct. 1910, pp. 323–324)

To know the final outcome of Freud's bodily and creative stoppage, let us listen to the conclusion of the essay, which metacritically describes its own publication as an act of forceful compromise between retention and discharge, between the reality and pleasure principles:

> The deficiencies of this short paper, which is preparatory rather than expository, will perhaps be excused only in small part if I plead that they are unavoidable. In these few remarks on the psychical consequences of adaptation to the reality principle I have been obliged to adumbrate views which I should have preferred for the present to withhold and whose justification will certainly require no small effort. But I hope it will not escape the notice of the benevolent reader how in these pages too the dominance of the reality principle is beginning [1911a, p. 226].

And so the essay had, as it were, a breech birth; its thought untimely born and its pleasure experienced in the breach.

Similarly, Jung's *Psychology of the Unconscious* was an agonistic composition replete with history and self-testimony. In this work, relying on mythology and the history of religion, Jung interpreted for several hundred pages a few daydreams and fantasies of a Miss Frank Miller, a young lady whom he had never seen. Whereas Freud used libido to designate only the sexual instinct, Jung now applied libido to psychic energy in general, a psychic energy manifesting itself in the form of universal symbols, the forerunners of Jung's archetypes. Significantly too, of all the myths treated, Jung stressed the myth of the hero, especially in his struggle for freedom and his contest with a gigantic beast. As Ellenberger (1970) aptly remarks, the original text 'terminated with a somewhat ambiguous remark that could apply to Freud's adversaries as well as to Freud himself: "I do not consider it the business of science to compete for the work, but rather to work toward the augmentation and deepening of knowledge"' (pp. 696–697).[53]

But let us turn back and follow, like a neurosis, the dramatic unfolding of what Plutarch might well have called parallel texts— Freud's and Jung's anthropological works. Soon after their return from the States in 1909, Jung avowed his obsession with eventually doing a comprehensive psychoanalytic study and asked Freud for 'a beam of light in that direction' (*FJL*, 14 Oct. 1909, pp. 251–252). Without casting that beam, Freud simply responded, 'I am glad you share my belief that we must conquer the whole field of mythology. Thus far we have only two pioneers: Abraham and Rank' (17 Oct. 1909, p. 255).

Thereupon Jung plunged into a study of archaeology and pursued the phylogenetic roots of neurosis with an enthusiasm that halted his correspondence (8 Nov. 1909, p. 258). Freud, surprisingly still caught up in periodicity theory, indirectly linked Fliess (with his 23-day periods) to Jung: 'It probably isn't nice of you to keep me waiting 25 days for an answer' (11 Nov. 1909, p. 259). There are more letters, and Freud exulted, 'I am delighted with your mythological studies. . . . These things cry out for understanding, and as long as the specialists won't help us, we shall have to do it ourselves' (21 Nov. 1909, p. 265). The wording here is extremely important, for a month later Freud repeated, with a nuance that disturbed Jung: 'I long for mythologists, linguists, and historians of religions; if they won't come to our help, we shall have to do all that ourselves' (19 Dec. 1909, p. 276). Jung took immediate umbrage: 'But most of all I was struck by your remark that you longed for archaeologists, philologists, etc. By this, I told myself, you probably meant that I was unfit for such work' (25 Dec. 1909, p. 279). In his answer opening the new year, Freud retracted and went completely over to Jung's side: 'Your displeasure at my longing for an army of philosophical collaborators is music to my ears. I am delighted that you yourself take this interest so seriously' (2 Jan. 1910, p. 282). And yet six months later Freud reverted to: 'I am becoming more and more convinced of the cultural value of ψ A, and I long for the lucid mind that will draw from it the justified inferences for philosophy and sociology' (5 July 1910, p. 340).

In this connection, Jung's memory of a conversation with Freud bears the greatest significance:

> I can still recall vividly how Freud said to me, 'My dear Jung, promise me never to abandon the sexual theory. That is the most essential thing of all. You see, we must make a dogma of it, an unshakable bulwark. . . .' In some astonishment I asked him, 'A bulwark—against what?' To which he replied, 'Against the black tide of mud'—and here he hesitated for a moment, then added—'of occultism.' First of all, it was the words 'bulwark' and 'dogma' that alarmed me. . . . But that no longer has anything to do with scientific judgment; only with a personal power drive.
>
> This was the thing that struck at the heart of our friendship. I knew that I would never be able to accept such an attitude. . . .
>
> My conversation with Freud had shown me that he feared the numinous light of his sexual insights might be extinguished by a 'black tide of mud.' . . . In my next book, *Wandlungen und Symbole der Libido*, which dealt with the hero's struggle for freedom, Freud's curious reaction prompted me to investigate further this archetypal theme and its mythological background. . . .
>
> After that second conversation in Vienna I also understood Alfred Adler's power hypothesis, to which I had hitherto paid scant attention. Like many sons, Adler had learned from his 'father' not what the father said, but what he did. Instantly, the problem of love (Eros) and power came down upon me like a leaden weight. Freud himself had told me that he never read Nietzsche; now I saw Freud's psychology as, so to speak, an adroit move on the part of intellectual history, compensating for Nietzsche's deification of the power principle. The problem had obviously to be rephrased not as 'Freud versus Adler' but 'Freud versus Nietzsche.' It was therefore, I thought, more than a domestic quarrel in the domain of psychopathology. The idea dawned on me that Eros and the power drive might be in a sense like the dissident sons of a single father, or the products of a single motivating force which manifested itself empirically in opposing forms [Jung, 1961, pp. 150–154].[54]

All together, these invaluable citations dramatically indicate the areas of dispute and delineate the shape of Jung's work to come: fascination with the occult, the depiction of the hero's struggle for freedom, and the stress on a single source of psychic energy symbolically conceived as a father of two dissident sons, Eros and power. In one stroke the son Jung dissented from his father Freud and elaborated an energy theory with the terminology of filial rebellion. This priceless mimetic play between the theoretician and theory summons up for us Yeats's well-phrased query, 'How can we know the dancer from the dance?'

Toward the end of 1910, the mythological sing-song tale continued. Jung lectured to the Zurich Society of Psychoanalysis on his forthcoming book about which he feared Freud's criticism.[55] Freud hastened to give encouragement: 'I don't know why you are afraid of my criticism in matters of mythology. I shall be very happy when you plant the flag of libido and repression in that field and return as a victorious conqueror to our medical motherland' (*FJL*, 22 Jan. 1911, p. 388).

But after that the tide turned. We hear no more of well-wishing, for it was Freud himself who was carrying the victorious banner in a secret night-march. On 12 February 1911, Freud declared that for some weeks he had been conceiving a larger synthesis but, significantly, omitted to say that it was *Totem and Taboo* (*FJL*, p. 391).[56] And then in the late summer came another quasi-cryptic note:

> Since my mental powers revived, I have been working in a field where you will be surprised to meet me. I have unearthed strange and uncanny things and will almost feel obliged *not* to discuss them with you. But you are too shrewd not to guess what I am up to when I add that I am dying to read your 'Transformations' [*Psychology of the Unconscious*] [*FJL*, 20 Aug. 1911, p. 438].[57]

Jung's response was anything but unmitigated joy:

> your letter has got me on tenterhooks because, for all my 'shrewdness,' I can't quite make out what is going on so enigmatically behind the scenes. Together with my wife I have tried to unriddle your words, and we have reached surmises which, for the time being at any rate, I would rather keep to myself [*FJL*, 29 Aug. 1911, p. 439].

Meanwhile the first half of Jung's *Psychology* had just appeared. Feeling that Jung agreed that the Oedipus complex is the root of religion, Freud avowed working on the same subject (*FJL*, 1 Sept. 1911, p. 441). But that feeling was not at all a restful one, for when

179

Freud used the pretext of the Weimar Congress in September to visit the Jungs, he did not at all mention Jung's opus (*FJL*, 30 Oct. 1911, p. 452).

In writing the second half of *Psychology of the Unconscious*, Jung was beset with some ambivalence. His wife, to whom he often said that Freud would not approve of Part Two, believed that some of her husband's parental complex was being solved, worked through, in its very writing (*FJL*, 6 Nov. 1911, p. 456). The last chapter, 'The Sacrifice,' was fundamentally dissident: unconscious sexuality is merely symbolic, and the true object of psychoanalysis in mythological terms is the 'sacrifice and rebirth of the infantile hero.' As Jung said, 'When I was working on my book about the libido and approaching the end of the chapter "The Sacrifice," I knew in advance that its publication would cost me my friendship with Freud. . . . I realized that the chapter "The Sacrifice" meant my own sacrifice' (1961, pp. 167–168).[58]

On 12 November 1912, Freud shared a troubling association: 'Some daemon has thus far prevented me from asking you whether you know Storfer of Zurich, whose essay on the special importance of parricide I published in the last number' (*FJL*, pp. 458–459). The link between Storfer, parricide, and Jung by the end of the letter, where Freud lauds Jung for his *Psychology of the Unconscious* and gets enmeshed in the old Fliessian quarrel of priority, is itself figurative of a father–son relationship:

> it is a torment for me to think, when I conceive an idea now and then, that I may be taking something away from you or appropriating something that might just as well have been acquired by you. When this happens, I feel at a loss. . . . Why in God's name did I allow myself to follow you in this field? [p. 459].

The conflict is fully ablaze, with the threatened son responding two days later: 'You are a dangerous rival—if one has to speak of rivalry. . . . You dig up the precious stones but I have the "degree of extension." . . . Naturally you will be ahead of me in certain respects but this won't matter much since you have anticipated by far the greatest part already' (*FJL*, p. 460). Jung's overextension of the libidinal concept and his loose use of mythological material drew fire from the father as they stepped ever closer to their point of no return. All in all, the year was a return of the repressed: the old conflicts rapidly emerged, with Freud, Jung, and their two works together forming a complex of actors and actions set in a murderous scene. While Freud was brooding over his *Totem and Taboo*, a narrative about youthful murderers, Jung was self-engrossed in a hero's sacrificial struggle. By early 1912, Jung's *Psychology of the Unconscious* was virtually finished which, sight unseen, was surmised by Freud to be a Declaration of Independence.[59]

And what did *Totem and Taboo* as writing mean for Freud? On a fundamental level, it is like his other writings, an extension of his body, a notion ever-abiding in Freud's awareness. As he wrote to Binswanger on 2 May 1909: 'I am panting a great deal under the burden of work, I am no longer too satisfied with my *corpus*, and am at present quite unproductive. I am already living on my past' (Binswanger, 1956, p. 11). The association is also in a letter of 29 May 1909 to Jung: 'I am counting the days till the holidays, when I shall be able to work in peace and also get my corpus back into shape' (*FJL*, p. 154). But *Totem and Taboo* also stands for the body of a woman, and here I raise a question I have deliberately overlooked in my exposition up to now: I have talked about the primal sons and the primal father, but not a word have I said about the woman whom that first patriarch jealously kept. Who is this carefully guarded woman? In a letter of 2 February 1910, Freud himself referred to Lady Psychoanalysis: 'For the [Nuremberg] Congress I now have the following: You on the development of ψ A (but mainly America, the rest is familiar to most of our people), me on the prospects for psychoanalysis, a happy combination since you represent the lady's future and I her past' (*FJL*, p. 292). As for *Totem and Taboo* in particular, it demanded so much of Freud's time that, starting out as a casual liaison, it took on all the demanding importance of a new wife. And then again, Freud claimed that the fourth and most cherished book of *Totem and Taboo* was none other than a veritable 'Princess.'[60] Collectively, therefore, *Totem and Taboo* was an extension of Freud's body, a parameter of identification on the one hand and, by projection, a female that constituted his object choice.

But what were the life and death wishes of *Totem and Taboo* as writing? In the first instance, Freud indicated that working on the last part of *Totem and Taboo* was evidence that his death, eagerly awaited by his Viennese opponents, was not yet realized. Besides being a vital sign, the opus was a lethal instrument hastening the final break with Zurich and purging psychoanalysis of 'all Aryan religiousness.'[61] With the papal wishes of Adler and Jung defeated, the psycho-analytic organization would again be unipolar and rid of its own Avignon heresy of a triple pontificate.[62] But, with the completion of *Totem and Taboo*, Freud's elation changed to doubt—a shift that Ferenczi and Jones interpreted as arising from Freud's living in his imagination the very experiences he described (the elation over killing and eating the father which was ensued by doubts). After all, it is a big step from wishing to kill the father in the *Interpretation of Dreams* to actually killing him in *Totem and Taboo* (Jones, 1955, p. 354).

Significantly, neither Ferenczi nor Jones referred to the father killing the son, the Abraham myth. It was in the light of this myth that Wittels saw *Totem and Taboo* as 'wreaking a scientific vengeance upon Jung, following the latter into the domain of folk-psychology, and there annihilating Jung on his own vantage ground' (1923, p. 191). While Stekel (1950, p. 143) also thought Jung might have been jealously offended for being surpassed on his own ground, the 'happy brothers' of the secret committee celebrated *Totem and Taboo* by treating Freud to a dinner which they called a totemic festival (Jones, 1955, p. 355).

But despite the committee's displacement, Freud's opus itself is an enactment of annihilation. There is first the annihilating which Freud Oedipally relived in killing his father, and the annihilating of the son Jung in accordance with the Abraham myth. And then there is the being annihilated in the totemic feast. In it not only did the sacrificing community of old, the god and the animal victim, have the same blood, but the god himself was represented twice over, as himself and as the totemic animal (1913a, pp. 136, 149). If we turn our attention to the writer Freud, we quickly summon up the reflection that he is constantly involved with the reader, who is given as a matter of course a substantial repast to digest. Surely we are justified in seeing elements of commensality and totemism in Freud's authorship, for he, his verbal offering, and the target audience are common members re-membered in each writing and, on the whole, throughout the corpus.

Notes

* First published in *Psychoanalysis and Contemporary Thought* (1979), 2: 551–593.

1 For brevity, the correspondence of Freud and Abraham (1907–1926) and Freud and Pfister (1909–1939) will be cited simply by a reference to the two correspondents (e.g., Freud and Abraham). *The Freud/Jung Letters* (Freud and Jung, 1906–1914) will be abbreviated by *FJL*. *The Minutes of the Vienna Psychoanalytic Society* (Nunberg and Federn, 1906–1915) will be cited as *Minutes*.

2 The story is told as if it happened only once, but it is a condensation of what was repeated countless times (see 1913a, pp. 142–143 n. and the more explicit statement in 1939, p. 81).

3 In *Moses and Monotheism* (1939, p. 81), Freud adds in his resumé that, if not driven out, the sons were either castrated or killed by the jealous father and that eventually the survivors took 'advantage of their father's increasing age.' That this jump in the assertion of detail is weighty indeed may be shown from Freud's letter to Ferenczi of 1 February 1912 (Jones, 1955, p. 453): 'We should greatly like to know whether the jealous Old Man of the Horde in Darwin's primordial family really used to castrate the young males before the time when he was content with simply chasing them away.' From the dynamic point of view, the omission of these details in *Totem and Taboo* is of course quite relevant. An in-depth study has yet to be made of the variants in Freud's slightly different resumés of the same conflict-laden material in his scientific works.

4 In his translation Strachey omits these last nine words of the citation: 'Ohne die Annahme einer Massenpsyche, einer Kontinuität im Gefühls-leben des Menschen . . .' (1913b, p. 90). For some ideas of *Totem and Taboo* anticipated in the *Minutes of the Vienna Psychoanalytic Society* but not indexed there, see: 13 February 1907 (v. 1, p. 113); 27 November 1907 (v. 1, p. 251); 25 November 1908 (v. 2, p. 70); 9 February 1909 (v. 2, p. 146); and 10 December 1910 (v. 3, p. 14).

5 For more on the primal horde theory's contemporaneous relevance to Freud's own circle, see Wittels (1923, pp. 192–193); Jung, in Bennet (1961, p. 44); Kanzer (1971, pp. 42–45); Schur (1972, p. 282); and R. Ostow (1977, pp. 169–172). Ellenberger (1970, pp. 527, 800) suggests modern Turkish history as a possible inspiration for *Totem and Taboo*: in 1908 a band of young Turks overthrew Abdul Hamid II, a cruel despot given to massacre, who wantonly retained for himself a harem with hundreds of wives guarded by eunuchs. I would also suggest that *Totem and Taboo* may well have been influenced phantasmally by a famous criminal affair that occurred in Vienna in 1910. A young army officer named Hofrichter 'poisoned four of his immediate superiors (by means of an aphrodisiac which they had had him procure for themselves), in order to accelerate his promotion' (*Minutes*, v. 3, p. 41 n). Excellent studies, general and anthropological, of *Totem and Taboo* are those by Freeman (1967), Neu (1974), and especially Nichols (1975).

6 See *FJL* (27 May 1911, p. 426; 6 Nov. 1911, p. 456).

7 See Freud and Pfister (4 Apr. 1911, p. 49) and *FJL* (2 Nov. 1911, p. 453). On this question, the history of psychoanalysis has yet to be written. Whether limited to Freud or going beyond him, the history would disclose hidden depths of economic factors and the aggressive drive affecting the relations between analysts and the development of the psychoanalytic movement.

8 See Jones (1959, pp. 197–198). In a possible reading of Freud's letter of

22 December 1912, addressed but not sent to Jung, Kanzer (1971, p. 32) concluded that Freud analyzed Adler. But Freud's letter of 3 January 1913 (*FJL*, p. 538) explicitly denies this.

9 On the other hand, Freud felt enough at ease with Wittels to accord him a unique experience in psychoanalytic annals, namely, to be present at an analysis conducted by Freud himself. As Wittels (1923, p. 138) wrote, during the time of Freud's alliance with Jung, 'it was my privilege during the greater part of a year to watch Freud at work, for I was present when he was analyzing a case of dementia praccox. It was because the patient was a dement, because her perceptions were so greatly dulled, that Freud could allow me to be there.'

10 On Ferenczi's visit, see Jones (1955, p. 55). On Rank see Anaïs Nin (1931–1934, p. 299), cited by Roustang (1976, p. 22).

11 See Freud's letter to Groddeck of 5 June 1917, cited by Roustang (1976, p. 18).

12 On Rank and Tausk, see Andreas-Salomé (1912–1913, pp. 332–333).

13 From the fact that in a letter of 20 October 1911 Freud told the Jungs that women always spoiled his friendships with men (*FJL*, p. 452)—a disclosure that sank into Emma Jung's memory—we can safely conclude that this includes Ida Fliess, whom Freud disliked (Jones, 1953, p. 287; Schur, 1972, p. 210).

14 See *FJL* (31 Jan. 1908, p. 116; 1 Sept. 1911, p. 442) and Freud (1914, p. 42).

15 See Freud and Abraham (3 May 1908, p. 34; 26 Dec. 1908, p. 64).

16 See *FJL* (9 Mar. 1909, p. 211; 18 Jan. 1911, pp. 384–385).

17 See *FJL* (27 May 1911, p. 426; 6 Nov. 1911, p. 456; 31 Dec. 1911, p. 476). The term Oedipus complex was first used in 1910, thereby standing alongside the older epithets father complex and nuclear complex (see Freud, 1900, p. 263 n).

18 See *FJL* (28 Oct. 1907, p. 95; 15 Nov. 1907, p. 98; 20 Feb. 1908, p. 122; 17 June 1910, p. 329).

19 See *FJL* (4 June 1909, p. 229; 14 Dec. 1909, p. 275; 25 Dec. 1909, p. 279). It is worthwhile noting that the Latin *famulus* (slave) is a cognate of *familia* (family). On the other hand, the old Germanic tribes distinguished between slaves and family members in a contemporaneously relevant way, for the latter were called *freondes*, those who are *free*, or literally in old English, those who are loved!

20 See *FJL* (2 June 1910, p. 325; 17 June 1910, p. 328).

21 See *FJL* (15 Oct. 1908, p. 172; 17 Jan. 1909, p. 196; 16 Apr. 1909, p. 218; 6 Mar. 1910, p. 300).

22 See *FJL* (7 July 1909, p. 240; 19 Dec. 1909, p. 277; 2 Feb. 1910, p. 292). On 8 May 1911, the 55-year-old Freud signed his letter to Binswanger, 'Your old Freud' (Binswanger, 1956, p. 32).

23 See *FJL* (29 Feb. 1912, pp. 488–489; 14 Nov. 1912, p. 518).

24 See *FJL* (10 Aug. 1910, p. 343), Jones (1955, p. 140), and Binswanger (1956, p. 31).

25 This sort of desperate 'posthumous' hope also obtained in the relationship with Fliess. After they no longer saw each other and a year after their friendly contact had ended, Freud suggested to Fliess the possibility of their doing a book together (Freud, 1887–1902, p. 335).

26 See *FJL* (3 Dec. 1908, p. 184; 11 Dec. 1908, p. 186).

27 In spite of this, unfortunately far too little is known of Federn. His son's biographical appreciation (1972) adds much information, but the mystery around Federn still persists; although he was Freud's substitute as acting president and his personal representative in scientific matters in Vienna, he was not a member of the famous Committee of Seven and perhaps was even unaware of its existence (pp. 19, 21). The secret was so well-kept that it was not divulged till five years after Freud's death by Hanns Sachs (1944).

28 See Freud (1914, p. 25). A complete work on the issue of priority in the beginning of psychoanalysis would make fascinating reading. With his 'Der Aggressionstrieb im Leben und in der Neurosen' (1908) in mind, Adler claimed the aggressive drive at his contribution to psychoanalysis (cf. Ansbacher, 1962; Bottome, 1939, p. 64). But Breuer had spoken of the aggressive and sexual drives in 1893 (pp. 200–201). Wittels (1923) 'in all humility' says his psychoanalytic explanation of the primitive horde predates Freud's by one year (p. 193 n). By virtue of his *Nervous Anxiety* (1912), Stekel claims the death instinct as his discovery (1950, p. 138); the editor of Andreas-Salomé's (1912–1913) journal sees in Ferenczi's (1913) notion of *Todestendenz* an anticipation of Freud's death instinct (p. 481); at any rate, Freud had a notion of the life instinct as early as 1910 (see Laplanche, 1975).

29 For the ideas in this paragraph, I am indebted to Selesnick (1963).

30 Both Jones and Jung have erroneously dated this first visit as taking place in February (see the corrective data in *FJL*, p. 24); in one place Jung even puts the first meeting in 1906 (Billinsky, 1969, p. 42).

31 See Freud and Abraham (3 May 1908, p. 34; 16 July 1908, p. 44; 23 July 1908, p. 46; 31 July 1908, p. 48) and *FJL* (13 Jan. 1910, p. 288; 19 June 1910, p. 330; 13 June 1912, p. 510).

32 See *FJL* (17 Oct. 1909, p. 254; 2 Jan. 1910, p. 282).

33 See Jung (1961, p. 156) and Bennet (1961, p. 44). Despite Freud's fainting, Jones (1955, p. 146) interprets the whole incident as Freud's victory over Jung; according to Jones, Jung was a teetotaler in the fanatic anti-alcoholic tradition followed by other Swiss, including Bleuler, and Freud's triumphant reaction to persuading Jung to drink was symptomatic of those wrecked by success. Countering Jones's interpre-

tation, Jung specified that he stopped taking alocholic beverages on joining the Burghölzli staff where thorough abstinence was the rule, and that he resumed taking alcohol with meals after resigning from the Burghölzi staff, i.e. six months prior to his transatlantic trip (Bennet, 1961, p. 37). Two points militate strongly against Jung's account: at the time Jung certainly gave the impression of being an abstinent, for both Ferenczi and Freud interpreted the fainting as a 'reaction to Jung's apostasy from anti-alcoholism' (Ferenczi's letter of 8 Dec. 1912, cited in Schur, 1972, p. 267). Second, Jung's letter of 30 April 1910 gives the impression that his apostasy was near the time of its writing (*FJL*, p. 313).

34 See *FJL* (9 Mar. 1909, p. 210). Jones (1955, p. 55) mistakenly gives the date of their New York arrival as 27 September instead of 29 August; he also errs in giving 1910 for 1911 as the year he himself read a paper at the International Congress of Medical Psychology (cf. pp. 74, 79).

35 There are slightly different accounts of this dream and its context in Bennet (1961, pp. 86–87) and Jung (1961, pp. 158–161).

36 In the light of this, Schur errs in contending that on this trip Jung probably could not tolerate Freud's narrating his dreams (1972, p. 254).

37 See *FJL* (3 Dec. 1912, p. 526; 18 Dec. 1912, p. 535). Cf. Billinsky (1969, pp. 42–43), Jung (1961, p. 158), and Bennet (1961, p. 40), the three accounts differing in minor details.

38 See Jung's letter of 23 July 1949 to Virginia Payne (Jung, 1906–1961, v. 1, p. 530).

39 It is worth citing one little-known anecdote about Jung's and Freud's success in the States. Stanley Hall and two colleagues at Clark had many interviews with a young girl claiming spiritualistic powers before discovering the underlying sexual motive, which took but one interview for Freud and Jung to see. As Hall wrote later: 'In a short interview with her they at once diagnosed the true nature of it all, and to my surprise she frankly confessed that her chief motive from the first had been to win the love of her adored one . . . The erotic motivation was obvious and the German savants saw little further to interest them in the case, and I was a trifle mortified that now the purpose so long hidden from us was so conscious and openly confessed' (cited in Ross, 1972, p. 393).

40 The letter is cited in Alexander and Selesnick (1965, p. 4).

41 Stekel's short account (1950, pp. 127–128) concurs with that of Wittels.

42 According to Stekel (1950, p. 129), Freud declared, ' "They begrudge me the coat I am wearing; I don't know whether in the future I will earn my daily bread." Tears were streaming down his cheeks. "An official psychiatrist and a Gentile must be the leader of the movement." ' Behind such a statement lies Freud's acute awareness of the conflict-laden history of science itself.

43 See Freud's letters of 28 September and 16 October 1910 to Bleuler (Alexander and Selesnick, 1965, pp. 2, 4).

44 At some points it is rather humorous to read the minutes of the Vienna Society right after the Congress. Objecting to the transfer of the psycho-analytic center to Zurich, Tausk and Wittels had recourse to a pathological oneupmanship to demonstrate that Vienna was more appropriate as a center. After Tausk described Vienna as a fittingly 'sick soil,' Wittels added that in Vienna 'each one of us has a neurosis, which is necessary for entry into Freud's teachings; whether the Swiss have, is questionable' (*Minutes*, 6 Apr. 1910, v. 2, p. 468).

45 See Lehmann's fine analysis (1978, esp. p. 187). In addition, I would only call attention to Stekel's reference to the same dream and his seeing an allusion to onanism in Savo*na*rola, an interpretation to which Freud did not demur (*Minutes*, 1 Mar. 1911, v. 3, pp. 184, 187).

46 Freud (1901, pp. 30–31; 1919, pp. 271–272) and *FJL* (27 Apr. 1911, p. 419; 21 July 1911, p. 436). I dare say that the place Enna which Freud initially referred to was unconsciously prompted as well by the name of Jung's wife, Emma. To critically map out Freud's associations would be a fascinating enterprise, starting with the idea that Enna is the *old* site of the present Castelvetrano, which brings in the association '*old* castle.'

47 My wording here is quite significant, for Jones baldly states that Adler last attended a meeting on 24 May (1955, p. 133); but Wolf comments on vol. 3 of the *Minutes*: 'The minutes of the meeting of 31 May, 1911, the last of the 1910–1911 season, are missing. One cannot help but be intrigued by this singular omission, inasmuch as only two weeks later Freud wrote Jung that he finally got rid of Adler (who had normally participted and had shown no signs of wishing to resign as late as the meeting on the 24th of May)' (1976, p. 684). And in his review of vol. 4 of the *Minutes*, Lichtenberg (1976, p. 694) indicates that the minutes are missing for the year's last meeting in May 1912, when, according to Jones, there was a bitter debate between Tausk and Stekel, with the latter then resigning. Here we must lament the absence of vital information in the published versions of primary psychoanalytic sources. Freud is certainly great enough to stand on his own, with all his human achievements and failings. He has no need of those who assign themselves superego and ego-ideal roles in purging Freudiana of any defect to be possibly found in his own character.

48 There is a remarkable passage in *On Aphasia* (1891, p. 62) which is totally neglected in biographical studies on Freud. Apart from indicating that Freud's inner thought was accompanied by slight lip movements, the passage shows how two nearly fatal experiences gave rise to a dual endopsychic perception of death, audial and visual. Indeed, visual and

audial perceptions of the same material characterize some of Freud's
dreams.

49 The various depictions of this episode do not tally concerning the order
and detail of events: see Bennet (1961, pp. 45–46); Binswanger (1956,
pp. 48–49); Jones (1953, pp. 316–317; 1955, pp. 145–147); Jung (1961,
pp. 156–157); Schur (1972, pp. 264–272); see also Jung's letter of 21
November 1953 to E. Bennet (Jung, 1906–1961, v. 2, p. 133). For
Freud's and Abraham's exchange on Amenhotep, see H. Abraham
(1974, pp. 43–46).

50 See Jones (1955, p. 99). But compare Freud's letter to Ferenczi which he
wrote one month after his grandson's death and in which he said that he
was depressed for the first time in his life (Jones, 1957, p. 92).

51 See Hannah (1976, p. 133). On the other hand, *Totem and Taboo* was the
influential source for Paul Federn's essay 'On the Psychology of
Revolution: The Fatherless Society' (1919), which connected the
Austrian Revolution of 1918 to universal Oedipal and parricidal wishes.
Freud in turn avowed that Federn's essay influenced him to write *Group
Psychology and the Analysis of the Ego* (1921) (see E. Federn, 1972).

52 For this dream and context, see Grinker (1975, p. 220). Concerning the
controversy over Jung's anti-Semitism, M. Ostow's revelation on his
vile conduct is conclusive (1977, p. 377).

53 *Psychology of the Unconscious* (1916) originally appeared as *Wandlungen
und Symbole der Libido*, published in two installments in the *Jahrbuch* in
1911 and 1912.

54 The dating of the conversation is problematic. Jones (1955, p. 140) and
Jung (1961, p. 150) would allow for the possibility of its taking place in
1910, but see the editorial notes in *FJL* (p. 216, n. 4; p. 309, n. 1).

55 See *FJL* (23 Dec. 1910, p. 383; 18 Jan. 1911, p. 385).

56 Hence Jones (1955, p. 350) errs in thinking that from the time Freud
announced to Ferenczi at the very end of 1909 a link between religion
and history nothing more was heard of the matter until August 1911.

57 This belies Jones's statement that Freud read this manuscript a year
before the Weimar Congress in September 1911 (1955, p. 351).

58 Jung never felt happy about this book, whose ideas came to him in
landslide fashion and which, in reaction to 'the constricting atmosphere
of Freudian psychology,' admittedly was written out rapidly without
regard to method and maturing reflection (Jung, 1950, p. xxiii).

59 See *FJL* (10 Mar. 1912, p. 494; 21 Apr. 1912, p. 500).

60 See Freud's letters to Ferenczi of 30 November 1911 and 12 June 1913
(cited in Jones, 1955, pp. 352, 354).

61 See Freud and Abraham (13 May 1913, p. 139; 1 June 1913, p. 141).

62 Cf. Freud's conversation in April 1913 with Binswanger: Adler and Jung
too 'wanted to be Popes' (Binswanger, 1956, p. 9). A full account of

religion either used as an analogy or personally reacted to by early analysts would prove a fascinating story. Falk (1977) has given a well-researched study of Freud's ambivalence towards Judaism. Jones, who was, apart from the small Swiss group, one of the very few Gentiles in the early history of analysis, uttered the most incredible statement for one so well-traveled and experienced as he: 'It has never been my fortune to know a Jew possessing any religious belief, let alone an orthodox one' (1959, p. 210).

References

Abraham, H. (1974) Karl Abraham: an unfinished biography. *International Review of Psycho-Analysis*, 1: 17–72.

Adler, A. (1908) Der Aggressionstrieb im Leben und in der Neurosen. *Fortschritte der Medizin*, 26: 577–584.

Alexander, F. and Selesnick, S. (1965) Freud–Bleuler correspondence. *Archives of General Psychiatry*, 12: 1–9

Andreas-Salomé, L. (1912–1913) *The Freud Journal of Lou Andreas-Salomé*, trans. S. Leavy. New York: Basic Books, 1964.

Ansbacher, H. (1962) Was Adler a disciple of Freud? A reply. *Journal of Individual Psychology*, 18: 126–135.

—— (1963) A reply. *Journal of Individual Psychology*, 19: 82.

Bennet, E. (1961) *C.G. Jung*. London: Barrie & Rockliffe.

Billinsky, J. (1969) Jung and Freud (the end of a romance). *Andover Newton Quarterly*, 10: 39–43.

Binswanger, L. (1956) *Sigmund Freud: Reminiscences of a Friendship*. New York: Grune & Stratton, 1957.

Bottome, P. (1939) *Alfred Adler: A Biography*. New York: Putnam's.

Breuer, J. (1893) Studies on hysteria. Section III: Theoretical. *Standard Edition*, 2: 183–251. London: Hogarth Press, 1955.

Ellenberger, H. (1970) *The Discovery of the Unconscious*. New York: Basic Books.

Falk, A. (1977) Freud and Herzl. *Midstream*, 23: 3–24.

Federn, E. (1963) Was Adler a disciple of Freud? A Freudian view. *Journal of Individual Psychology*, 19: 80–82.

—— (1972) Thirty-five years with Freud. *Journal of the History of Behavioural Science*, 8: 7–33.

Federn, P. (1919) Zur Psychologie der Revolution: die vaterlose Gessellschaft. In: *Der Aufsteig, Neue Zeit- und Streitschriften*, Nos. 12–13. Vienna: Anzengruber.

Ferenczi, S. (1913) Stages in the development of the sense of reality. In: *Sex in Psychoanalysis*. New York: Basic Books, 1950, pp. 213–239.

Freeman, D. (1967) *Totem and Taboo*: A reappraisal. *The Psychoanalytic Study of Society*, 4: 9–33. New York: International Universities Press.

Freud, S. (1887–1902) *The Origins of Psycho-Analysis: Letters to Wilhelm Fliess, Drafts and Notes*, ed. M. Bonaparte, A. Freud, E. Kris. New York: Basic Books, 1952.

—— (1891) *On Aphasia*, trans. E. Stengel. New York: International Universities Press, 1953.

—— (1900) The interpretation of dreams. *Standard Edition*, 4, 5. London: Hogarth Press, 1953.

—— (1901) The psychopathology of everyday life. *Standard Edition*, 6. London: Hogarth Press, 1960.

—— (1909) Family Romances. *Standard Edition*, 9: 235–241. London: Hogarth Press, 1959.

—— (1910) Leonardo da Vinci and a memory of his childhood. *Standard Edition*, 11: 57–137. London: Hogarth Press, 1957.

—— (1911a) Formulations on the two principles of mental functioning. *Standard Edition*, 12: 213–226. London: Hogarth Press, 1958.

—— (1911b) Psychoanalytic notes on an autobiographical account of a case of paranoia (dementia paranoides). *Standard Edition*, 12: 1–82. London: Hogarth Press, 1958.

—— (1913a) Totem and taboo. *Standard Edition*, 13: 1–161. London: Hogarth Press, 1955.

—— (1913b) Totem und Tabu. *Gesammelte Werke*, 9: 1–94. Frankfurt: Fischer, 1973.

—— (1914) On the history of the psychoanalytic movement. *Standard Edition*, 14: 1–66. London: Hogarth Press, 1957.

—— (1919) James J. Putnam [Obituary]. *Standard Edition*, 17: 271–272. London: Hogarth Press, 1955.

—— (1921) Group psychology and the analysis of the ego. *Standard Edition*, 18: 65–143. London: Hogarth Press, 1955.

—— (1939) Moses and Monotheism. *Standard Edition*, 23: 1–137. London: Hogarth Press, 1964.

—— and Abraham, K. (1907–1926) *A Psycho-analytic Dialogue: The Letters of Sigmund Freud and Karl Abraham*, ed. H.C. Abraham and Ernst L. Freud. New York: Basic Books, 1965.

—— and Jung, C. (1906–1914) *The Freud/Jung Letters*, ed. W. McGuire. Princeton: Princeton University Press, 1974.

—— and Pfister, O. (1909–1939) *Psychoanalysis and Faith: The Letters of Sigmund Freud and Oskar Pfister*. New York: Basic Books, 1963.

Graf, M. (1942) Reminiscences of Professor Sigmund Freud. *Psychoanalytic Quarterly*, 11: 465–476.

Grinker, R. (1975) Reminiscences of Dr. Roy Grinker. *Journal of the American Academy of Psychoanalysis*, 3: 211–221.

Hannah, B. (1976) *Jung: His Life and Work.* New York: Putnam's.

Jones, E. (1953) *The Life and Work of Sigmund Freud, Vol. 1: The Formative Years and the Great Discoveries, 1856–1900.* New York: Basic Books.

—— (1955) *The Life and Work of Sigmund Freud, Vol. 2: Years of Maturity, 1901–1919.* New York: Basic Books.

—— (1957) *The Life and Work of Sigmund Freud, Vol. 3: The Last Phase, 1919–1939.* New York: Basic Books.

—— (1959) *Free Associations.* New York: Basic Books.

Jung, C.G. (1916) *Psychology of the Unconscious: A Study of the Transformations and Symbolisms of the Libido,* trans. B. Hinkle. New York: Dodd, Mead, 1927. [Rev. ed.: Symbols of Transformation. In: *Collected Works*, vol. 5. London: Routledge & Kegan Paul, 1956.]

—— (1921) Psychological types. In: *Collected Works*, vol. 6. Princeton: Princeton University Press, 1971.

—— (1950) Foreword to the fourth Swiss edition of *Psychology of the Unconscious.* In: *Collected Works*, vol. 5. London: Routledge & Kegan Paul, 1956.

—— (1961) *Memories, Dreams, and Reflections,* ed. A. Jaffé. New York: Pantheon, 1963.

—— (1906–1961) *C.G. Jung: Letters,* ed. G. Adler, 2 vols. Princeton: Princeton University Press, 1973–1974.

Kanzer, M. (1971) Freud: the first psychoanalytic group leader. In: H. Kaplan and B. Sadock (eds.), *Comprehensive Group Psychotherapy.* Baltimore: Williams & Wilkins, pp. 32–46.

Laplanche, J. (1975) Pulsion de vie—1910. *Psychanalyse à l'université*, 1: 185–186.

Lehmann, H. (1978) A dream of Freud in the year 1910. *International Journal of Psycho-Analysis*, 59: 181–187.

Lichtenberg, J. (1976) Book review of *Minutes of the Venna Psychoanalytic Society*, vol. 4. *Journal of the American Psychoanalytic Association*, 24: 689–696.

Mahony, P. (1979) Friendship and its discontents. *Contemporary Psychoanalysis*, 15: 55–109.

Neu, J. (1974) Genetic explanations in *Totem and Taboo.* In: R. Wollheim (ed.), *Freud: A Collection of Critical Essays.* Garden City, N.Y.: Anchor Books, pp. 366–393.

Nichols, C. (1975) The history of psychoanalytic anthropology: from Freud to Róheim. Unpublished doctoral dissertation, Brandeis University, Mass.

Nin, A. (1931–1934) *Journal.* Paris: Stock, 1969.

Nunberg, H. and Federn, E. (eds.), (1906–1915) *Minutes of the Vienna Psychoanalytic Society,* vols. 1-4. New York: International Universities Press, 1962–1975.

Ostow, M. (1977) Letter to the editor. *International Review of Psycho-Analysis*, 4: 377.

Ostow, R. (1977) Autobiographical sources of Freud's social theory: *Totem and Taboo, Group Psychology and the Analysis of the Ego, and Moses and Monotheism Revisited. Psychiatry Journal of the University of Ottawa*, 2: 169–180.

Rieff, P. (1951) The meaning and history of religion in Freud's thought. In: B. Mazlish (ed.), *Psycho-analysis and History*. Englewood Cliffs, N.J.: Prentice-Hall, pp. 23–44.

Ross, D. (1972) *G. Stanley Hall: The Psychologist as Prophet*. Chicago: University of Chicago Press.

Roustang, F. (1976) *Un destin si funeste*. Paris: Editions de Minuit.

Sachs, H. (1944) *Freud: Master and Friend*. Cambridge, Mass.: Harvard University Press, 1945.

Schreber, D.P. (1903) *Memoirs of My Nervous Illness*, trans. I. Macalpine and R.A. Hunter. London: Dawson, 1955.

Schur, M. (1966) Some additional 'day residues' of 'The Specimen Dream of Psychoanalysis.' In: R. Loewenstein *et al.* (eds.), *Psychoanalysis — A General Psychology*. New York: International Universities Press, pp. 45–85.

—— (1972) *Freud: Living and Dying*. New York: International Universities Press.

Selesnick, S. (1963) C.G. Jung's contributions to psychoanalysis. *American Journal of Psychiatry*, 120: 350–356.

Stekel, W. (1912) *Conditions of Nervous Anxiety and Their Treatment*. London: Paul Trench, Trubner, 1923.

—— (1950) *The Autobiography of Wilhelm Stekel*, ed. E. Gutheil. New York: Liveright.

Wittels, F. (1923) *Sigmund Freud: His Personality, His Teaching and His School*. New York: Dodd, Mead, 1924.

Wolf, E. (1976) Book review of *Minutes of the Vienna Psychoanalytic Society*, vol. 3. *Journal of the American Psychoanalytic Association*, 24: 683–689.

9

Kafka's 'A Hunger Artist' and the symbolic nuclear principle*

From the examination of Freud's prose we are easily led to approach aesthetic discourse itself—after all, it was Greek literature par excellence that served to stimulate Freud's fertile mind and even to furnish him with immemorable terms; and we, joining forces with a host of his contemporary colleagues, admire his prose not only for its scientific but also for its artistic qualities. Sheerly aesthetic discourse, however, presents its own challenges for comprehension, and in my exploration of them I shall follow a path indicated by Victor Rosen[1] and attempt to trace further the relationship between content and form in aesthetic discourse, beginning with Kafka's classic piece of German fiction. I might say immediately that I recognize the potential perilousness in using such terms as content and form— meaning, for example, possesses as well as confers structure; then again, on another level of reference, plot may be readily relegated to either content or form. Still in all, in spite of their problematic dichotomy, the terms content and form continue to retain a heuristic value for many critics, myself included.

Responding to Ernst Kris's lament that psychoanalysis had yet to address itself to a psychology of style and honestly recognize the necessarily circumscribed limits of his own efforts in a vast interdisciplinary domain, Rosen defined style as 'a progressing synthesis of form and content in an individually typical manner according to the individual's sense of "appropriateness." Style is conceived as an expression of the organizing function of the ego' (1977, pp. 287–288). To see this delineation within a grand perspective, I suggest that style might be considered ideally as content appropriately elaborated or extended by form; as such, style

193

becomes a distinctive characteristic of human discourse, whether it be sustained clinically, oneirically or aesthetically. Elucidatory of the oneiric context, there is Freud's contention that '*The form of a dream or the form in which it is dreamt is used with quite surprising frequency for representing its concealed subject-matter*' (*S.E.* 4: 332).

We might observe that however profitable the application of Freudian dream theory to literature has been, the dream theory itself does not account for all mental functioning. More particularly, Freud's theory of jokes must be used to supplement the dream theory as an approach to the understanding of literature; to do otherwise entails reductionism. Freud's distinction is relevant here: 'Dreams serve predominantly for the avoidance of unpleasure, jokes for the attainment of pleasure; but *all* our mental activities converge in *these two aims*' (*S.E.* 8: 180, italics mine). In avoiding unpleasure, dreams manifest greater regression and unconscious activity, as exemplified by the lack of logical connections, causality, and the like. Contrarily, unlike dreams, jokes are made to be intelligible and do not 'create compromises . . . [or] evade the inhibition' (*S.E.* 8: 172). On the other hand, dreams and jokes are similar in that a preconscious thought sinks down and is given over to unconscious revision. Now these processes evident in dream-work and joke-work are also found in 'art work,' to use a parallel term. Yet art-work stands apart insofar as preconscious and conscious ideas are also given a pre-eminent preconscious and conscious elaboration. Consequently, art is shaped by the singularization, however varied, of ego ideals. This contrasts with the radical egocentricity of drives in themselves and of dreams as a whole, as Freud was wont to insist upon.

In my outlook on the art or literary object, I have been greatly influenced by Robert Waelder's profound essay, 'The Structure of Paranoid Ideas,'[2] an essay recognized by Loewenstein and others as a pioneering attempt to establish the isomorphism between symptom and defence mechanism. It is profitable to pay repeated attention to Waelder's exposition and especially to where it focuses on two defences, projection and denial:

> Projection is denial with a special countercathexis. Since the mechanism consists in disclaiming, the countercathexis has the form of a claim.
> But there is one more connection to be considered. Not only has the countercathexis the same formal structure which the defensive operation had. The return of the warded-off material, too, is bound to have the same formal characteristics. This relation, which may be of general significance, may be called the

194

isomorphism of symptom and defence mechanism. If the defence was denial, the return of the disclaimed has the form of a claim. . . . The original defence mechanism would determine the form in which the warded-off material returns (isomorphism). It may be that further generalizations are possible and that *all* pathological processes, neurotic, psychotic, psychopathic, have the same basic structure, i.e., conflict-defence and countercathexis-return of the warded-off (pp. 173 and 176).

Reflection on this passage quickly leads us to reject the sometimes postulated correspondences between literary content and form on one side, and psychoanalytic drives and defences on the other; drives and defences are traceable in literary content and also in literary form. But since dynamically, defences are always unconscious, we must also summon up synthetic ego functions to account for the literary object. The isomorphism of defence and symptom may be considered analogous to that of sublimation and the workings of artistic workings of the synthesizing ego. Depending upon the artist and the containment of his pathology, these factors may figure combinatorily in varying degrees in both the content and form of his creation.

Creative geniuses are able to achieve a rich intrication of form and content, and hence in their art-work, both form and content attain a higher complex integration than is present in dream-work, joke-work, or in the free association of clinical discourse. At least in the instance of less extended literary works, it is critically enlightening and feasible to posit a single, symbolic nuclear principle that in large measure governs the content and form and shapes both their conscious and unconscious elements. To demonstrate my thesis, I shall immediately take Kafka's 'A Hunger Artist' as an example. After a brief justification of my choice of text, I shall proceed to a selective *explication de texte* and then to a psychoanalytic investigation, both methodologies reinforcing each other in the postulation of a centrally informing symbolic principle.

In a recent book on applied psychoanalysis, two critics have justly said that 'Kafka's "A Hunger Artist" is perhaps one of the most powerful, perfectly told tales ever written.'[3] Most of the power of Kafka's story, I would add, comes from the author's technique of broadening levels of meanings, establishing a continuum among those levels, and subjecting them to many reversals in the literary and psychoanalytic sense of the term. A clarification of Kafka's technique of inclusivity and expansiveness brings to light other dimensions affected by his utilization of reversals.

195

Kafka's majestic short story has attracted a great deal of stimulating criticism which, according to its orientation, has advanced a multitude of biographical, historical, and aesthetic perspectives.[4] The very nature of Kafka's fiction, beset internally as it is by countless thematic balances and modifications, promotes an ever-eddying textual criticism. This notwithstanding, I still feel that much of essential importance remains to be said about the meaning and technique of 'A Hunger Artist.'

One of Kafka's principal techniques of inclusivity or broadening levels of reference lies in his structuring of vertical reference. Specifically, the hunger artist is polyvalent, occupying a mediating and Janus-faced position within the triadic hierarchy of meaning that maps out the story:

1. the religious ascetic the creative artist	the immaterial, ethereal level
2. the hunger artist	(a) the immaterializing level (fasting of itself)
	(b) the worldly level (the artist's sensationalism)
3. the leopard	the physical level

The originality of this frame of reference is that it introduces an upward and downward thrust between levels, thereby departing from the uni-directional upward reference so widespread in conventional allegory. Furthermore, the levels in the above schema do not exist in absolute isolation from one another. Accordingly, Kakfa has achieved a quasi-anthropomorphological description of the leopard's awareness, thus pushing the animal up towards level 2, whereas the groanings and animalistic rage of the caged artist turn him down towards level 3.[5] Levels 1 and 2 are spanned by the ambiguity of *Künstler* in its double meaning of artiste and artist.[6] The movement between levels may also be appreciated through I. A. Richards' analytical categorization of metaphor into tenor or idea and vehicle or image. When in the end, the hunger artist unimpededly extends his fasting, he literally wastes away into a diminished insignificance that must be searched out with sticks poked into a pile of straw. In other words, as the vehicle or the physical level diminishes, the tenor monopolizes the meaning and there is an upward thrust in the story; with the dwindling of the very percept, the reader himself is induced into a commentary of a radically conceptual nature. This dramatic evolution of partial allegory into near pure allegory is a rare literary achievement[7] and stands apart from the frequent non-dramatic presentation of allegory as a *donné*.

196

Kafka's great genius manifests itself in the choice of artist on level 2. A less talented writer might conceivably have selected as protagonist an artisan of pottery who would put more 'soul' into his artifacts as he improved, with the banal result that the substantiality of the artifact would be maintained till the very end. By contrast, Kafka shows his genial narrative gift in creating a type of artist who, by the literal emaciation of his body into death, becomes an inevitable and relentlessly overwhelming conceptual indicator. In this light, hunger is radically economic within the immaterial-physical hierarchy: a refined tenor succeeds a wasting body. But the very summit of narrative brilliance and suggestive reversibility is instanced by the jarring juxtaposition of the extreme effeteness ending the story (the death of the artist) alongside the vital physical level (the rampant leopard).[8]

The three-leveled hierarchical scheme in 'A Hunger Artist' raises the age-old question of allegory, a theoretical question ideally receiving sustained study in its own right. Be that as it may, the nature of allegory will never be fully defined without our first settling the domain of literary allusion, its techniques and properties, a domain that is even more unexplored. It would seem, at any event, that as allusion becomes less sporadic and at the same time *refers to* a higher 'Platonic' plane of meaning, it tends to become allegorical. We might have better said 'embraces' instead of 'refers to,' for a mock epic, on the other hand, contains a sustained allusion to a higher level which is simultaneously rejected. Kafka's technique of poly-reference at times is rather close to that of the mock epic (as in *The Castle* and, par excellence, *Metamorphosis*). But even if Kafka is to be associated with allegory proper, we must grant that Kafka's penchant for thematic modifiction, remodification, and ironical inversions breaks him off from the main allegorical tradition.[9] Kafka's originality lies in the fact that his allegory to an extent operates as a dystopia, an upside-down world where the ideal is debased or demystified and where iconoclasm is wanton, as opposed to traditional allegory in which there is a realm, immediate or distant, where the ideal remains intact.

It has been said that 'A Hunger Artist' is strictly a literal story, but to this one may object that since a story may be coherently comprehended on the literal level, the possibility of other levels is not at all obviated. And in fact, there is allegory in Kafka's story but it is continual, not continuous. What demands even more interpretative tact is that the two more abstract domains—religious and aesthetic—are not necessarily concurrent, for at certain times they may succeed each other or just overlap. And even where there is a double reference there may not be a weight equally distributed among its individual terms, much like the distributional variability of the overdetermined dream image. In the text at hand, the artist's eventual confession that he would have eaten if he found the right food certainly applies in a critical sense more to the absolutist claims of all religions than to the Romantic artist's self-asserted mythic vocation. On the other hand, a firmer reference to aesthetic creativity is found in the statement that children inside or outside school have not been prepared for the lesson of fasting (7).[10]

In the realm of religious and ascetic references, the most remarkable are those which play freely with biblical narrative and relate to Christ.[11] First, the two lady assistants to the faltering martyr replace Simeon who helped carry the Cross, and secondly recall the two Marys present at the crucifixion, an event alluded to again in Kafka's story. The termination of the forty-day fast is announced by the impresario who is a parody of Christ's harbinger, John the Baptist. Although a herald, the impresario is untrue to his subject and does not understand him: 'The impresario came forward, without a word—for the band made speech impossible—lifted his arms in the air above the artist, as if inviting Heaven to look down upon its creature here in the straw, this suffering martyr...' (3). The passage combines the scenes of Christ the Infant laid in straw and His baptism by John. The third chapter of Matthew's gospel depicts the latter scene, rendered so familiar by religious iconography: 'And Jesus, when he was baptized, went up straightway out the water: and lo, the heavens were opened unto him.' An ironical reversal is added. In Matthew and Luke, the baptism is immediately followed by Christ's fasting for forty days, whereas in 'A Hunger Artist,' the baptismal parody concludes the forty-day fast. Kafka's subsequent portrayal of the artist fuses iconographic representations of Christ both falling beneath the Cross and also crucified:

> his head lolled on his breast as if it had landed there by chance; his body was hollowed out; his legs in a spasm of self-preservation clung close to each other at the knees, yet scraped on the ground as if it were not really solid ground, as if they were only trying to find solid ground; and the whole weight of his body, a feather-weight after all, relapsed onto one of the ladies (3).

In a more general sense, the grand public did not believe in the hunger artist, living or dead. Kafka's dying protagonist who begs forgiveness is the ironic contrast of the dying Christ forgiving the spectators.

Contributing an added dimension to the ironies in the vertical technique of hierarchical inclusivity is the technique of horizontal expansion, which deftly manipulates the particular as a universal. This technique of expansion operates in two ways: the hunger artist can be both an individual and class figure; second, certain events centering around him, though occasional in occurrence, are softly focused so as to appear typical. More precisely, the term 'hunger artist' acquires a general dimension in occurring four times without the definite article, contrasting with over fifty occurrences with the definite article. The overall result, a stylistic *coup de grâce*, is the illusory union variously created between the definite and indefinite, the general and particular. After the singular and indefinite 'a' in its title, the story opens with a generic statement explicitly referring to hunger artists as a class and ascribing a certain experience suffered by them all: 'During the recent decades the interest in hunger artists has lessened' (my translation). Subsequently in the first paragraph of the German version, Kafka thrice precedes 'hunger artist' by the definite article, yet in each case the epithet is generic in nature: 'At one time the whole town took a lively interest in the hunger artist . . . everyone wanted to see the hunger artist at least once a day . . . and then it was the childrens' special treat to see the hunger artist.'[12] Then, in the course of the second paragraph, there is a delicate shift to the *particular* hunger artist or protagonist of the story. An amateurish trait would have been to write 'a hunger artist' or 'the hunger artists' to designate the class. But Kafka does nothing of the kind; he deftly moves with grammatical legerdemain from the general to the particular. And yet the hunger artist is surely individualized, for not every one of his peers would sing, like to tell jokes, and so forth.

The other two occurrences of 'a,' in paragraphs six and eight, are limited in tonal influence. If Kafka desired indefiniteness as the predominant tone, he would have certainly employed 'a' in place of 'the' in the penultimate paragraph where the artist is submerged in a pile of straw. Instead, Kafka retains the major though not exclusive stress on particularity with the definite article. In this way, although the particular hunger artist is the cynosure of the story, as an allusive and inclusive force, he expands both in horizontal and vertical directions, representing other hunger artists and also those of a 'higher' productivity.

Attendant with the skilful gliding between the particular artist and the artist class there is the element of the double nature, unique or occasional, and typical, of some episodes. Periodicity is surely the keynote of the hunger artist's life—his fasts are broken with small regular intervals of recuperation (4). Similarly, the band music and fanfare announcing the termination of his fasts is a recurrent ritualistic event ('But then there happened yet again what always happened'). In the course of this ritual, however, an episode took place which, upon second look, was by no means invariable. When the artist collapses, the two lady assistants react in their own personal ways. However, the particularization of their reactions within a cyclical chain of events fades into an impression of generalization. The detail of the nearby attendant in readiness along with the generalizing pressures of the muted style tones down the transition from the typical to the non-typical and in that manner unites the two poles. Likewise, one may see aspects of the same technique in the elaborated incident of the artist's outrage, where the typical and predictable (he raged especially when fasting a long time) dominates the particular.

In terms of point of view as well, 'A Hunger Artist' reveals an inclusive soft focus and ultimately involves both the narrator and reader in the fabric of its reversals. In the first place, the narrator adopts a shifting partiality, favouring the hunger artist while he is alive:[13]

> Of course there were people who argued that this breakfast was an unfair attempt to bribe the watchers, but that was going rather too far (2) . . . and never yet, after any term of fasting—this must be granted to his credit—had he left his cage of his own free will (3). And when once in a time some leisurely passer-by . . . spoke of swindling, that was in its way the stupidest lie even invented by difference and inborn malice, since it was not the hunger artist who was cheating, he was working honestly, but the world was cheating him of his reward (8).

But subsequent to the artist's death, the narrator presents the bias of the circus spectators in a somewhat favorable light: 'Even the most insensitive felt it refreshing to see this wild creature leaping around that cage that had so long been dreary' (10).[14] Narrative soft focus is also found in the ambiguity or doubtfulness of the narrator's omniscience. It is impossible to tell whether he is totally omniscient and therefore merely revealing the partial knowledge of the protagonists or whether he is partially omniscient and thereby participating in the partial knowledge of the protagonists.[15] There are three outstanding instances of such ambiguity:

> Yet for other reasons he was never satisfied; it was not perhaps mere fasting that had brought him to such a skeleton thinness that many people had regretfully to keep away from his exhibitions, because the sight of him was too much for them, perhaps it was

dissatisfaction with himself, that had worn him down (3). For meanwhile the aforementioned change in public interest had set in; it seemed to happen almost overnight; there may have been profound causes for it, but who was going to bother about that (5) . . . perhaps they might even have stayed longer had not those pressing behind them in the narrow gangway . . . made it impossible (7)

A note of indefiniteness also occurs with respect to the reader-audience. Its presence is somewhat implied or felt by the narrator's use of 'of course' (2, 6, 7). Once, however, the audience is directly addressed—in the second person-singular and it is not clear whether the address issues from the reflecting artist, the narrator, or both: 'He might fast as much as he could, and he did so; but nothing could save him now, people passed him by. Just try to explain to anyone the art of fasting!' (8). Briefly, the twentieth-century fascination for Kafka's works is to some degree due to their unmooring, their peculiar indefiniteness and inclusive shifting perspective which on the one hand releases from traditional stable perspectives and, on the other hand, as a result of their suggestive formal nature, command further speculation on the part of the reader.

Given Kafka's technique of inclusivity and expansiveness, we are now in a better position to pursue the material which he has subjected to reversal, both in its psychoanalytical sense of defense and in the literary sense as a principle of narrative structure. As I indicated before, much of Kafka's fiction is a mixture of allegory and dystopia or upside-down utopia. If the traditional thrust of allegory is upward, in reference to abstractions, morality, religion, and the like, the Kafkaesque allegory has a downward movement, de-idealizing abstract forces, exposing their corruption and attendantly showing their unattainability. *The Trial* spectacularly testifies to such a reversed conception, and somewhat in the same category is 'A Hunger Artist' with its various reversals, ironies; it presents no resting place or solution except death, for any other solution is inverted and begins another series of problems.

The standard analytical commentary on reversal is in Freud's metapsychological paper 'Instincts and Their Vicissitudes' (*S.E.* 14: 126–140). There, Freud lends special attention to two defenses: reversal into the opposite and turning around upon the subject's self. They are among the ego's very oldest defenses[16] and may here be conveniently assimilated into the one rubric, reversal. In treating reversal, Freud has recourse to two pairs of component instincts (sadism and masochism, voyeurism and exhibitionism) and what he calls the total ego activity of love (p. 137). Reversal may involve:

1. A change of instinctual aim, as from activity to passivity. e.g. instead of my torturing another, the other tortures me.
2. A change of object, while the instinctual aim remains the same—this is reflected by the Greek middle voice, e.g. instead of torturing another, I torture myself.
3. A reversal of content, in the one instance of love giving way to hate. In effect, writes Freud, this topic is quite complicated and he posits three opposites for love: love-hating, love-being loved, and love and hate taken together as antithetical to unconcern or indifference.

Now, the artist is not only a simple exhibitionist (he stares into vacancy while others are looking at him) but can simultaneously be an exhibitionist-voyeur (he looks at others while they are looking at him) or then again, there's a reversal into sheer voyeurism: he triumphantly looks at the tired watchers eating after a sleepless night. The masochistic element in this voyeurism is clear, for on the other hand, the artist is depressed at seeing the meat destined for the caged animals, to which he feels inferior; similarly, he is pained by the self-asserting starers. In parallel fashion, the fasting artist is not only masochistic, but is also sadistic; he goes to great lengths to keep the watchers sleepless throughout the night, and he wants the public to maintain at considerable inconvenience their interest in his fasting past the forty-day limit.

Indeed, the story puts forth various combinations and reversals of the four component instincts: the lady assistants who, in striving for the exhibitionistic post of honor, coldly exploit the artist's exhibitionism; the spectators who sadistically delight at the distress of a lady assistant; the circus visitors that fear the leopard's roar yet in rapt voyeurism crowd around his cage to look at him; the artist's delusional madness that he can fast indefinitely, with the final result that he neglects to keep up-to-date the notice board and dwindles from sight underneath the straw, to the complete undoing of exhibitionism. And then again, concern may give way to indifference, as when the public forgets the artist; or concern may give way to a combination of both hatred and indifference as in the case of the accusation of the malicious passer-by.

The mechanism of reversal not only applies to the story's thematic elaboration of the component instincts but also the irony Kafka uses to structure the narrative. The public would rather suppress or repress than be fully aware of its caprices, a fact brought out by the story's very last sentence which ironically reverts to the story's first sentence which sequentially complements it:

But they braced themselves, crowded round the cage, and did not want ever to move away.

During these last decades the interest in professional fasting has markedly diminished.

What is more, exhibitionistic demonstrability of the artist's fasting is ultimately self-defeating and self-punitive, for the public's voyeuristic capability is unequal to the artist's exhibitionistic powers. Only he himself can be adequate witness to his performance, but no one will believe him. Verifiability of his fasting exceeds the spectators' masochistic tolerance of inconvenience. All this adds up to the consideration that breaking a public record feeds on public acknow-ledgment and acclaim, and without that response, record-breaking occasions further isolation.

Hence, the artist is prisoner of his enterprise. It is possible that his very thinness is counterproductive and keeps people away; his melancholy is misunderstood as caused by fasting whereas the logical reverse was true: although he truthfully says that fasting is easy, he is accused of being modest or deceiving, and when he sings to prove he's not eating for the neglectful watchers playing cards at some distance away, they admire his hypocrisy and cleverness that much more. Even the paradoxical possibility of being intriguing because of his temporary unpopularity boomerangs against the artist: 'People grew familiar with the strange idea that they could be expected, in times like these, to take an interest in a hunger artist, and with this familiarity the verdict went out against him' (8). The most poignant reversal, in a dramatic sense, occurs at the end of the story when the artist undergoes a change of character. He rejects the surface heroism of his past fasting as essentially an involuntary act. Though maintaining his dying decision to fast, he is no longer proud about it. This final humility from an otherwise deranged forsaken character is taken as craziness itself by the overseer who continually reverses his logical position:

> 'Forgive me, everybody,' whispered the hunger artist . . .
> 'Of course,' said the overseer, and tapped his forehead with a finger to let the attendants know what state the man was in, 'we forgive you.'
> 'I always wanted you to admire my fasting,' said the hunger artist.
> 'We do admire it,' said the overseer, affably.
> 'But you shouldn't admire it,' said the hunger artist.

'Well then we don't admire it,' said the overseer, 'but why shouldn't we admire it?'

'Because I have to fast, I can't help it,' said the hunger artist.

'To me you look strange,' said the overseer, 'and why can't you help it?'

'Because,' said the hunger artist, lifting his head a little and speaking, with his lips pursed, as if for a kiss, right into the overseer's ear, so that no syllable might be lost, 'because I couldn't find the food I liked. If I had found it, believe me, I wouldn't have made any scene and would have stuffed myself like you or anyone else.'[17]

It is an ironic reversal that the artist's physical diminution is concomitant with the diminution of his fame. Ultimately visuality in all its forms fails as a compensation for orality. The narcissistic relation between eye and mouth finally collapses, to be succeeded by aurality and a quasi-osculation. The sadistic impresario gives way to the overseer who, befitting his partial role as superego, with his head turned sidewards, listens to the artist's final confession.[18]

Summarily, in Kafka's story, reversal in its psychoanalytic and non-psychoanalytic sense is the nuclear symbolic principle out of which much of the content and form are elaborated. It keynotes the gliding of opposite meanings into each other, the story's use of biblical allusion, the dramatization of the four component drives, the technique of including the general in the particular and vice versa, and lastly, the story's overall structure, whose beginning is also to be understood as following its ending. I shall now retreat from reference to twentieth-century German textuality and go back to two texts in English Renaissance literature where I shall once more work with my thesis about a nuclear symbolic principle.

Notes

* First published in *American Imago* (1978), 35: 357–374.

1 Victor Rosen, 'The Psychology of Style.' In: S. Atkin and M. Jucovy (eds.), *Style, Character and Language*. New York: Jason Aronson, 1977.

2 *International Journal of Psycho-Analysis*, (1951), 32: 167–177.

3 Morton Kaplan and Robert Kloss (1973, p. 80).

4 A bibliography of secondary criticism dealing with 'Ein Hungerkünstler' is furnished by Meno Spann in 'Franz Kafka's Leopard,' *Germanic Review* (1959), 34: 87 fn. Among subsequent analyses one may single out: H.M.

Waidon, 'The Starvation-Artist and the Leopard,' *GR*, 35 (1960): 262–269; Meno Spann, 'Don't Hurt the Jackdaw,' *GR*, 37 (1962): 68–78; Herbert Deinert, 'Franz Kafka—Ein Hungerkünstler, *Wirkendes Wort*, 13 (1963): 78–87; Ingeborg Henel, 'Ein Hungerkünstler,' *Deutsche Vierteljahrschrift für Geistesgeschichte*, 38 (1964): 230–247; A. Foulkes, 'Kafka's Cage Image,' *Modern Language Notes*, 82 (1967): 462–471; Paul Neumarkt, 'Kafka's A Hunger Artist: The Ego in Isolation,' *American Imago*, 27 (1970): 109–122.

5 From a point of view of narrative development, there are other factors too that prepare for the final appearance of the leopard. The modulated anticipations range from the indirect (the designated watchers were usually butchers) to the direct (the caged artist was dressed in black tights, with his ribs sticking out).

6 This dual meaning of *Künstler* as artist and artiste was noted by Waidon (1960), p. 269.

7 A fascinating analogue to the starvation artist is Malbecco, Spenser's allegorical character of jealousy (*Faerie Queene*, Book III. *ca.* 109). Figuring forth the insubstantiality of jealousy, Malbecco languishes away into a near-nothingness; reduced to feather-weight, he is frustrated in a suicidal jump for he merely floats into the valley below; ultimately, he forgets his manhood and acquires the name 'Gealosie' itself (stanza 60).

8 Henel comments incisively (1964, p. 238):

> Only in the single moment when the value of hunger itself is contested does the vitality of the hunger artist break out, a vitality which he otherwise does not possess. With animal fury he seeks to justify the hunger that denies everything animal. At this point Kafka carries to the extreme the paradox of living from hunger and creates a situation of uttermost irony.

9 Cf. Günther Anders (1951, p. 40):

> The *allegorical writer* brings his conventional (theological, mythological, or the like) translation mechanism into operation so that it replaces *concepts by images*. The true symbolist takes the part as the whole, i.e., he has an object represented by another, because they are ostensibly consubstantial. Kafka does neither one nor the other. What he translates in images are not concepts but special situations . . . *he draws on language and its already existent figurative nature*. He takes metaphorical words literally.

Leaving certain statements aside, I agree with Anders to some extent: Kafka is concerned with revealing situations. But at least in some of his ironical inversions, it seems to me that he is concerned chiefly with disordering time-honored ideological systems and that his starting point, as such, is *Begriffe* (concepts).

10 For purposes of convenience, I shall habitually locate references to Kafka's short story by paragraph number in brackets. All citations are from *The Penal Colony* (1969, pp. 243–256). I should like to instance several shortcomings of this largely laudable translation by Willa and Edwin Muir:

(a) *Thin* does not capture the suggestion of *stomach* (*Magen*) in *Magerkeit*, for an empty stomach is the material cause of the faster's thinness; the same shortcoming recurs in the use of thinness for *abgemagert* (3). In this light, Kafka splendidly describes the surprise of the 'open-mouthed' children (1), an epithet ironically underlining the non-oral essence of the spectacle.

(b) The effort to perform 'beyond human imagination' does not contain the physical note of *Unbegreifliche* (the ungraspable) which is imagistically related to artist's extending his arms from the cage in order that they be felt and to his subsequent disappearance beneath a pile of straw.

(c) 'Blenching ladies' is a pale substitute for 'totenbleiche . . . Damen' (3), as *death* (*der Tod*) is an underlying current throughout the short story.

(d) *Obstinate* is a deficient rendering for *harnäckigste* (hard-necked, 3) which is adjectively ironic for an artist whose head at the end of a fasting performance was too heavy for his 'strengthless neck.'

(e) The reduction of the artist to a mere 'impediment on the way to the menagerie' misses the profundity of the German *Hindernis* (7), which is a notational pun on *die Hunde* 'hind or doe'. Thereby the German text punfully highlights the difference between the fierce animality of the leopard and the doe-like frailty of the artist, 'ein immer kleiner werdendes Hindernis.' Similarly, that the impresario *hurried* over Europe doesn't do justice to the German *jagte*, literally 'hunted!'

11 There is a continuum between the story's deliberate inversion of historical fact and the elusiveness of verifiable fact within the story itself. The cage is but one manifestation of isolation both of persons and of truth. Only the starvation artist is the true witness of his fast; his truthful statement about the easiness of fasting is deemed hypocritical; his melancholy is misinterpreted not only by the roguish impresario but even by some well-meaning people (4); his final fasting record is unknown, even to himself—the ultimate isolation of person from fact; even the old figure on the counting board, unchanged for many days, is doubted by a passer-by. Lastly, the overseer judges the artist insane in this deathbed confession, his greatest moment of truth.

12 I find Deinert's heading too simplified, based on the proposition that

'This short story, however, is called A Hunger Artist and deals with a hunger artist' (1963, p. 79).

13 This favoritism was nevertheless modified, for the character of the hunger artist was anything but perfect, even within the realm of asceticism. If fasting was easy for him, he had difficulty in other areas, both somatic and psychic. He suffered from the stench of the animals; their nocturnal restlessness and their roaring at mealtime unnerved him; both the comfortable straw and accumulated fatigue made him reluctant to stand up at the end of his fast. If fasting for some time did not make him melancholy, it at least made him irritable (4). From a more psychic point of view, he did not have courage enough to read the circus contract: proudly used to widespread acclaim, he could not accept working for a village fair; he found distrust of his fasting unendurable; he even engaged in almost conscious self-deception. Vanity is the keynote of his quest for fame: he made no secret that fasting was the easiest thing for him, but on the other hand he wanted kudos and admiration for it; he fasted not to teach but to astound the public. With all this in mind, I find it hard to appreciate Professor Steinhauer's conclusion that the hunger artist is an ascetic saint and that he 'wants admiration for the ideal of fasting, not for his personal triumph' (1962, p. 40).

14 For Deinert (1963, pp. 86–87), the end of the story clearly demonstrated that neither the leopard nor the artist is a hero and that they both live compulsively; Ingeborg Henel (1964, pp. 241–242) is also rather harsh toward the artist. But in fact, in his last moments the starvation artist rose to heroic grandeur. He forsook admiration and insisted that his fasting should not be esteemed. His last looks were firm, not proud; he was purged finally while the spectators and the overseer continued to live a life of oversight.

15 Technically, the problem here pertains to the ambiguities of 'style indirect libre' or 'erlebte Rede.' For a convenient and comprehensive summary of German, French, and English scholarship on this field, see Dorrit Cohn (1966). After a fine structural analysis of the problems involved in 'erlebte Rede,' Cohn pointedly concludes: 'The degree of association or dissociation between an author and his creature is not always so easy to establish . . . In this respect, the narrated monologue often sustains a more profound ambiguity than the other modes of rendering consciousness; and the reader must reply on context, shades of meaning, coloring, and other stylistic devices in order to determine the overall meaning of a text' (p. 112). Overlooking the complexities stemming from 'erlebte Rede' and point of view, critics have variously distorted the text with strained interpretations. The leopard is severely denigrated by Von Wiese, Waidon and Steinhauer, while Spann asserts

that the leopard had 'full possession of all the life values the hunger artist lacked' (1962, p. 74).

16 Anna Freud (1966, 2, p. 52).

17 I have somewhat shortened this passage and in two instances I have changed the Muirs's deficient translation. For their 'What a fellow you are' and 'made no fuss' I have substituted 'To me you look strange' and 'made no scene' respectively. In the German text the *Aufseher* 'overseer' addresses the discovered artist with the comment: 'Da sich mal einer'; subsequently the artist says if he found the right food, he wouldn't have been any *Aufsehen*, or 'scene' colloquially. Hence the original text linguistically unites food, sensationalism, and the overseer.

As fundamental support of the all-decisive exhibitionism and voyeurism, Kafka makes superb use of recurrent light and sight references, which are often bypassed in the Muir translation. The scene of the watchers who *deliberately* removed themselves and obviously *afforded* the artist the chance to cheat loses the visual suggestivity of the German 'ab*sich*lich' and 'in offenbarer Ab*sicht*' (2). The adjectival disparateness of the English 'dim night lighting' (2) and the miserable (2) and troubled artist (4) lacks the photic unity of the corresponding terms: *trüben Nachtbeleuchtung*, *trübselig*, and *trüber*. Similarly, the English *proceedings, moment, caution* (3), *glory, pointing out* (4) and *actions* (7) do not have the visually imagistic continuity of the original *Gesehen, Augenblick, Vorsicht, Glanz, erklären*, and *Absicht*. In the terminating paragraph, the professional dimming eyes are countered by the eager onlookers surrounding the lively leopard, whose vitality is thrice qualified by *schien*. The English translation *seemed* has lost much of the visual reference which it formerly had, and which still exists in *scheinen* and its other current meaning *to shine*.

18 See O. Isakower (1939).

References

Anders, G. (1951) Kafka: *Pro und Contra*. Munich: C.H. Beck.

Cohn, D. (1966) Narrated monologue: definition of a fictional style. *Comparative Literature*, 18: 97–112.

Deinert, H. (1963) Franz Kafka—Ein Hungerkünstler, *Wirkendes Wort*, 13: 78–87.

Foulkes, A. (1967) Kafka's cage image. *Modern Language Notes*, 82: 462–471.

Freud, A. (1936) *The Ego and the Mechanism of Defense*. The Writings of Anna Freud, 2. N.Y.: International Universities Press.

Freud, S. (1915) Instincts and their vicissitudes. *Standard Edition*, 14: 126–140. London: Hogarth Press, 1957.

Henel, I. (1964) Ein Hungerkünstler. *Deutsche Vierteljahrschrift für Literaturwissenschaft und Geistesgeschichte*, 38: 230–247.

Isakower, O. (1939) On the exceptional position of the auditory sphere. *International Journal of Psycho-Analysis*, 20: 340–348.

Kaplan, M. and Kloss, R. (1973) *The Unspoken Motive: A Guide to Psychoanalytic Criticism*. N.Y.: Free Press.

Kafka, F. (1967) *Erzählungen*. Berlin: Schocken.

—— (1969) *The Penal Colony: Stories and Short Pieces*. N.Y.: Schocken.

Mahony, P. (1974) 'La Ballade des pendus' of François Villon and Robert Lowell. *RCLC*, 1: 22–37.

Michaelson, L. (1968) Kafka's hunger artist and Baudelaire's old clown. *Studies in Short Fiction*, 5: 293–295.

Neumarkt, P. (1970) Kafka's 'A Hunger Artist': the ego in isolation. *American Imago*, 27: 109–122.

Rubenstein, W. (1952) Franz Kafka: a hunger artist. *Monatshefte*, 44: 13–19.

Spann, M. (1959) Franz Kafka's leopard. *Germanic Review*, 34: 85–104.

—— (1962) Don't hurt the jackdaw. *Germanic Review*, 37: 68–78.

Spenser, E. (1968) *Edmund Spenser's Poetry*, ed. H. Maclean, N.Y.: Norton.

Stallman, R. (1964) 'A Hunger Artist.' In: A. Flores and H. Swander (eds.), *Franz Kafka Today*. Madison, Wisc.: Wisconsin University Press.

Steinhauer, H. (1962) Hungering artist or artist in hungering: Kafka's 'A Hunger Artist.' *Criticism*, 4: 28–43.

Waidon, H. (1960) The starvation artist and the leopard. *Germanic Review*, 35: 262–269.

Shakespeare's Sonnet 20 and its symbolic nuclear principle★

With a surprising amount of certitude we can infer the development of Shakespeare's Sonnet 20 from its nuclear conception to its final existence as an elaborated fusion of content and form. More particularly, warded-off homosexual strivings and the frustration over the phallicized identity of an object give rise to linguistically expressed derivatives of absence and overcompensating excess. The upshot is a beautiful expansion of a symbolic nuclear principle into the lyric's lexical, syntactical, logical, and prosodical structures.

Sonnet 20 reads as follows:

> A woman's face with nature's own hand painted,
> Hast thou the master mistress of my passion,
> A woman's gentle heart but not acquainted
> With shifting change as is false women's fashion,
> An eye more bright than theirs, less false in rolling:
> Gilding the object whereupon it gazeth,
> A man in all hues in his controlling,
> Which steals men's eyes and women's souls amazeth.
> And for a woman wert thou first created,
> Till nature as she wrought thee fell a-doting,
> And by addition me of thee defeated,
> By adding one thing to my purpose nothing.
> But since she pricked thee out for women's pleasure,
> Mine be thy love and thy love's use their treasure.[1]

The surface plot of the poem is simple enough. Dame Nature fell in love with one of her female creatures, and to overcome her own frustration turns that creature into a man. This transsexual, a cynosure for both admiring sexes, has masculine and feminine traits. To the regret of the poet-speaker who is resigned to Platonic love, Dame Nature has destined the male transsexual for the physical pleasure of women. The richness of the poem, however, eludes this short summary, and accordingly I shall give sequentially a lexical, syntactical, logical, and prosodic analysis.

Lexicality

Much more than is apparent at first reading, the poem's lexicality is thoroughly saturated with sexual references and with bisexuality that is indicated either in a juxtaposed or a condensed manner. This is best seen if spelled out in a line-by-line selective analysis.

1. *nature's . . . painted*. One of the greatest antitheses preoccupying modern thought—nature and culture—was comprehended during the Renaissance period as an opposition between nature and art. The oxymoronic unification of these poles (nature's, painted) inaugurates a whole series of sexual oxymoron, of bisexuality, in the poem.

2. *master mistress*. As has been often noted by commentators, this epithet may be interpreted as having two nouns of equal value or, on the other hand, as consisting of a noun (mistress) being modified by the adjective *master*. But what I find important is the ambiguity itself, permitting a unisexual or a bisexual rendering. As well, *master* and *mistress* were also used interchangeably in the game of bowls to refer to that object of passionate attention, the first small bowl thrown out at the beginning of the game.[2]

3. *gentle*. The Latin etymology of this word, *gens*, included both sexes and meant tribe or race; *gentle*, moreover, occurred frequently in such Elizabethan lexical composites as *gentleman* and *gentlewoman*.

acquainted. Booth suggests, though with too much timidity, a pun on *quaint*, which also signified the female genitalia.[3]

4. *shifting*. There is a play on *shift* designating (a) a trick; (b) a change of clothing; (c) a smock or woman's chemise.[4] These shiftings and fashions of false women are to be compared with the fashioning of Lady Nature (lines 1, 9–10).

5–6. *eye . . . gilding*. Because of its shape, its moisture, and its garniture of hair, *eye* was used in the Renaissance as a yonic symbol.[5] But also throughout Elizabethan poetry *eye* was a homonymic pun on *I*, which iconically is a phallic referent. There is also an allusion to

Renaissance photic theory whereby the eye was supposed to emit beams which then alit upon an object. Shakespeare writes that the Young Friend's eye gilds (brightens; enriches), i.e. covers over with gold or yellow. In sum, *eye* is bisexual semantically and, in an allusive way, iconically as well.

7. *A man in hue*. Although *hue* has been variously interpreted as color, complexion, form, appearance, I follow Ingram and Redpath[6] who reject the first two choices, for they would contradict the poem's opening and reduce it to absurdity. The latter two meanings—the more current ones till the middle of the seventeenth century—give the correct picture: the Friend's female features are nevertheless embodied in a manly form or hue which has at its command the hues or excellences of both sexes.

controlling. Besides being a synonym for *restricting* and *dominating*, this word is paranomastic for *cunt-rolling*.[7] *Controlling* also relates to its original source of contre-roll, a copy of a roll of accounts that was kept for purposes of verification; hence the Friend's hue becomes a standard against which all other hues, male or female, must be judged.[8]

8. *steals men's eyes*. Seymour-Smith offers the following meanings which are on the right track but do not go far enough:

> (i) attracts the gazes of all men, by stealing them from women; (ii) *steels* the gazes of men, so that they do not look desirously. (A reference, in one word, to the Friend's sexual attractiveness and to his spiritual power to subdue lust.)[9]

But the second meaning *steels* itself is ambiguous, viz. makes resolute against lust and also turns into steel or hardens the phallacized erectile eyes that gild! *Steals* as well puns homonymously on *stales* or urinates;[10] furthermore, as a noun *stale* meant prostitute and as a verb, to render unpalatable to sexual curiosity.[11]

women's souls amazeth. Soul also refers to a stout stick or staff, which was spelled variously as *sowel, soul, soule* and *sole*, and was used as a phallic reference elsewhere by Shakespeare;[12] in its primary sense, *soul* ought to be understood not as a spiritual element but rather as the seat of emotions, for throughout the poem there is a derogatory note when *woman* appears in the plural.[13] It is as if the singular poet-speaker splits off femaleness, seeing it positively and sublimatorily in the unitary example of the friend and valuing it negatively as an eroticized bad object in the pluralized person of women. With impressive documentation, Green establishes *amazeth* as a reference, via labyrinth, to vulva;[14] he might have also added that mazes were labyrinthine designs with figures symbolically lost within them which were habitually used by Elizabethan printers to fill in the typographically empty spaces at the ends of chapters, books, and so on. There is also in *amazeth* the echo of a notational pun on amazon, the mythological strong woman who cut away one *mastos* or breast in order to practice archery well.

10. *a-doting*. This is a verbal play on *dot* or dowry.

11–12. *addition . . . adding*. This sole tautology in the poem is quite appropriate, mimetically signifying a kind of overkill.

12. *one thing*. Pace Wilson,[15] *thing* refers not only to the male but also to the female pudendum.[16] According to a certain mathematical theory extending from the ancient times up to the Renaissance, the number one was no number, a proposition at the basis of Shakespeare's sonnets 8, 135 and 136. Hence in this extra sense, the 'one thing' for the speaker is for his 'purpose nothing.' *Nothing* as a term in itself is a yonic symbol,[17] and therefore in a double way one thing equals nothing, both mathematically and in a sexually symbolic manner.

purpose. Here there is a notational pun on *puss*, meaning whore.[18]

13 *pricked*. Beside referring to the prick or peg at the center of an archery target,[18] the word means selected, adorned, and as well contains an Elizabethan colloquial term for the penis.

14. *thy love's*. As Booth most insightfully observes, '*thy love's* can mean not only "of your lovemaking and of the passion you feel" but also "your beloved's"—i.e. "of him who has your love," "my." '[19] Therefore in the whirligig of mediated sexual activity, not only does Lady Nature via women make love with the friend but also the poet via the friend makes love with other women.

use. Current term for sexual intercourse.

treasure. Contrary to modern pronunciation, *treasure, nature,* and *measure* rhymed with *pastor*.[20] In the context of lines 13–14, *use, measure* and *treasure* variously echo *usary*, which also meant sexual intercourse at the time. In the closing couplet, therefore, phonology weaves in with semantics to eroticize or re-eroticize love at any level, physical or Platonic. To cap it all, such Elizabethan writers as George Peele, John Lyly and Shakespeare himself punfully related *women* and *we men*.[21]

In Sonnet 20 the lexical references to bisexuality and the interchange of sexual identification are numerically remarkable. The saturating presence and absence of phallus reads as a page which on either side says See verso. Phallic ambivalence is played out in a somersault blur of things and no-things and in the thinnest interface between abstinent resignation and overbrimming vicarious pleasure. The wealth of conscious and unconscious meaning in such a text is particularly suited to a psycho-analytical approach, an approach enhanced by the perceptions of Ferdinand de Saussure, the founder of modern linguistics. The second Saussure so to speak, the investigator of Latin anagrams,[22] found in them a supplementary sign system, though guided by rigid conventions. Working within this Saussurean model but suggestively pushing it much further, Jonathan Culler argues for the 'otherness of meaning': 'man is a creature who lives among signs and must try not only to grasp their meaning but especially to understand the conventions responsible for their meaning.' Within this framework,

> since signifieds are so intangible we might well feel justified in granting priority to the signifier, which can actually appear before us as a written word, promising meaning and provoking us to set off in pursuit of it. But if we do this we must remember that it is only the promise of determinable signified—meanings determined by convention—which makes a form a signifier.[23]

Syntactical structure

The nucleus of the poem—to repeat, a frustration over a phallicized object giving rise to derivatives of absence and overcompensating excess—is grammatically evident in the numerous inversions, ellipses, and in the manipulation of parataxis and hypotaxis.

I hold syntactical inversion to be intimately related with anal eroticism; the sonnet's very textuality bears allusions to homo-sexuality. As Ernest Jones remarked, anal eroticism results in

> the tendency to be occupied with the reverse side of various things and situations. This may manifest itself in many different ways: in marked curiosity about the opposite or back side of objects and places—*e.g.* in the desire to live on the other side of a hill because it has its back turned to a given place; in the proneness to make numerous mistakes as to right and left, east and west, to reverse words and letters in writing; and so on.[24]

Commenting on the passage, Abraham adds: 'There is no doubt that

214

the displacement of libido from the genital to the anal zone is the prototype of all these "reversals." '[25]

Many traces of this anal eroticism are evidenced in the extraordinary number of syntactical inversions in Sonnet 20. As a matter of fact, among Shakespeare's first thirty-eight sonnets it is the only one that begins with the grammatical object (face) and even its subject and verb (Hast thou) are inverted; in line 2, *painted* is also dislocated. The inversion in line 5 is a standard one in English (as is . . . fashion). There's one inversion in line 8 (souls amazeth); multiple inversions affect the whole of lines 9 and 11; inversions also have displaced *nothing* (line 12) and *Mine* (line 14).[26]

If syntactical inversion in Sonnet 20 is an elaboration of anal eroticism, ellipsis or the omission of words is a mimetic residue of castration anxiety. The various ellipses (italicized) may be listed as follows:

Thou hast A woman's gentle heart . . .	(line 3)
. . . as *it* is *with* . . .	(line 4)
Thou hast An eye . . .	(line 5)
Thou art A man . . .	(line 7)
. . . thing *which is* to . . .	(line 11)
. . . use *be* their . . .	(line 14)

Two points deserve especial attention. First, the grammatical traces of castration, viz. ellipsis, mainly pivot around two verbs, *to be* and *to have*, and it is precisely the *having* of a phallus in Shakespeare's poem that determines not only one's personal *being* but also the kind of *having* of the other. Secondly, the cluster in lines 11 and 12 of inversion, ellipsis and tautology is without parallel in the rest of the poem and thereby aptly underscores the bone of contention which is the semantic purport of those two lines.

As for paratactic syntax, the poem contains its two kinds: the absence of conjunctions and somewhat telegraphic style of the octave and the use of conjunction but deprived of its logical value (the *And* of line 9). This latter biblical use of *and* as a sort of phonetic glue and the former type of parapraxis are the syntactical forms most closely conforming to primary process. The hypotaxis or hierarchized syntax and judgment of subordination that characterize the couplet conform to secondary process. On the surface level, then, the poem moves from absence of conjunction to undercutting of conjunction (the *And* is really a *nothing!*) to the logical use of conjunction respected at least for its surface value.

Logical structure

The structure of the poem's logical argument in itself is significant; it is characterized by binarity and inversion, which are mimetic traces of the bisexual and anal erotic matter suffusing the sonnet. Progressing in seven two-line units, the sonnet's organization as sonnet is exceptional; this couplet-like quality cuts across its organization as three quatrains and couplet. It is also noteworthy that the three quatrains are laced together by half and slant rhymes.

The logical structure may be also looked at in a different way. The first lines, in the present tense, constitute a blazon or catalogue of the friend's traits that make him the poet-speaker's master mistress. After the encomium of the octet comes a temporal inversion, a *narratio* as a flashback in the past tense (lines 8–12); the resolution of the closing couplet separates into an antecedent expressed in the past (line 13) and a consequent expressed in the present (line 14). Summarily, due to the binarity and inversion marking its logical structure, the poetic construct in its progression not merely talks about but incorporates and mimetically enacts its themes.

Prosodical structure

With the exception of Sonnet 87 (whose main theme also concerns excess), Sonnet 20 by having fourteen hypermetric lines is unique among Shakespeare's 154 sonnets. The eleventh syllables, then, comprise one more trace of overcompensating excess affecting the poem's various structures. But there is something even more outstanding in the poem's prosody: all the endings save *thing*[28] (line 12) are unstressed. In Elizabethan England *masculine* was applied to rhymes that ended in a stressed syllable (*OED* 3b). Hence the endings of Sonnet 20 doubly function as signifiers; they are *additions* but the additions are unstressed and therefore feminine; the notable exception of *nothing* serves to dramatize this ambiguity. The poem is a beautiful demonstration, on the strictly prosodic level, of signifiers referring to other signifiers, all this being in the line endings. There is yet another contrast: all the terminal words linguistically are form words and semantically are very important as opposed to the initial words of the fourteen lines which for the most part are unstressed, monosyllabic and of lower semantic value. Thereby frontal and terminal linear positions play off with factors of absence and presence, accentuation and non-accentuation, voidness and excess, all of which comprise messages on the sub-semantic level and constitute an elaboration of the sonnet's overt statements.

In conclusion, the mimetic quality of Sonnet 20's lexical, syntactical, logical and prosodical elements comprises a meaningful network that subtends the surface or manifest statement. As the poem's symbolic nuclear principle, the fetishized intensity of the representation of the phallus and the attendant castrated reaction emanate into multiple antithetic traces of absence and presence. Passing on to the next chapter, we shall complicate our set task by comparatively examining two poems of Shakespeare's formidable contemporary, Ben Jonson.

Notes

★ First published in *American Imago* (1979), 36: 69–79.
1 For the text of the sonnet I have used J. Dover Wilson's (1966) edition, *Shakespeare's Sonnets*.
2 See M. Friedman (1971).
3 *Shakespeare's Sonnets* (1977, p. 163).
4 See the entry under *shifts*, James Henke (1975, 2: 268).
5 See Henke (1975, 2: 147) and also the entry under *eye* in Eric Partridge (1968, p. 102).
6 *Shakespeare's Sonnets* (1964, pp. 49–50). There's also a possible punning on *hue-you*, but because we are not sure whether the *h* was pronounced, we are confined to conjecture (see Kökeritz, 1953, p. 77). If indeed the *h* was not aspirate, it would hitch up with Shakespeare's punning with *you-ewe* (Kökeritz, 1953, p. 210); in turn, the ewe or female sheep was also used to designate whore (Henke, 1975, 2: 147).
7 See Booth (1977, p. 164). For other homonymic punning on *cunt*, cf. the entries under *conscience* and *constable* in Partridge (1968, pp. 84–85) and Henke, the latter also giving significant entries under *conference, conflicts, consumes, content,* and *converse* (1975, pp. 117–118).
8 Dover Wilson (1966, p. 118).
9 *Shakespeare's Sonnets.* (1966, p. 124).
10 Kökeritz (1953, p. 148).
11 Partridge (1968, pp. 189–190) and Henke (1975, 2: pp. 279–280).
12 Green (1974, pp. 67–72).
13 See Melchiori, (1976, pp. 111–112).
14 Green (1974, pp. 74–75 and plates).
15 Dover Wilson (1966, p. 117).
16 Henke (1975, 2: p. 292) and Booth (1977, p. 164).
17 See Henke (1975, 2: p. 221); Pyles (1949); Jorgensen (1954).

18 Friedman (1971).
19 *Shakespeare's Sonnets* (1977, p. 165).
20 Kökeritz (1953, p. 271).
21 Green (1974, pp. 80–81).
22 See Starobinski (1971).
23 These citations are from pp. 112–113 and 117 of Culler's (1976) excellent study.
24 Jones (1950, p. 423).
25 Abraham (1927, p. 390). Cf. p. 391:

> Certain cases of neuroses in women, in which an unusually strong castration complex is expressed, reveal to us best the deeper meaning of such a tendency to reversal. We find in them that it springs from two main motives—a displacement of the libido from 'in front' to 'behind', and the wish for a change of sex.

26 *Controlling* (line 7) may be equally a noun or a participial adjective; if it is the latter, it is also displaced.
27 I have given here just one possible way of filling in the ellipsis.
28 Shakespeare and his contemporaries pronounced this word as *nó thíng* and therefore quite differently from the modern nóthing.

References

Abraham, K. (1927) *Selected Papers*. London: Hogarth.

Culler, J. (1976) *Saussure*. London: Fontana.

Freud, S. (1919) Preface to Reik's *Ritual: Psycho-Analytic Studies, Standard Edition*, 17: 257–263. London: Hogarth Press, 1955.

—— (1925) An autobiographical study. *Standard Edition*, 20: 7–74. London: Hogarth Press, 1959.

Friedman, M. (1971) Shakespeare's 'Master Mistris': image and tone in Sonnet 20. *Shakespeare Quarterly*, 22: 189–191.

Green, M. (1974) *The Labyrinth of Shakespeare's Sonnets*. London: Charles Skilton.

Henke, J. (1975) *Renaissance Dramatic Bawdy (Exclusive of Shakespeare: An Annotated Glossary and Critical Essays)*, 2 vols. Salzburg: Universität Salzburg.

Jones, E. (1950) *Papers in Psycho-analysis*, 5th edition. London: Baillière.

Jorgensen, P. (1954) Much Ado about Nothing. *Shakespeare Quarterly*, 5: 287–295.

Kökeritz, H. (1953) *Shakespeare's Pronunciation*. New Haven: Yale University Press.

Melchiori, G. (1976) *Shakespeare's Dramatic Meditations*. London: Clarendon Press.

Partridge, E. (1968) *Shakespeare's Bawdy*, 2nd edition. London: Routledge.

Pyles, T. (1949) Ophelia's nothing. *Modern Language Notes*, 54: 322–323.

Shakespeare, W. *Sonnets* (1944) 2 vols., ed. H. Rollins. Philadelphia: Lippincott.

—— (1961) ed. D. Bush and A. Barbage, Baltimore: Penguin.

—— (1963) ed. M. Seymour-Smith. London: Heinemann.

—— (1964) ed. W. Ingram and T. Redpath. London: University of London Press.

—— (1964) ed. G. Willen and V. Reed. New York: Thomas Crowell.

—— (1966) ed. D. Wilson. Cambridge: Cambridge University Press.

—— (1968) ed. G. Kittredge, rev. I. Ribner. London: Blaisdell.

—— (1969) ed. B. Smith. New York: New York University Press.

—— (1977) ed. S. Booth. New Haven: Hale University Press.

Starobinski, J. (1971) *Les Mots sous les mots: Les anagrammes de Ferdinand de Saussure*. Paris: Gallimard.

11

Ben Jonson's 'best pieces of poetry' and a comparison of their symbolic nuclear principle*

Our subject consists of two poems composed by Ben Jonson on the deaths of two of his children. It might be of note that Jonson himself was a posthumous child, born one month after his father's demise. Although we know little of Jonson's early life, we are certain that he married in 1592 at the age of twenty, that in May of the following year he had his first daughter, and that some six months later she died from the plague; a subsequent son, born in 1596, lived for seven years before he too was fatally stricken by another of London's all too frequent plagues.

We shall proceed by first explicating each epitaph and then comparing them both in terms of their overt themes with their differing symbolic nuclear principles. Perhaps we may begin with Jonson's 'On My First Son' whose more memorable lines, in spite of some enlightening commentaries,[1] contain much that demand further explanation:

Farewell, thou child of my right hand, and ioy;
My sinne was too much hope of thee, lou'd boy,
Seuen yeeres tho' wert lent to me, and I thee pay,
Exacted by thy fate, on the iust day.
O, could I loose all father now. For why
Will man lament the state he should enuie?
To haue so soone scap'd worlds, and fleshed rage.
And, if no other miserie, yet age?
Rest in soft peace, and, ask'd, say here doth lye
BEN. IONSON his best piece of *poetrie*.
For whose sake, hence-forth, all his vowes be such,
As what he loues may neuer like too much.[2]

Readers have universally admired the poem's controlled muted tones, but what has been neglected is the precise frame of the speaker's mind. The bereaved father tries to struggle through and overcome his mourning; yet he still finds himself guilty about his ambitions for his son, whose death on one level is felt to be fitting punishment for paternal injustice. Jonson's narcissistic identification with his son, meanwhile, undergoes a secondary shift: the inaugural paternal protectiveness (the first eight and a half lines) is followed by a stance in which the father now addresses his son as a superego and ego-ideal.

A scrutiny of Jonson's epitaph in terms of its rich local detail will further our thematic examination. 'Farewell' as a notational pun on 'fare or travel well'[3] anticipates the double Hebraic meaning of *Benjamin*: 'child of the right hand' and 'child of good omen.' The boy, who was actually named Benjamin, is a source of his father's 'joy' in a polysemous sense: physically, narcissistically, and morally. During his son's life, the father was unjust, had too much hope for him, and to that extent did not allocentrically bid him to fare well; thus the son is now urged to fare well as contrasted to his father who in one way fared badly and who did not live up to the righteousness etymologically contained in his own name. The vocative 'lou'd boy' applies differently to the past and present, to being either ill-loved in the past and being contritely loved in the present. In line with the contriteness, 'I thee pay' signifies simultaneously I pay by means of you and I pay for you (by my poem and by my sorrow); in addition, the payment references are foreshadowed in *fare*, which also at that time meant the cost of conveyance (*Oxford English Dictionary* 4b). 'Exacted,' which is a notional pun on 'exact' or 'just,' modifies 'thee' or even the whole clause 'I thee pay.' Reread as such, the compounded meaning becomes: the father is required or exacted to pay; the son is exacted or extracted (*OED* 5) out of life. Tying in with the elaborate complexity of 'right' or just hand and 'exacted,' 'just day' comes to mean the Day of Immediate Judgment and Justice, the right day, the day for the just and righteous; it is the eminent day of reckoning for that which was 'too much' (lines 2 and 12). 'Loose,' orthographically interchangeable with 'lose' in the Renaissance, gives rise to two meanings: may I forget (*OED* 5d) fatherhood, or abandon fatherhood. The next sentence is an extraordinary example of technical virtuosity: whereas world's rage refers to wars and the like, and the flesh's rage refers to erotic strivings, pestilence is mutually shared by both terms—a fine lexical overdetermination, for the son died in a plague![4] Next, the father's unrest, along with the violent and disintegrating rage wrought by the world, stand off from the 'soft peace' of afterlife. The son is then told to be the father's spokesman, a delicate allusion to 'fate' of line 4, which etymologically comes from the Latin *fari*, to speak. But far more remarkable punning begins with Jonson's use of 'lie,' whose double meaning of 'prevaricate' and 'repose' constituted such a hackneyed figure in English Renaissance poetry. Obliquely counteracting the Platonic alliance of poetry with falsehood, Jonson summons as spokesman his best poem, his own created son of rectitude and truth (cf. the Greek *po[i]esis*: creation; also, poetry). As a creation, the boy lies under the epitaph poem and is even better than it!

Finally, as Wesley Trimpi has analysed so well, the closing of the poem is a superb translation of Martial's line, 'Quidquid ames, cupias non placuisse nimis':

> Jonson translates the line by making a distinction between 'love and like,' which were ordinarily used redundantly in a formulaic combination. The apparently casual association of the two, when a distinction is being made, increases the reader's perception of the antithesis. Jonson makes 'what' (he loves) the object of both love and like, whereas Martial makes it the object of love but the subject of please.[5]

I further add that the distinction in Martial suffers as well because desire is given over to three forms: *ames, cupias, placuisse*. Jonson reduces this cluttering effect by translating the subjunctive *ames* into the noun form 'vowes,' thus enhancing and isolating the antithesis between the remaining two verbs: self and object-love are most clearly set against each other.

Like the epitaph for his son, Jonson's 'On My First Davghter' on the surface expresses emotion in a reserved Horatian manner. Both in its own right and as a comparative instrument the elegy merits a greater evaluation than has customarily been assigned it:

> Here lyes to each her parents ruth,
> MARY, the daughter of their youth:
> Yet, all heauens gifts, being heauens due,
> It makes the father, lesse, to rue.
> At sixe moneths end, shee parted hence
> With safetie of her innocence;
> Whose soule heauens Queene, (whose name shee beares)
> In comfort of her mothers teares,
> Hath plac'd amongst her virgin-traine:
> Where, while that seuer'd doth remaine,

This graue partakes the fleshly birth,
Which couer lightly, gentle earth.

Immediately one may note that modifying the resignation over object loss there is a preoccupation with the posthumous fate of the little girl's body and soul.

Before further thematic commentary, however, some preliminary lexical explications are in order. 'Ruth,' primarily meaning sorrow, carries a suggestion of the biblical Ruth who also, though in a completely different way, took leave of her parents.[6] At any rate, the grieved narrator is rendered 'father lesse, to rue.' Because of the ambiguity of 'lesse' as an adjective as well as an adverb, two meanings emerge: primarily, the father rues less; secondarily, the lamenting parent is merely a husband and no longer a father. 'She parted' means she left the earth and also her soul parted from her body. In line 8, 'teares' are also definable as poems of lament pinned onto a hearse. Finally, the antonymy between 'seuer'd' and 'remaine' in the following line contrasts with the synonymous relation between 'lightly' and 'gentle.'

The most fascinating aspect of the poem's subject matter, however, pertains a sexual aspect of mourning. Reflecting a medieval outlook, Jonson was thoroughly guilty about the sexual origin and life of man, a guilt expressed in unmistakable tones:

I know my state both full of shame and scorne,
Conceiv'd in sinne, and unto labour borne.
                    ('To Heauen,' lines 17–18)

Now if his six-month-old daughter died of the plague in November 1593, it was exactly a year after Jonson's marriage and she could well have been the first fruit of her parents' pristine sexual activity, their 'youth.' This explains all the more why Jonson attended greatly to the virginity of his daughter. She bore the same name as Christ's mother and became part of her 'virgin-train.' She also was given, punfully, a litany attribute of heaven's queen: *ros caeli*, heaven's due (line 3). This notwithstanding, Jonson was wary, mostly unconsciously one could say, about the short-lived virginity of the buried cadaver, as a close reading of the poem will undeniably demonstrate. In ths connection we may call to mind the foreboding threat to the reluctant virgin in Marvell's 'To His Coy Mistress': 'Then worms shall try / That long-preserved virginity.' On the physical level, Jonson's daughter was not secure in the grave, where there was a danger to her 'innocence' (etymologically, the state of not being harmed). An alarming note takes hold in line 10:

Where, while that seuer'd doth remaine

This leads to the last couplet, which carries strong notes of the fear of physical defloration, the violator being figured forth as the earth. The intense physicality of the epithet 'fleshly birth' should be understood with reference to line 2: the daughter is corpulent, and her origins were carnal—'the daughter of their fleshly youth.' One must bear in mind too that the adjective ascribed to earth—gentle—is cognate with genesis and generation. But some of the other lexical items are more telling. Backdropped against the reference to 'safetie of her innocence,' the notion of hymeneal perforation is semantically suggested directly by 'couer lightly' and indirectly by 'seuer'd,' whose meaning phonetically resonates in *'parted'* and *'partakes.'* Given this abundant coherence of submerged material, we are more than justified to continue searching out the thread of erotic allusions. 'Partakes' signifies shares or eats; 'parted' hints also to the body itself parting in two; 'beares' homonymously puns on 'bare,' and 'teares' also means rips. Within this context, it is now clear that the 'Here lies' of the poem's beginning, though the most conventional of formulas, is enlisted in the service of sexual expression.

Another way of exposing the psychological and aesthetic value of Jonson's final couplet is through its source in Martial v, 34. At the end of his epitaph on the six-year-old Erotion, Martial declared:

Mollia non rigidus caespes tegat ossa: nec illi,
terra, gravis fueris: non fuit illa tibi.
(I translate: let not the harsh turf cover her
soft bones: nor you, earth, be heavy—she has not
been such on you)

Jonson's definitive editors hold that Jonson's final couplet is one of 'unadorned plainness' and that 'To the graceful fancy of the Martialesque epitaph it makes no approach whatsoever.'[7] I could not be in greater disagreement. The eroticization of 'soft bones' into 'fleshly birth' is anything but plain. Aesthetically the suggestive force of Jonson's verbs, furthermore, avoids the blandness of the double occurrence of the Latin verb 'to be,' *fueris* and *fuit.* Jonson's 'gentle earth' certainly is a vocative, but it is also a submerged request: Please be gentle, o earth. And there is yet the most extraordinary distinction in Jonson's poem, a syntactic distinction with far-reaching psychoanalytical implications. The syntax is concerned with the abodes of the girl's body and soul. First of all, we must pay close attention to the referential complexity of the most syntactically difficult line in 'On My First Daughter':

Whose soule heauens Queene, (whose name shee beares)

      ↓   ↓

    daughter   daughter

The grammatical parallelism of the units *whose* plus noun, though with different semantic referents (daughter and heavenly queen), skilfully joins the two Marys by grammatical parallelism and semantic fusion or blurring. By comparison, the last two lines of the poem, dealing with the girl's body in earth, are syntactically direct and simple. Jonson can permit syntactical intertwining only between heaven's queen and his daughter who in this contact remain virginal. In this comparative sense, the absence of 'mimetic' intertwining syntax and by the same token the presence of simple syntax constitute a defense in the last couplet which expresses the father's fear of the contact between earth and his daugher. In their original Greek and Latin etymologies respectively, syntax and relation are very close—they deal with placement, rapport; and this they do in a spectacularly 'interrelated' manner in Jonson's memoriam. If the closing syntax is simple, its psychoanalytically reactive import is complex—*pace* Jonson's editors.

After these separate analyses, we have now arrived at a second stage, a comparative reading of the two poems. Through a superficial literary reading, Jonson's editors overlook the libidinal nature of both poems and glibly say the one on the son is 'the more masculine production.' A comparison of the two epicedes, in fact, does lead us into the deeper layers of Jonson's sexuality. The risk of haphazard comparisons is diminished by the fact that the poems present parallel tetradic structures:

Son	*Daughter*
I. lines 1–2. Identification of the child and the father's emotional reaction.	I. lines 1–2. Identification of the child and the parents' emotional reaction.
II. lines 3–5. The exacted payment does not lessen the father's sorrow.	II. lines 3–4. The due payment makes the father lament less.
III. lines 6–8. By dying, the son avoided miseries.	III. lines 5–6. By dying she left with her innocence.
IV. (a) line 9. Wish that the son rest in peace. (b) lines 10–12. Son as spokesman for father's feelings and resolutions.	IV. (a) lines 7–10. The mother is comforted that her daughter is honored in heaven as a virgin. (b) lines 11–12. Daughter's precarious state in her earthly grave.

We can use and build on this outline to make several things clear. The very first sections show a momentous difference in voice and address, indicating Jonson's closeness to his son and intriguing removal from his daughter. In the Son poem, Jonson refers to himself in the first person, his son as addressee in the second, and to his wife not at all. By contrast, the poet never addresses his daughter directly; she is in the third person as well as her father and mother, who figures prominently. The result is that the communicative structure, besides indicating a closer relationship between father and son, serves as a defensive distanciation against the father's Oedipal desires towards the daughter.

Through the commercial imagery in the second section of each elegy, the poet leaves evidence of his stronger ego attachment to his son. Whereas Jonson accepts the celestial gift of his daughter is due back to heaven, he speaks of the filial loan as exacted from him. The grammar also bears traces of this relative attachment:

It makes the father lesse to rue
O could I loose all father now.

Whereas the first statement is a declarative statement of fact, the second is a subjunctive, a wish not realized: I wish I could abolish my paternal attachment. Again, the metonymic 'all father' is parentally closer than 'the father.' It is also of the utmost relevance that Jonson, who all along in the poem to his daughter, refers to himself in the third person, does not do it in this instance. 'The father' instead of 'her father' or 'me, father' is another use of grammar enlisted in the service of Oedipal defence, though this time the defence is a double one.

With the third sections of his elegies, the poet tries to console himself with the advantages of his children's deaths. The son's departure is portrayed negatively; he *avoided* miseries—including rage, which is what Jonson precisely fears about his daughter's corpse. The daughter's departure is given a positive and even pleonastic description: she left with the safety of her innocence, a resounding instance of defensive overdetermination. In contrast to the perfect parallelism of the first three sections, the subdivided fourth parts, as the outline indicates, are in chiastic relation with each other. This significant reversal underscores what is really the most important and most censored for Jonson, and thus reserved for the very last. In effect, the fourth parts of each poem deal with reconciliation and experience of overcoming the loss. In the final lines, we have Jonson's wish projected onto his son on one hand, and his wish for the comfort of his daughter on the other. In the deepest

226

sense, the words of the Son poem are applicable to the daughter, though Jonson would not dare say it: he liked her too much.

These thematic differences are further reflected in the syntactic difficulties peculiar to each poem. In the Son epicede, the most troublesome grammatical structures concern the father himself (lines 5 and 12), whereas in the other poem, the syntactically difficult lines deal with the daughter alone (line 10) or together with 'heauens Queene' (line 7). When it comes to verb tense and mood, it's the son that is the focus of complexity. In the Daughter poem, nearly all the verbs are in the present indicative; in the other poem, the verbs are in the past, present, present perfect, future, indicative, conditional, subjunctive and imperative.

Jonson's relation to the son is in terms of *être*, and to the daughter in terms of *avoir*. He narcissistically merges with his son by paraphrasing their common name (line 1) and then by having the son repeat their name (line 10)—the very verbal repetition is an enactment of narcissism and an interesting variant of the Greek myth of Narcissus and Echo. Whereas in the Greek myth the nymph Echo pined away for love of Narcissus until nothing was left of her but her voice, in Jonson's epitaph, the father and son are one in name, in creation, in poetry. Alongside the classical myth, there is also the religious allusion to their being God the Father and Son figures. Biblically, Christ is associated with the Divine Right Hand and, on Judgement Day, is to sit 'at the right hand of the Father.' The explicit references concerning the right hand and the 'just day' are quite to the point, as well as the fact that Jonson's son turns into his projected superego, his spokesman, his Logos, his Word, on earth. This terrestrial God the Father and Son compare to the two heavenly Marys in the other poem. As the two essential notes in the context, *terrestrial* and *heavenly* subtly spatialize Jonson's emotive reaction to spiritual transformation. Though a muted Christ figure, the son strangely enough receives less spiritual affirmation than his sister. He is vaguely described as merely 'lent' whereas she is explicitly called one of 'heauens gifts.' We read too that the boy has not outrightly attained the heavenly status of his sister placed in the 'virgin-traine.' In a global though non-sexual sense, the boy is more earthbound than the girl; in the grave, he elicits a bragging identification from his father. On a sexual level, however, it is the earthbound and buried daughter that elicits her father's erotic and anxious concern.

One can hardly overstress the active post-mortem role that Jonson assigns to his son. The boy is addressed as an active participant—he is confidently asked to be a kind of moral preacher to the inquisitive passerby. The daughter on the contrary is pictured as passive, defenceless, and as such elicits her father's protective pleas. She is not ever given the quasi-active status as an auditor; in the poem about her, only earth is addressed directly and at that, with a message which is quite to the point: cover her lightly. Furthermore, Jonson makes no issue of his son's body being separated from his soul. The son's integration, in other words, is a far cry from his sister's split entity, her soul in heaven comforting her mother and her interred body discomforting her father.

The foregoing examination has gradually equipped us to undertake a penetration into the poems in terms of their nuclear symbolic principle. Described phasically, Jonson's attitude to his children is marked by anality—the connections between anality and financial or commercial attitudes have been too well traced to be repeated here. Yet Jonson's anal attitude is not the same for each. Toward his daughter, he is anally expulsive and genitally anxious: he readily relents to heaven's creditor call and he fears the sadism of the personified grave and earth. In the Son poem, Jonson reacts ambivalently, in a partially anally retentive manner and in a partially expulsive one. The payment has been exacted from him; he wishes that he could loose or loosen himself. He remains a masochistic suffering victim of the world's rage from which the son has been forcibly drawn, and then he includes an element of softness in a wish for his son: 'Rest in soft peace,' a telling overdetermined pleonastic translation of the Latin which, omitting the 'soft,' simply says 'resquiescat in pace.' It must also be borne in mind that the father's final position is not a fully committed resolution; instead, he projects into his withdrawn son the desire that his father will be not indissolubly attached to future objects!

We may now attempt a more precise delineation of the symbolic nuclear principle which determined to a great degree the overall conception and development of Jonson's epitaphs. Let us start with the Daughter poem, which is relatively uncomplicated in this regard. Qualifying Jonson's mournful resignation is his ambivalent concern over his belief about the posthumous separation of his daughter's soul from her body: ambivalent, for on one hand he envisaged her virginity being celebrated in heaven, and on the other hand, he unconsciously felt the separation of her body from her soul to be a prototype of another kind of severance, the posthumous defloration of his daughter's body. Hence the covert dispersion of references to severance throughout the poem; hence the temporary hesitation in understanding the existential import of 'Where, while that' (line 10) and relating it to an antecedent; hence, the reactive, syntactical interweaving and semantic blurring between the two Marys in line 7.

The symbolic nuclear principle governing the Son poem is even more imposing in its elaboration. In a way, the poem begins with an epi-epitaph: the father writes an introductory epitaph that ends with a traditional note on peace; there follow three words of transition ('and asked, say') which leads into another epitaph with the most conventional of openings ('Here lies'). The result of all this is that there is a quasi-juxtaposition of epitaph formulae, 'Rest in . . . peace,' 'Here lies,' but in reversed order. That reversal, similar to the reversals qualifying as anal character traits as we have seen in the previous chapter, is indicative of Jonson's anally determined ambivalence. Succinctly put, Jonson's 'sphincter morality' shapes his mourning as a partial resignation over bereavement; anal retentiveness is masked over by pseudo-release. Provisionally we may clarify the poem by visualizing it more or less as a series of containers: there is the poem as a whole which, as an epitaph, is over the tomb; then within the poem the first eight and a half lines serve as a container for the three and a half succeeding ones; and then inside the latter lies Jonson and also his poetry.

But our provisional clarification becomes less satisfactory upon closer inspection, for the contained epitaph proves elusive. Where actually is the buried son? Under his father's epitaph? Under his own epitaph? Are his assigned words to be read or to be heard by the passersby? These questions give even more irony to the double identity of Benjamin junior as son and poem (again, in Greek the identification of poetry and creation). The text then destructures, detextualizes itself, curling like a Möebuis strip and showing the unstable relationship between contents and discontent. The contained epitaph, with its symbolic significance of being placed at the end, is not entirely contained as fiction; Jonson has not wholly released it into a fictional setting. That is, the contained epitaph, both in terms of its terminal location and its resistance to imaginative specificity testifies to Jonson's anal retentive reaction toward his son's death. The concluding epitaph, we can finally say, is quasi-contained within the fictional elaboration of the preceding poem and as such, is like a compromise formation. Though his son has departed, Jonson never fully *loosens* his relationship, and it is that reaction that created the symbolic nuclear principle informing his grander conception of the two epitaphs. To rephrase the governing principle of 'On My First Son' as a Cretan sophism: though the son lies and tells the truth under the epitaph, where do he and the poem lie?

Notes

★ First published in *American Imgo* (1980), 37: 68–81.
1 The most interesting focus of recent criticism has been on the import of its closing couplet. The general reading of this couplet is neatly set forth, though unsympathetically, by Beaurline (1966, p. 67): 'Most readers think that *like* is a weaker form of love, and they imagine that Jonson ends with a cynical turn of thought: he vows that he'll not love as intensely in the future because he has lost his son.' On the other hand, both Beaurline himself and Wesley Trimpi (1962, p. 183) align Jonson's orientation with his specific source in Martial (VI, 29). Thus, according to Beaurline, Jonson's declaration 'means about the same as Martial's line: whatever he loves may never please him too much, may never be the object of self-congratulation. His love has been disciplined so that it will never be a smug or selfish love' (1966, p. 68). Both Francis Fike (1969, pp. 217–219) and W. David Kay (1971, pp. 132–136) give a Christian reading to the last couplet and link it to the religious statements found in the beginning; I cannot see why both readings should not be entertained simultaneously.
2 Citations of Jonson's poetry are from the Herford and Simpson edition.
3 First glossed by Fike (1969, p. 205).
4 The series of fricatives in line 7 is phonically appropriate for the pandemic rage, and the escaped syllable in 'scap'd' is an apt instance of highly artistic elision which skilfully captures the semantics of the very word.
5 Trimpi (1962, p. 183).
6 It's worth remarking that the thematic complexity of the first two couplets is tightened through the polyptoton of its bracketing rhymes, 'ruth' and 'rue.'
7 *Ben Jonson*, 2: 380. Just as erroneous is Trimpi's assertion that 'The feeling is not complicated' (1962, p. 180).

References

Abraham, K. (1927) *Selected Papers*. London, 1927.
Beaurline, L. (1966) The selective principle in Jonson's shorter poems. *Criticism*, 8: 64–74.
Brown, N. (1959) *Life Against Death*. Middletown, Conn.: Wesleyan University Press.
Fike, F. (1969) Ben Jonson's 'On My First Sonne.' *The Gordon Review*, 11: 205–220.
Freud, S. (1908) Character and anal eroticism. *Standard Edition*, 9: 167–175.

—— (1917) On transformations of instinct as exemplified in anal eroticism. *Standard Edition*, 17: 125–133. London: Hogarth Press, 1955.

Jones, E. (1950) *Papers in Psycho-Analysis*. 5th edition. London: Ballière.

Jonson, B. (1925–52) *Ben Jonson*, ed. C. Herford, P. and E. Simpson, 11 vols. Oxford: Clarendon Press.

Kay, W. (1971) The Christian wisdom of Ben Jonson's 'On My First Sonne.' *Studies in English Literature*, 11: 125–136.

Lacan, J. (1966) *Ecrits*. Paris: Editions du Seuil.

Parfitt, G. (1968) The poetry of Ben Jonson. *Essays in Criticism*, 18: 18–31.

—— (1969) Ethical thought and Ben Jonson's poetry. *Studies in English Literature*, 9: 123–134.

—— (1971) Compromise classicism: language and rhythm in Ben Jonson's poetry. *Studies in English Literature*, 11: 109–124.

Trimpi, W. (1962) *Ben Jonson's Poems*. Stanford: Stanford University Press.

Villon's 'La Ballade des Pendus' and its symbolic nuclear principle*

Villon's 'La Ballade des pendus' (The Ballade of the Hanged) has received the highest praise, being classified as 'perhaps the most intensely dramatic of all French medieval poems'[1] and even as 'one of the most moving of all lyric poems to have been written in the French language.'[2] Readers are invariably impressed by the hanged victims' painful awareness of corporeal disintegration. Indeed, they appear to express a helplessness before an array of powers: the power of the potentially vindictive spectators, the power of legal government, the power of natural forces (the winds, rain, sun, and predatory birds) and the decisive power of eternal judgement. But there are more resistant meanings in 'La Ballade des Pendus':

> Freres humains qui après nous vivez,
> N'ayez les cuers contre nous endurcis,
> Car, se pitié de nous povres avez,
> Dieu en aura plus tost de vous mercis.
> Vous nous voyez cy attachez cinq, six;   5
> Quant de la chair, que trop avons nourrie,
> Elle est pieça devorée et pourrie,
> Et nous, les os, devenons cendre et pouldre.
> De nostre mal personne ne s'en rie,
> Mais priez Dieu que tous nous vueille absouldre.   10
>
> Se freres vous clamons, pas n'en devez
> Avoir desdaing, quoy que fusmes occis
> Par justice. Toutesfois, vous sçavez
> Que tous hommes n'ont pas bons sens rassis;
> Excusez nous, puis que sommes transsis,   15

Envers le fils de la Vierge Marie,
Que sa grace ne soit pour nous tarie,
Nous preservant de l'infernale foudre.
Nous sommes mors, ame ne nous harie;
Mais priez Dieu que tous nous vueille absouldre.   20

La pluye nous a debuez et lavez,
Et le soleil dessechiez et noircis;
Pies, corbeaulx, nous ont les yeux cavez,
Et arrachié la barbe et les sourcis.
Jamais nul temps nous ne sommes assis;   25
Puis ça, puis la, comme le vent varie,
A son plaisir sans cesser nous charie,
Plus becquetez d'oiseaulx que dez a couldre.
Ne soiez donc de nostre confrairie;
Mais priez Dieu que tous nous vueille absouldre.   30

Prince Jhesus, qui sur tous a maistrie,
Garde qu'Enfer n'ait de nous seigneurie:
A lui n'ayons que faire ne que souldre.
Hommes, icy n'a point de mocquerie;
Mais priez Dieu que tous nous vueille absouldre.[3]   35

I have translated Villon's 'La Ballade des pendus' as follows:

Human brothers, who live after us,/ Do not have your hearts
hardened against us,/ For, if you pity us poor men,/ God will
sooner have mercy on you./ You see us tied here, five, six./ As for
the flesh which we fed too much,/ It is in pieces, devoured and
rotten,/ And we, the bones, are becoming ashes and dust./ Let no
one laugh at our ill,/ But pray God that He wish to absolve us all.

If we call you brothers, you ought not/ To have disdain,
although we died/ By justice. However, you know/ That all men
are not endowed with good sense;/ Plead, since we are gone,/
With the Son of the Virgin Mary,/ That his grace not be dried up
for us,/ And that He preserve us from the infernal thunder./ We
are dead, let no soul molest us;/ But pray God that He wish to
absolve us all.

The rain has scoured and washed us,/ And the sun dried and
blackened us;/ Magpies and crows have pecked out our eyes,/ And
tore out our beards and eyebrows./ At no time ever are we seated;/
Now here, now there, as the wind varies,/ And without stop, it
drives us about at its pleasure—because of birds, more pitted than
thimbles./ Do not then be of our fraternity;/ But pray God that He
wish to absolve us all.

233

May Prince Jesus, who has supremacy over all,/ Take care that hell does not have dominion over us;/ May we have nothing to do or to account for there./ Men, here is no matter at all for mockery;/ But pray God that He wish to absolve us all.

The range of elements in Villon's short thirty-five line poem comprises an impressive catalogue: life and death; a cosmology extending from earth to hell to heaven; a temporality embracing the past, present, and future; the realms of the physical, the psychical and spiritual; the definite and indefinite; the limited number of condemned, the presumably greater number of spectators, and then all mankind; the world of the inanimate and animate; the egocentric and allocentric; affective tones of fear, pity, sympathy, irony, contriteness, and fraternal love; and finally, description, invocation and exhortation. This striking scope of elements—one could easily go on to name more—is moulded, subtlized, dramatized, and intensified in great part as a result of Villon's handling of the interlocutory frame. Whereas complexity in many lyrics arises from their figurative density, the richness of meaning in Villon's ballade stems prominently from the relationship between speaker (or voice) and addressee; rather than possess a tropical richness in itself, the language of Villon's poem in large part receives it from the interlocutory frame. Our initial task, then, is to explore that frame, and at the same time we can be reasonably assured that we will be concurrently on the right path to trace the poem's symbolic nuclear principle.

David Kuhn, one of the standard authorities on Villon, held that 'in the fiction of the poem, a hanged man speaks for all the "human brothers" '[4]—perhaps here Kuhn was guided by the poem's iconographic tradition and the famous woodcut, attached to the poem from the very beginning, which showed but one hanged victim on the Parisian gibbet. But the truth of the matter is that the very identity of the speaker in 'The Ballade of the Hanged' is somewhat vague, for it is not at all clear whether the speaking voice is singular and therefore representing the hanged group, or whether the voice is choral, i.e. the group itself is speaking. Neither is the definite number of the hanged given—there may be five or six. Accumulatively, such indefiniteness serves to underscore the alienation of the plightful voice.

For purposes of convenient reference, however, let us assume that the voice has a plural identity. Our next concern then has to do with the intriguing nature of their existence, for if we listen closely to how they speak, we realize that we experience a shifting identity. Accordingly the speakers may be simply ravaged bodies—they refer

234

to themselves as 'us, the bones.' Second, the speakers may be souls, and thus they refer to their having departed (*transsis*). Third, as combined entities, they address the spectators as 'human brothers.' In sum, there is a shifting nature or instability inherent in the very fictivity of the speakers in the poem.

Without resolving anything more about the speakers' identity for the moment, let us pass on to the challenge encountered when we try to demarcate the addressee. Quite clearly, in the octave of the first three stanzas, the addressee merely consists of those who look ('you see us'). But in each stanza, the penultimate and last or refrain lines, which constitute a syntactic unit, contain an evolving referent and addressee (whereas poets frequently achieve variation in meaning by changing one or more words in a refrain, Villon succeeded with the feat of effecting a semantic change in identical refrains or, paradoxically speaking, effecting a non-repetitiveness in repetition). In Villon's refrain specifically, 'tous nous' (us all) accumulates meaning until, by line 35, it includes the hanged, the spectators, and mankind in general. This triple reference is to be found in the previous refrains but at various emerging levels, ranging from suggestion to secondary to primary and surface meaning. At first, only the spectators are exhorted, are spoken *to* in the first three stanzas; those same spectators, along with others, are spoken *about* in the epithet 'tous nous' (us all).

Another way of analyzing the epithet *tous nous* (us all) lies in considering its components individually. In the first three stanzas, excepting the refrains, *nous* is utilized exclusively to refer to the hanged; the spectators are indicated by *vous* (see esp. lines 1–5, 11, 13, 15, 19 and 29). The sole use of *tous* is logically distributed, alluding to all mankind; hence *tous hommes* (all men, line 14) is an instance which contributes, albeit quietly, to the evolving amplification of *tous nous*. But with the closing of the poem, the pronominal components of the refrain epithet *tous nous* are linearly separated and appear in order of occurrence in the beginning of the envoi (lines 31–32). We quickly comprehend that *tous*, having progressed from an intensifier to a pronoun with independent status, means all mankind (line 31), while *nous* primarily refers to the hanged and secondarily includes the immediate spectators (line 32). Yet *tous* and *nous*, though epithetical components that are now separated, are nevertheless bound to each other by virtue of a certain syntactical and semantic dexterity: they are both set in displaced prepositional phrases found in parallel location before *seignurie* (dominion) and *maistrie* (supremacy), which in turn are rhyming synonyms. The fractionalization of the pronominal construct, then, is partly a linear effect, preparing for the last line where the epithet is found intact once more. Opposed to its previous occurrences, the *tous nous* in the last refrain now embraces the hanged, the spectators, and mankind all as primary references.

Coming to the suferficially simple last five lines of the envoi, we observe that there are two addressees. The first is another hanged victim, Jesus; the second is all mankind (*hommes*). The latter nomination, emphasizing the primordial and bare existence of man as man, is obviously a wider reference than the 'human brothers' (*freres humains*) invoked in line 1. In parallel fashion, the more individualized 'Let no one laugh at our ill' has been transformed into the generalizing and more inclusive declaration 'here is no matter for mockery.' With the penultimate line, the voice directly addresses mankind at large—in effect, all who read the poem as well. In the addressee situation, therefore, there has been a transition from the internal to the external interlocutorship, from spectators to readers. Summarily, in the envoi, whereas the explicit addressee or second person extends from Jesus to all mankind, the *tous nous* (us all) in its potential as a first, second, and third person referent has semantically evolved so that addressers, addressees, and personal referents are fused. In that way, we see, the speakers' traumatizing state of fragmentation and alienation is held in check.

Let us now view from another angle the manoeuvres enlisted by the speakers to control the helplessness of their plight. On one hand, they invoked both human and divine understanding and mercy. They resorted to somewhat of a superior position in counseling the onlookers to pray, to demand pardon also for themselves, a pardon forthcoming that much 'sooner' on the express condition that they themselves show clemency to those condemned by legal authority.

The greatest superior of the hanged, however, is manifest in the irony undercutting the overt comradery of the following asservation:

> Toutesfois, vous sçavez
> Que tous hommes n'ont pas bons sens rassis
> (However, you know/ That all men are not endowed
> with good sense).

Do the spectators *know*? According to strict logic, Villon's universal statement is a sophistical one, being either distributed or undistributed. Hence it may mean *no* man has good judgment, or some men have no *good* judgment. Guided by this ironical strategy, Villon put this logically ambiguous statement after the speakers' declaration that they were killed *Par justice*. Now if all men lack judgment, the hanged possibly were not killed by justice but by injustice. And on the other hand, the hanged have judgment where the spectators do not, for implicitly throughout the poem the latter are asked to have good judgment.

All these attitudes entertained by the voice are gnomically found in the initial appellation *Freres humains*. On the simple descriptive level, the spectators are brothers insofar as they are part of humanity. The crux, though, is whether the *Freres humains* is a mere vocative or whether in fact it also contains a submerged imperative: that is, do be human brothers and become pitiful. In this regard we must perceive that line 3 reads, '*If* you pity us.' The dual interpretation of *Freres humains*, then, is not just a speculative or capricious one, but is highly significant, and indeed is further underscored in the poem. Thus the second stanza begins with a hedged utterance, 'If we call you brothers'; in contrast, the next stanza avoids any initial fraternal address, only to end with a somewhat derisive pun, 'Do not be then of our fraternity (*confrairie*).'

Since one of the rhetorical ends of the poem is that the spectators *become* brothers, the inaugural *freres* is not a fait accompli. In that light, the poem's four stanzas constitute a piece of deliberative rhetoric which attempts to persuade the spectators, as I have said, to render sympathy. But what is important here to note is that Villon with masterful irony turned the begging of a question into a bold and successful tactic: dramatically, the vocative, which inaugurates the poem and which is voiced by the hanged, should be one of the resolutions made by the spectators. The adjective *humains* participates in the charged meaning of *freres*: whether it be in medieval Latin, English or French, *humain* could signify either 'benevolent' or 'having the characteristics of a rational being.'[5] The ironical strategy of the poem dictates that both meanings are applicable and not applicable to the speakers and to their terrestrial addressees. It becomes clear, then, that the speakers, afflicted by alienation and reduced to being part objects in a most visual sense, strive to reacquire self-esteem by identifying with the spectators, an identification which is controlled by irony. Such a dynamic constellation comprises the poem's symbolic nuclear principle.

However subtle be Villon's mastery of the interlocutory frame in order to contain anxiety in the fantasized scene, his use of phonemic structures is even subtler. Spatially the poem contrasts the presence of hereness (*ici*) of the victims on the gibbet and an elsewhere, be it the location of the spectators or the posthumous destiny of the victims. The phonemic cluster *ci* (here) echoing throughout words in each stanza stress the spatiality:

st. 1	endurcis	st. 2	se
	se		occis
	mercis		rassis
	cy		transsis
	six		

st. 3	noircis	envoi	icy
	sourcis		
	assis		

Of all these lexical items, it is *transsis* (gone, departed) that captures much of the poem's spatial tension. Although phonemically incorporating *ci*, *transsis* bears the opposite meaning, i.e. away from here. And the hanged demand pardon precisely because they are departed.

From the speakers' point of view, their anxiogenic hereness stands apart from a threatening whereness. Stressing that threatening spatiality is the *où* (where) which echoes throughout the poem:

st. 1	nous	st. 2	vous
	nous		toutesfois vous
	nous		tous
	vous		nous
	vous nous		pour nous
	nourrie		nous . . . fouldre
	pourrie		nous . . . nous
	nous		tous nous . . . absouldre
	pouldre		
	tous nous . . . absouldre		

st. 3	nous	envoi	tous
	nous		nous
	sourcis		souldre
	nous		tous nous . . . absouldre
	nous		
	couldre		
	tous nous . . . absouldre		

Going deeper into the poem, we realize that the recurrent *ou*, if not accented, is the disjunctive *or*. We realize even further that the disjunctive and spatial obstacle between speakers and addressees is overcome through the unifying epithet *tous nous* (us all). The final answer, then, to the spatial problem of departing from here (*transsis*) is that there be a community (*tous nous*) prayer for absolution (*absouldre*); with absolution, the posthumous whereness is no longer a source of fear. The word *absouldre*, let us note, comes from the

238

Latin *solvere*, 'to melt'; such a meaning must be brought to bear on the distanciation involved in the spectators' hard (*endurcis*) heart and the speakers' bony remains, for with absolution for all, they will not be alienated from one another. To put it succinctly, the spatial concepts *ici/où* (here/where), which point to the speakers' anxiety and which ring throughout the ballade, are highlighted by their lexical assimilation into *transsis* and *absouldre* that respectively specify and resolve in a semantic sense the problems posed by space.

In similar fashion, the antipodal nature of the possible reactions of the spectators—disdain or pity—is phonemically woven into the poem. The disdain of course is represented by the rhyme *s'en rie* (laugh at), and doubly so in the word *mocque/rie* (mockery); *rie*, moreover, echoes as a rhyme ending three times in each of the four stanzas. But what is even more striking, the ideal outcome that the spectators should pray and not laugh is further stressed by the phonemic assimilation of *rie* (laugh) in the reiterated supplication *priez* (pray)!

To conclude: Villon contains the trauma of fragmentation and various kinds of exclusion by means of integrative subtleties in both the interlocutory and phonemic organizations of the poem. The desire for rapprochement that semantically defines those organizations is modulated by irony, which keynotes the speakers' refusal to assume a servile position. In the elaboration of the poem's symbolic nuclear principle, we might add, Villon succeeded masterfully in exploiting the rhymes and refrains, the strategic points of the ballade.

Notes

★ First published in an expanded and somewhat altered form in the *Canadian Review of Comparative Literature* (1974), 1: 22–37.
1 Fox (1962, p. xx).
2 Ibid., p. 28.
3 For the text of Villon, see Villon (1923).
4 Kuhn (1967, p. 454). Cf. also the confusion of Siciliano (1934, p. 278).
5 Whereas modern French retains the double meaning, modern English from about 1700 has orthographically distinguished between 'human' (characteristic of mankind) and 'humane' (benevolent).

References

Fox, J. (1962) *The Poetry of Villon*. London: Thomas Nelson.

Kuhn, D. (1967) *La Poétique de François Villon.* Paris: Armand Colin.

Siciliano, I. (1934) *François Villon et les thèmes du moyen âge.* Paris: Armand Colin.

Villon, F. (1923) *Oeuvres: édition critique avec notices,* ed. L. Thausne. Paris: Picard.

13

Women's discourse and literature: the question of nature and culture*

In examining the content and form of woman's expression in terms of whether any differences may be exclusively due to culture and not to nature, I want to emphasize that my simple aim is to advance several considerations and to sharpen the focus of some initial questions. Right away I admit that the vastness of the subject makes me uncomfortable, reminding me of the anecdote of the driver who asked directions from a Vermont farmer and was told: 'Well, now, if I wanted to go where you want to go, I wouldn't start from here.'[1] Speaking for myself, I can start only from where I am and from what I have, with the restless solace that my thinking on the subject continues to change.

Nature vs. art, a dichotomy dominant in Greek and Roman thought as well as in Renaissance culture, has now evolved into nature vs. culture, a challenging antithesis for all contemporary sciences. We all are familiar with the aporias encountered by investigators who try to arrive at laws which are not culture-bound, and we can readily think of the glib generalizations and naive assumptions of former ages in their facile descriptions of the so-called innate in the human being and the harmony of that innateness with world order. Disillusionment about such preordained order and harmony, Freud told us, imposed three narcissistic wounds on the human race. The first of course was the heliocentric finding by the Polish astronomer Nicolaus Copernicus in the sixteenth century, which demonstrated that our planet was not the center of the universe. The second blow was Darwinism, which destroyed the illusion that we forever maintained a detached and superior position in the animal kingdom. The third revolutionary decentering was

241

psychoanalysis itself, showing us how our reason is enslaved by our drives.[2] We are now undergoing a fourth truthful upheaval, one which would have shaken Freud himself, namely, the uncovering of our neurotic, androcentric, phallocentric, and phallogocentric history.

A difference among feminists who actively take a stand against the androcentric tradition is that American women stress the history of their social oppression whereas French feminists emphasize unconscious repression.[3] When it comes to the question of discourse proper, many of my reflections were stimulated by the differences of opinion among French female writers. Some, such as Catherine Clément, Marguerite Yourcenar,[4] Simone de Beauvoir and Julia Kristeva,[5] deny that there is a special female literary language *per se*. On the other hand, others such as Hélène Cixous,[6] Luce Irigaray[7] and Claudine Herrmann[8] conceive of a special female language which is related to the female body.[9] As I understand them, to write like a true woman means avoiding linear rationality and centeredness and instead, endorsing decentralization, fragmentation and multiplicity. On this matter, let us listen for a minute to Hélène Cixous:

> Nearly the entire history of writing is confounded with history of reason, of which it is at once the effect, the support, and one of the privileged alibis. It has been one with the phallocentric tradition . . . By writing her self, woman will return to the body which has been more than confiscated from her . . . Women must write through their bodies, they must invent the impregnable language that will wreck partitions, classes, and rhetorics, regulations and codes . . . There is always within her at least a little of that good mother's milk. She writes in white ink [1976, pp. 879, 881, 886].

Faced with such dramatic introspective comments as the foregoing, I could not escape the divisive question: Which commentators were accurately describing the role of women's body in their writing? I eventually became confirmed in my initial assumption that the two apparently mutually exclusive positions could be reconciled, but for a while I was caught up in stressing the sheerly cultural element in woman's language and in the linguistic evaluation of that language.

Otto Jespersen's pioneer essay, 'The Woman,' written in the second decade of this century,[10] shows us that linguistics itself is subject to an androcentric ideology. After cavalierly congratulating women for their 'instinctive shrinking from coarse and gross expressions' (1921, p. 246), Jespersen's chauvinism becomes ever more gross:

Men will certainly with great justice object that there is a danger of the language becoming languid and insipid if we [note the implied readership!] are always to content ourselves with women's expressions . . . Men thus become the chief innovators by which we sometimes see one term replace an older one . . . Most of those who are in the habit of reading in foreign languages will have experienced a much greater average difficulty in books written by males than by female authors, because they contain many more words, dialect words, technical terms, etc . . . we have here a trait that is [partly] independent of education [pp. 247–248].

To cap it all, when Jespersen attempts to demonstrate that women characteristically express themselves in broken sentences, he cites as primary sources excerpts of female dialogue drawn from fictional literature written by male authors (1921, pp. 250–251).

Since Jespersen we have met with a great deal of research on women's language and its social determinants, taking account of such variables as the channel of communication, the setting and participants, the subject, purpose, genre, lexicality, grammar and phonology. As part of the micropolitical structure, language both conveys and enacts all kinds of social inequalities, including that between the sexes. This inequality manifests in discourse through the phenomenon whereby 'personal information flows opposite to the flow of authority,' for example, individuals in a corporation are more self-disclosing to the immediate superior than to their own immediate subordinates.[11]

A contentious study in this area is Robin Lakoff's *Language and Woman's Place* (1975), which proposes that the differences in the speech of the North American woman constitute a very genderlect, and indeed of an inferior, second-class kind. According to Lakoff, woman's insecurity in her genderlect is shown not only in her rising final intonational patterns but also in the frequency of tag questions (e.g. It's true, isn't it?). It may be countered, however, that tag questions and rising finals, rather than showing lack of confidence, demonstrate that the nature of woman's discourse is essentially a dialogue, an opening out onto the other, and hence opposed to the declarative, authoritative style of many males.[12]

For purposes of contextualization, we might for a moment refer to two historical examples of the subversive impact of male discourse. First, in a series of writings which deserve to be better known, Ong shows how Latin as a male sex-linked language has left its imprint even on today's culture.[13] Briefly, from the sixth to the ninth century of our era, Latin changed from being a mother tongue to becoming a vernacular such as Italian, Spanish, French or Roumanian. To be sure, Learned Latin continued, but only as a chirographically controlled language taught in an extradomestic, extrafamilial setting. Prior to the sixth century, Latin had been spoken by millions, literate or illiterate. But thereafter, with the rise of the vernacular, Latin, now Learned, would be spoken only by those who could write it. For roughly a millennium in European history, right up to the seventeenth century, women were mostly unilingual whereas educated men were bilingual, using the vernacular as well as Latin. In this context, learning Latin had the trappings of a puberty rite, *un rite de passage*. To master it one had to depart from home where women were retained and go to school, an institution restricted to male teachers and pupils. Discipline and beating accompanied the teaching of Latin, which permitted access to abstract tribal lore. Besides being a linguistic badge of male identity, Latin served as a sex-restrictive passport into a world where males controlled the educational, diplomatic, medical, clerical and legal life.

Girls typically learned at home rather than in schools, and indeed, throughout the Middle Ages and Renaissance the vernacular romances were in large part kept alive by a female audience. With the advent of the nineteenth century, a configurational pattern emerged between the entrance of women into institutions of formal education and the gradual yielding of Latin before the status of the mother tongue in those institutions. Within this perspective we better understand the rise of Anglo-American New Criticism in the 1920's and 1930's. The sensitivity of this criticism to ambiguity and multiple denotation and connotation grew out of vernacular soil; a poetics focusing on nuanced connotation could hardly emerge in direct response to a language learned from books. In sum, we are justified in perceiving a line of development extending over 1,500 years from the emergence of male-sexed Latin to the rise of New Criticism in our own time.

As the second example of the subversiveness in male discourse, suffice it to mention briefly Freud's Irma dream which I analyzed in Chapter 5. I might re-emphasize, however, that the dominating male doctor is factual, logical, and accusatory while his female patient is subordinately pleading, suffering, illogical, defensive, and pained by an unfulfillable wish addressed to a self-righteous male authority.[14] As we reflect on this capital instance of grammatical subversiveness in one of the foremost books written in modern times, we become more aware of the all-pervasiveness and sometimes very hidden reaches of male dominating discourse, only to find ourselves today at the beginning of a long process of detection and uprooting that will take many decades to come.

The socio-cultural considerations of my last two examples might urge us to ask again but with greater urgency, Are there any innate psychological differences specific to women, and related to these differences, is there a quintessentially female discourse? In the three-tiered schema of soma, psyche, and discourse, we quickly discard any one-to-one correlation but if we pause to reflect on the possible correlation of overall Gestalts or of selected differentia, we do not meet with experiential circumstances that facilitate sure inductions. Some recent research has claimed that the defense systems of three-year-old children differ according to their sex and that little girls' defenses have a more pronounced orientation toward introjection. But to such a conclusion one may object that already at three or four the processes of acculturation and socialization have already left a decisive impression. And one might object even more vigorously by alluding to filmic studies showing how parents react differently according to the sex of a child within the very instants following its birth.[15]

A promising path out of this problematic morass has been opened up by such genderologists as Robert Stoller[16] and others. Using sex strictly in a biological sense, they understand, for example, female sexuality as a factorial of hormones, chromosomes, gonads (ovaries), external genitals (vulva and vagina) and internal apparatus (uterus and tubes). Although this biological anlage forms part of gender identity, it is not the main component. Gender identity is mainly psychological in nature, arising from learning experiences beginning with sex assignment at birth and including subsequent parental attitudes and the child's developing body ego. Stoller finds in women a core gender identity called primary femininity, formed in the first few years of life. This finding is a far cry from Freud's contention that there is no real femininity until the phallic phase; but more than that, since the mother is the first object, girls tend to be more confident of their femininity than boys of their masculinity. Criticising Freud's 'penile semantics'[17] and his tenet about a child's primary identification with the father, the French psychoanalyst Colette Chiland explained:

> Regression to a primary identification with the mother carries a danger for both sexes . . . One can understand that envy of femaleness should be more deeply repressed than penis envy, that phallic over-cathexis of the visible penis should protect against the invisible and fruitful power of the maternal belly.[18]

Evidence for the early gender identity comes from some of the most serious research to date. A nine-year study of some seventy children showed that genital awareness emerges from sixteen to nineteen

245

months of age,[19] an observation harmonizing with the data of John Money and Ankle Ehrhardt of the Johns Hopkins Psychohormonal Research Unit, who found that beyond the age of eighteen months successful sex reassignment is problematic; more to our interest, they found that language development was the chief factor determining that cut-off period.[20] Said in other words:

> Imprinting regarding gender identity and gender-role differentiation is closely linked with the timing of language acquisition. The baby begins to develop a gender-differentiated self-concept under the stimulus of sex-coded social interaction at approximately the same time that he/she begins to acquire native language. This timing is illustrated in the case of babies with ambiguous genitalia. Neonatal freedom to decide on a sex of rearing congruent with surgical and hormonal options diminishes with each month of age until it is nearly impossible to reverse a decision after the 18th month. Up until that time, the best option can be chosen, even if it requires a reannouncement of the sex assigned at birth. After 18 months of age, sex reassignment is as potentially disastrous as it would be to an ordinary adult.[21]

This coincidence of language and gender acquisition shares a common timing with the end of the mirror stage at approximately eighteen months when, for Lacan, the child recognizes that his parents do not respond fully to his inarticulate demands and enters into the problematic sexualization and discourse of the Symbolic Order.[22]

Language acquisition around this time is extraordinarily metaphorical for the child, whose very act of enunciation, regardless of the content, is full of symbolic value. In my thinking here I have been influenced by that remarkable essay, 'Psycho-physical Problems Revealed in Language,' written by Ella Freeman Sharpe. Sharpe endorses the notion that we cannot study metaphor very long without arriving at the borderline of sanity and that metaphor is as ultimate as speech and, conversely, speech is as ultimate as thought. In this view, metaphor evolves in language only when the bodily orifices are controlled:

> At the same time as sphincter control over anus and urethra is being established, the child is acquiring the power of speech, and so an avenue of 'outer-ance' present from birth becomes of immense importance. First of all the discharge of feeling tension, when this is no longer relieved by physical discharge, can take place through speech. The activity of speaking is substituted for

the physical activity now restricted at other openings of the body, while words themselves become the very substitutes for the bodily substances.[23]

At the base of this kaleidoscopic interchange is the mouth, the very cradle of perception.[24] These various factors explain the libidinalization of the act of utterance itself at various phases set off as the oral, urethral,[25] anal,[26] phallic, and genital.[27] Likewise silence, which serves to punctuate the smaller and larger units of discourse, has also been identified in varius libidinal phases ranging from the early oral to the genital.[28] The combination of these multiple factors surely has a direct impact on a woman's freedom in creativity and on the symbolic relationship to her literary product but, as far as I can see, has no necessary or predictable specific manifestation on any particular formal elements of composition.

In dealing with the global effect of positive identity on woman's discourse and writing, we cannot neglect the concept of inner space invoked by Erikson.[29] For Erikson, anatomy is destiny to the extent that 'it determines not only the range and configuration of physiological functioning and its limitations but also, to an extent, personality configurations' (1963, p. 285); accordingly part of female psychology may be grounded in the sense of inner space. Although Erikson makes a welcome theoretical shift of emphasis away from the negative Freudian stress on the loss of an external member, a position which leaves womanhood at best with a 'ubiquitous compensation neurosis,' he is equally guilty of an unjustified inferential leap. For his contention that the richly convex parts of female anatomy suggest 'fullness, warmth, and generosity' and that 'the very existence of the inner productive space exposes women early to a specific kind of loneliness, to a fear of being left empty or deprived of treasures, of remaining unfulfilled or drying up,' Erikson was taken to task by Kate Millett who amusingly pursued his fancy: 'By rough computation, a woman menstruates some 450 times in her life. One begins to grasp the multiple sorrow of this many bereavements, that many children she didn't bear . . . a demographer's nightmare.'[30] The concept of inner space, nevertheless remains highly valuable, though we must be vigilant about any subversive metaphorical extension. The use of woman's inner space to justify enclosing her within a domestic setting and industrial or professional service roles is unwarrantable either socially, morally, or linguistically.

Apart from the inner space specific to woman there is a series of other psychological factors which, though common to both sexes, enables us to appreciate the vicissitudes of the body image in woman's writing. The varying body image in altered and deepened states of consciousness can affect writing much as it can affect clinical free associations, to which literature has often been compared. The manifestation of the body image varies in accordance with the four Jungian types.[31] That is to say, although we are directed by the functions of thinking, feeling, intuition, and sensation, individuals differ as to the predominance of any one; and in particular, the somatically drenched free associations of the sensation type are characteristically of another order than the clinical discourse of the intellectual type. Apart from these factors, the developmental capacities, the phase of libidinal arrest and libidinal fixation,[32] early trauma, the valence of introjects, and the capacity and quality of partial regression also determine a female writer's estimate about the union of her own body and literary corpus. The resultant constellation of these factors and the primordial relationship of language with other body products may in some general sense influence a writer's tropes, especially if they are shaped by primary rather than secondary process. We must not forget, furthermore, that the designed or unintentional presence of body image in one's writing is influenced by that phenomenon whereby 'in the process of writing, voyeurism is changed into exhibitionism.'[33] Object relations bear not only on the effect of writing but also its origin. Here we can do no better than to listen to the concise lucidity of Julia Kristeva:

> For men, artistic creation has its roots in the pre-oedipal stage and the dominant relationship of female to male. What happens to men who are artists is that while in the process of creation, they bring back the emotional trauma of their own mother–son relationship. In fact it is this psychological structure which is at the base of Western Art, and is particularly obvious in avant-garde art. Women on the other hand experience the incestuous relationship somewhat differently. For them there is a kind of identification with the mother and a realization that the daughter's body like that of the mother is maternal.[34]

Kristeva's provocative comments on creativity and discourse become further pertinent with our recourse to an uncanny etymology. Over 4,000 years ago, in the kingdom of Lagesh, the word *freedom* appeared for the first time in recorded history. *Freedom* in that ancient Sumerian language is written *Amargi*, which literally means 'return to the mother' (S. Kramer, 1963). The matrix of mother and freedom can tell us endlessly about our own native tongue (in the unique experience of psychoanalytic treatment, we learn our mother tongue twice).

In conclusion, if we let our minds freely roam through the foregoing discussion, the following distinctions impose themselves. Women's literature necessitates analysis not only of its content and form but also of the symbolic meaning attributable to the very act of its expression, be it in writing or in speech. If there be genderlect differences in the content and form, we may generally look to socioeconomic phenomena as the decisive factors. Lexical, morphological, and syntactical features may constitute a genderlect, then, but that genderlect is a question of nurture, not nature. But when we turn to certain linguistic productions, ranging from 'primitive' free association to aesthetic discourse, we soon meet with considerations which are of similar order to that of early language acquisition. Body image and inner space are prominent determinants of the symbolic meaning underlying the enunciation *qua* enunciation of these special linguistic productions. As we remember, the biological anlage forms a part, albeit minor, of core gender identity; nature is present, but subordinate to nurture. One last point remains. Although alliable with lexicality, the use of tropes nevertheless, especially when characterized by primary process and instinctual motivation, may give evidence of early gender identity formation and partake of the same symbolic meanings inherent in certain enunciatory acts.

Notes

★ First published in *Contemporary Psychoanalysis* (1983), 19: 444–459.

1 The anecdote comes from Erik Erikson (1963, p. 265).

2 Uncannily enough, Freud alludes to the three narcissistic blows three times: (*Standard Edition*, 16: 285); 'A Difficulty in the Path of Psycho-analysis' (*Standard Edition*, 17: 136–143; 'The Resistances to Psycho-analysis' (*Standard Edition*, 19: 221).

3 Cf. Elaine Marks (1978).

4 See the responses to a distributed questionnaire, reported in *La Quinzaine Littéraire*, Aug. 1974, pp. 27–30.

5 See 'China, Women and the Symbolic: An Interview with Julia Kristeva' by Josette Féral (1976) *Sub-stance*, 13: 9–18.

6 Cf. her 'The Laugh of Medusa' (1976); Christiane Makward's (1976) 'Interview with Hélène Cixous,' *Sub-stance*, 13: 19–37; 'Rethinking Differences: An Interview,' *Homosexualities and French Literature: Cultural Contexts/Critical Texts*, ed. G. Stambolian and E. Marks (1979). Ithaca, N.Y.: Cornell University Press, pp. 70–86.

7 See esp. Irigaray (1974).

8 See 'Le sexe du langage,' *Quinzaine Littéraire*, Aug. 1974: pp. 25–27 and Herrmann (1976).

9 'Concerning the related issue of sexual taboo words, Elaine Schowalter promotes the need of women to create their own lexicon for the body: Women beginning to experiment with sexual vocabulary violate these cultural taboos; and of course, our sexual vocabulary has become so brutalized and misogynistic that it presents serious obstacles to the woman artist. But a literature which attempts to deal comprehensively with female experience must create a vocabulary for the body. We have been trained to think of our bodies in prepositions, like Donne: "License my roaming hands and let them go/ Before, behind, between, above, below." The process of naming will be awkward for a while, perhaps, but it is fundamental to an autonomous female art' ('Literary Criticism: A Review,' *Signs*, 1975, 1: 451–452.

10 The essay is chapter 13 in Jespersen (1921).

11 See the comments of N. Henley and E. Goffman (1975) cited in the survey by Thorne and Henley (1975, pp. 14–15, 26, 190). A summary follow-up to this encyclopaedic source is Kramer, Thorne, and Henley (1970). Cf. also Yaguello (1978).

12 See the statement of Ellen Morgan cited by Thorne and Henley (1975, p. 25) and the stimulating book review by Sally McConnell-Ginet (1975).

13 Among Ong's works, cf. esp. *The Barbarian Within* (1962, pp. 210–212); *In the Human Grain* (1976, p. 21); *The Presence of the Word* (1967, pp. 76–77, 241–255); *Rhetoric, Romance and Technology* (1971, pp. 65–66, 113–141); *Interfaces of the Word* (1977, pp. 25–31, 216–217).

14 That Irma and Freud's wife were pregnant makes his chauvinism that much more chauvinistic.

15 With the ability of current technology to detect the sex of the fetus and with our knowledge that the fetus reacts to sensory data from both inside and outside the womb, consideration of exogenetic factors must be pushed back to the pre-natal horizon. And in keeping with the not so utopic eventuality of predetermining an offspring's sexual identification, our prospect will be turned back to the time of preconception and, to pun seriously, we must then revise our preconception about preconception. Yet before this regression issue as to where would innate begin and how would we conceive it, epistemological reflection about innateness is turned out of whack; a start is no longer *ab ovo*, and questions about precedence among chickens and eggs become cheaper by the dozen.

16 For recent summary articles by Stoller, see his 'Primary Femininity' (1977) and 'Femininity' (1980).

17 Cf. Joel Fineman (1966).

18 Chiland (1980).

19 See Galenson and Roiphe (1980). As a demonstration of the marked

influence of a mother's sexual fantasies on her child, the authors cited the repetitive intense genital cleansing by some mothers in contrast to the nigh complete avoidance of that area by others.

20 See their *Man and Woman, Boy and Girl* (1972).
21 Baill and Money (1980, pp. 51–52).
22 Cf. Stuart Schneiderman's (1980) Introduction to *Returning to Freud*.
23 Ella Sharpe, *Collected Papers on Psycho-analysis* (1968).
24 René Spitz, 'The Primal Cavity': A Contribution to the Genesis of Perception and Its Role for Psychoanalytic Theory' (1955).
25 Robert Fliess, 'Silence and Verbalization' (1949).
26 Karl Abraham (1927, p. 380).
27 Fliess (1949, p. 28). Cf. Annie Anzieu (1977, p. 156):

L'organisation linguistique du langage féminin inclut la représentation inconsciente de soi, déterminée par la cavité génitale. Alors que chez l'homme on peut reconnaître aisément que puissance verbale est équivalent de puissance phallique.

28 Cf. Fliess (1949, pp. 23–25); C. Van der Heide (1961); Merloo (1964, p. 21); Mahony (1979).
29 'Womanhood and Inner Space' (1963). For an elaboration of different kinds of inner space (oral, anal, genital, mastic, etc.) among both women and men, see Judith Kestenberg (1968) and Tor-Bjorn Hågglund *et al.* (1978). Cf. esp. p. 74: 'As a psychic trait, motherhood bases itself obviously quite equally on *identification and the psycho-physical development of the inner space*. It is more prominently manifest in women than in men but it, nevertheless, not totally bound to sex nor only to its own biological species.'
30 *Sexual Politics* (1971, p. 218). Over a decade after his first article, Erikson resumed his thinking in 'Once More the Inner Space' (1975, pp. 225–247). Although he is now more cautious, I believe that he is still guilty of overstatement and metaphorical extension. But in one place he insightfully supplements the Freudian penis envy assigned exclusively to women with inter-male penis envy as well as 'probably . . . a deep envy for the maternal capacity' (p. 238). The point is well taken and serves to correct a Western prejudice as old as Aristotle which gives a one-sided male description of woman's insufficiency. I think it would not only be amusing but profitable to turn the tables around and define man exclusively in negative terms, as lacking maternal inner space, and then to measure the impact of a discourse extended along these lines. At any event, the envy of penis, breast and uterus exists in *both* sexes. Erikson speaks inconsistently of body part (penis envy) and function (maternal capacity); were he to have drawn a tight logical parallel and thereby to have spoken about penis functions, he would have realized other complications in his linkage.

31 See Jung (1921). Unfortunately most analysts of non-Jungian orientation have neglected the potential applications of this book.
32 Cf. Erikson's well-said distinction:

> In our general clinical usage we employ the term fixation alternatively for that infantile state in which an individual received the relatively greatest amount of gratification and to which, therefore, his secret wishes persistently return and for that infantile stage of development beyond which he is unable to proceed because it marked an end or determined slow-up of his psychosexual maturation. I would prefer to call the latter the point of *arrest*, for it seems to me that an individual's psychosexual character and proneness for disturbances depends not so much on the point of fixation as on the *range* between the point of fixation and the point of arrest, and on the *quality* of the interplay [1954, p. 5].

33 Bergler (1949, p. 189).
34 Interview, *Sub-stance*, 13: 16.

References

Abraham, K. (1921) Contributions to the theory of the anal character. In: *Selected Papers on Psycho-analysis*. London: Hogarth Press, 1927, pp 370–392.

Anzieu, A. (1977) Des mots et des femmes. *Nouvelle Revue Française de Psychoanalyse*, 16: 151–168.

Baill, C. and Money, J. (1980) Physiological aspects of female sexual development: conception through puberty. In: M. Kirkpatrick (ed.), *Women's Sexual Development*, New York: Plenum, pp. 61–76.

Bergler, E. (1949) *The Basic Neurosis: Oral Regression and Psychic Mechanism.* New York: Grune & Stratton.

Chiland, C. (1980) Clinical practice, theory and their relationship in regard to female sexuality. *International Journal of Psycho-Analysis*, 61: 359–366.

Cixous, H. (1976) Interview. *Sub-stance*, 13: 9–18.

—— (1976) The laugh of Medusa. *Signs*, 1: 875–893.

—— (1979) Rethinking differences: an interview. In: G. Stambolian and E. Marks (eds.), *Homosexualities and French Literature: Cultural Contexts/ Critical Contexts*. Ithaca, New York: Cornell University Press, pp. 70–86.

Erikson, E. (1954) The dream specimen of analysis. *Journal of the American Psycho-Analytic Association*, 2: 5–56.

—— (1963) Womanhood and inner space. In: *Identity: Youth and Crisis*. New York: Norton, 1968, pp. 261–294.

—— (1975) *Life History and the Historical Moment*. New York: W.W. Norton.

Fineman, J. (1966) Psychoanalysis, bisexuality, and the difference before the sexes. In: M. Nelson and J. Ikenberry (eds.), *Psychosexual Perspectives*. New York: Human Science Press.

Fliess, R. (1949) Silence and verbalization: a supplement to the theory of the analytic rule. *International Journal of Psycho-Analysis*, 30: 21–30.

Freud, S. (1916–1917) *Introductory lectures on psycho-analysis. Standard Edition*, 16. London: Hogarth Press, 1963.

—— (1917) A difficulty in the path of psycho-analysis. *Standard Edition*, 17: 137–144. London: Hogarth Press, 1955.

—— (1925) The resistances to psycho-analysis. *Standard Edition*, 19: 213–222. London: Hogarth Press, 1961.

Galenson, E. and Roiphe, H. (1980) Some suggested revisions concerning early female development. In: M. Kirkpatrick (ed.), *Women's Sexual Development*. New York: Plenum, pp. 83–106.

Hågglund, T.B. *et al.* (1978) Some viewpoints on women's inner space. *Scandinavian Psychoanalytic Review*, 1: 65–77.

Herrmann, C. (1976) *Les voleuses de langue*. Paris: Editions des Femmes.

Irigaray, L. (1974) *Speculum de l'autre femme*. Paris: Editions de Minuit.

Jespersen, O. (1921) *Language: Its Nature, Development and Origin*. London: Macmillan.

Jung, C. (1921) Psychological types. *The Collected Works of C.G. Jung*, vol. 6. Princeton: Princeton University Press, 1971.

Kestenberg, J. (1968) Outside and inside, male and female. *Journal of the American Psycho-Analytic Association*, 16: 457–520.

Kristeva, J. (1976) China, women and the symbolic: an interview. *Substance*, 13: 9–18.

Kramer, C., Thorne, B. and Henley, N. (1970) Perspectives in language and communication. *Signs*, 3: 638–651.

Kramer, S. (1963) *The Sumerians: Their History, Culture and Character*. Chicago: Chicago University Press.

Lakoff, R. (1975) *Language and Woman's Place*. New York: Harper & Row.

McConnell-Ginet, S. (1975) Our father tongue; essays in linguistic politics. *Diacritics*, 5: 44–50.

Mahony, p. (1977) Towards a formalist approach to dreams. *International Review of Psycho-Analysis*, 4: 83–98.

—— (1979) The boundaries of free association. *Psycho-analysis and Contemporary Thought*, 2: 155–198.

Marks, E. (1978) Women and literature in France. *Signs*, 3: 832–842.

Mcrloo, J. (1964) *Unobtrusive Communication: Essays in Linguistics*. Assen, Netherlands: Van Gorcum.

Millett, K. (1971) *Sexual Politics*. New York: Avon.

Money, J. and Ehrhardt, A. (1972) *Man and Woman, Boy and Girl*. Baltimore, Maryland: Johns Hopkins University Press.

Ong, W. (1962) *The Barbarian Within*, New York: Macmillan.

—— (1967) *The Presence of the Word*. New Haven: Yale University Press.

—— (1971) *Rhetoric, Romance and Technology*. Ithaca, N.Y.: Cornell University Press.

—— (1976) *In the Human Grain*. New York: Macmillan.

—— (1977) *Interfaces of the Word*. Ithaca, New York: Cornell University Press.

Schneiderman, S. (1980) *Returning to Freud*. New Haven: Yale University Press.

Schowalter, E. (1975) Literary criticism: a review. *Signs*, 1: 445–455.

Sharpe, E. (1968) *Collected Papers on Psycho-analysis*. London: Hogarth Press.

Spitz, R. (1955) The primal cavity: a contribution to the genesis of perception and its role of psychoanalytic theory. *The Psychoanalytic Study of the Child*, 10: 215–240.

Stoller, R. (1977) Primary femininity. In: H. Blum (ed.), *Female Psychology*. New York: International Universities Press, pp. 58–78.

—— (1980) Feminity. In: M. Kirkpatrick (ed.), *Women's Sexual Development*. New York: Plenum Press, pp. 127–146.

Thorne, B. and Henley, N. (1975) *Language and Sex: Difference and Dominance*. Rowley, Massachusetts: Newbury House.

Van der Heide, C. (1961) Blank silence and the dream screen. *Journal of the American Psycho-Analytic Association*, 9: 85–90.

Yaguello, M. (1978) *Les mots et les femmes*. Paris: Payot.

Index

255